RAIL ATLAS
OF
BRITAIN

Compiled by **S. K. Baker**

Oxford Publishing Co. Oxford

© Oxford Publishing Co.

1st Edition 1977 SBN 86093 009 2

2nd Edition 1978 SBN 86093 046 7

Maps Drawn by Paul Karau

Printed by S & S Press Ltd. Abingdon
Bound by Kemp Hall Bindery Oxford

Film work and plates by Knight Publishing

Typesetting by Gem Graphic Services

Published by
Oxford Publishing Co
8 The Roundway
Headington Oxford

PREFACE TO FIRST EDITION

The inspiration for this atlas was two-fold; firstly a feeling of total bewilderment by 'Llans' and 'Abers' on first visiting South Wales four years ago, and secondly a wall railway map drawn by a friend, Martin Bairstow. Since then, at university, there has been steady progress in drawing the rail network throughout Great Britain. The author feels sure that this atlas as it has finally evolved will be useful to all with an interest in railways, whether professional or enthusiast. The emphasis is on the current network since it is felt that this information is not published elsewhere.

Throughout, the main aim has been to show clearly, using expanded sheets where necessary, the railways of this country, including the whole of London Transport and light railways. Passenger lines are distinguished by colour according to operating company and all freight-only lines are depicted in red. The criterion for a British Rail passenger line has been taken as at least one advertised passenger train per day in each direction. On passenger routes, to assist the traveller, single and multiple track sections, with crossing loops on single lines have been shown. Symbols are used to identify both major centres of rail freight, such as collieries and power stations, and railway installations such as locomotive depots and works. Secondary information, for example junction names and significant tunnels, with lengths if greater than one mile, has been added in areas where clarity would not be significantly affected.

The author would like to express his thanks to members of the Oxford University Railway Society and to Nigel Bird, Chris Hammond and Richard Warson in particular for help in compiling and correcting the maps. His cousin, Dr Tony McCann deserves special thanks for removing much of the tedium by computer sorting the index, as do Oxford City Libraries for providing excellent reference facilities.
June 1977

PREFACE TO 1979 EDITION

This 1979 edition of the Rail Atlas of Britain incorporates the many changes which have taken place in the railway network since the first edition; both minor changes and major new works, such as the Tyne and Wear Metro, are shown. There is also more private siding information, and two extra insets have been provided, clarifying the complex areas of Aberdeen and Sheffield.

The author would like to thank those friends who have helped him to collect material for this new edition, and also everyone who has written to him, expressing their appreciation of the Atlas, and supplying much useful information.
Sheffield, South Yorks   Stuart K. Baker
October 1978

CONTENTS

KEY TO ATLAS

		Surface	Tunnel	Tube
British Rail — Passenger	Multiple Track			
	Single Track			
London Transport *(Line indicated by code)* Also Greater Glasgow and Tyne & Wear	Multiple Track	C	C	C
	Single Track	C	C	C
Preserved & Minor Passenger Railways	Multiple Track			
	Single Track			
Freight only lines — *(British Rail & Others)*	No Single/ Multiple Distinction			

Advertised Passenger Station: Saltburn

Crossing Loop at Passenger Station: Newtown

Crossing Loop on Single Line: *Murthly*

Unadvertised/Excursion Station: Warrenby*

			LM ER
Major Power Signalboxes	PRESTON	B.R. Region Breaks	
Carriage Sidings	C.S.	Colliery *(including opencast site)*	▲
Freight/Marshalling Yard	TINSLEY	Power Station	△
Freightliner Terminal	FLT	Oil Refinery	●
National Carriers Depot	NCL	Oil Terminal	○
Locomotive Depot/Stabling Point	■ BS	Cement Works or Terminal	■
British Rail Engineering Ltd.	BREL	Quarry	□
Junction Names	*Haughley Junc.*	Other Freight Terminal	

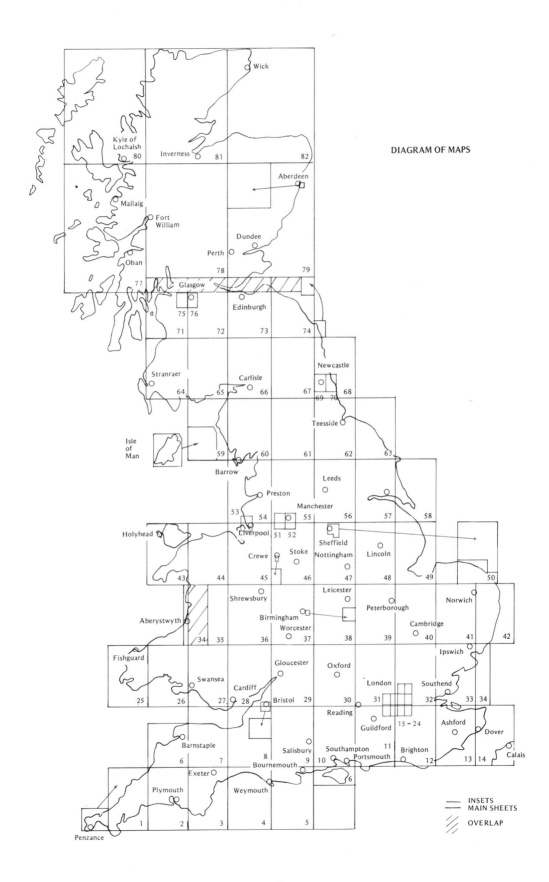

DIAGRAM OF MAPS

INSETS
MAIN SHEETS
OVERLAP

(iii)

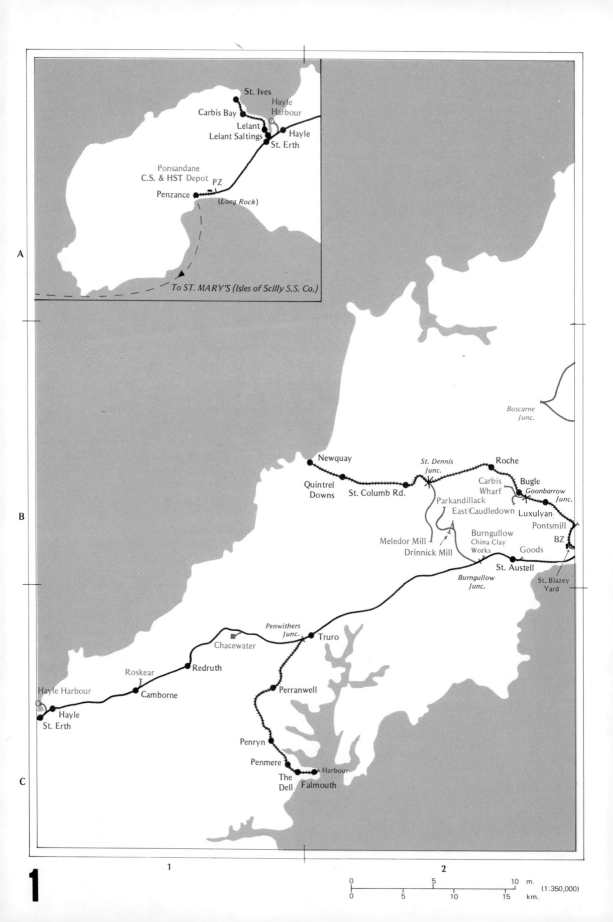

St. Ives
Carbis Bay
Lelant
Hayle
Harbour
Lelant Saltings
Hayle
St. Erth

Ponsandane
C.S. & HST Depot
PZ
Penzance
(Long Rock)

To ST. MARY'S (Isles of Scilly S.S. Co.)

A

Boscarne
Junc.

Newquay
Roche
Quintrel
Downs
St. Columb Rd.
St. Dennis
Junc.
Carbis
Wharf
Bugle
Goonbarrow
Junc.
Parkandillack
East Caudledown
Luxulyan
Pontsmill
BZ

B

Meledor Mill
Drinnick Mill
Burngullow
China Clay
Works
Goods
St. Austell
St. Blazey
Yard
Burngullow
Junc.

Penwithers
Junc.
Truro
Chacewater
Roskear
Redruth
Perranwell
Hayle Harbour
Camborne
Hayle
St. Erth
Penryn
Penmere
Harbour
The
Dell
Falmouth

C

1

2

0   5   10 m.
0   5   10   15   km.

(1:350,000)

1

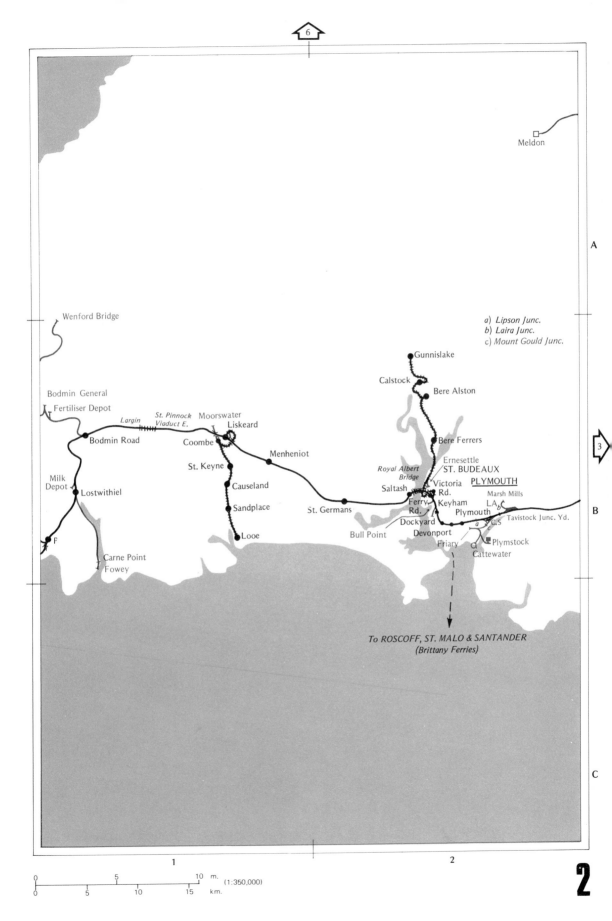

A

Meldon

Wenford Bridge

a) *Lipson Junc.*
b) *Laira Junc.*
c) *Mount Gould Junc.*

Gunnislake

Calstock

Bere Alston

Bodmin General
Fertiliser Depot

Largin   *St. Pinnock Viaduct E.*   Moorswater

Bere Ferrers

Liskeard

Bodmin Road   Coombe

Menheniot

Royal Albert Bridge   Ernesettle
ST. BUDEAUX

St. Keyne

PLYMOUTH

Milk Depot

Saltash   Victoria Rd.

Lostwithiel

Causeland

Marsh Mills

Ferry Rd.   Keyham   LA   b

Sandplace

St. Germans

Dockyard   Plymouth   C.S

a   c

Bull Point

Tavistock Junc. Yd.

P

Devonport

Friary

Looe

Carne Point
Fowey

Plymstock
Cattewater

To ROSCOFF, ST. MALO & SANTANDER
(Brittany Ferries)

3

B

C

1   2

0   5   10 m. (1:350,000)
0   5   10   15 km.

2

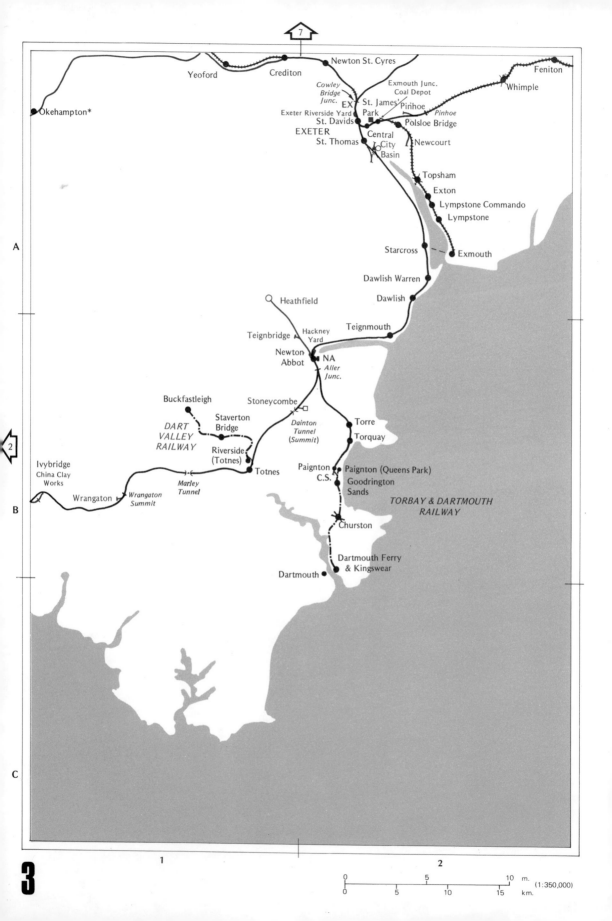

Okehampton*

Yeoford

Crediton

Newton St. Cyres

Feniton

Whimple

Cowley
Bridge
Junc.

Exmouth Junc.
Coal Depot

EX

St. James'
Park

Pirihoe

Exeter Riverside Yard

Pinhoe

St. Davids

Polsloe Bridge

EXETER

St. Thomas

Central
City
Basin

Newcourt

Topsham

Exton

Lympstone Commando

Lympstone

Starcross

Exmouth

Dawlish Warren

Dawlish

Teignmouth

Heathfield

Teignbridge

Hackney
Yard

Newton
Abbot

NA

Aller
Junc.

Buckfastleigh

Stoneycombe

Staverton
Bridge

DART
VALLEY
RAILWAY

Dainton
Tunnel
(Summit)

Torre

Torquay

Riverside
(Totnes)

Ivybridge
China Clay
Works

Marley
Tunnel

Totnes

Paignton

C.S.

Paignton (Queens Park)

Goodrington
Sands

TORBAY & DARTMOUTH
RAILWAY

Wrangaton

Wrangaton
Summit

Churston

Dartmouth Ferry
& Kingswear

Dartmouth

2

A

2

B

C

1

2

0   5   10   m.
(1:350,000)
0   5   10   15   km.

3

Axminster

Maiden
Newton

Colyton
SEATON TRAMWAY (2' 9")　　Colyford
Axmouth
Seaton

8

5

A

B

C

2

0   5   10   m.
                        (1:350,000)
0   5   10   15   km.

4

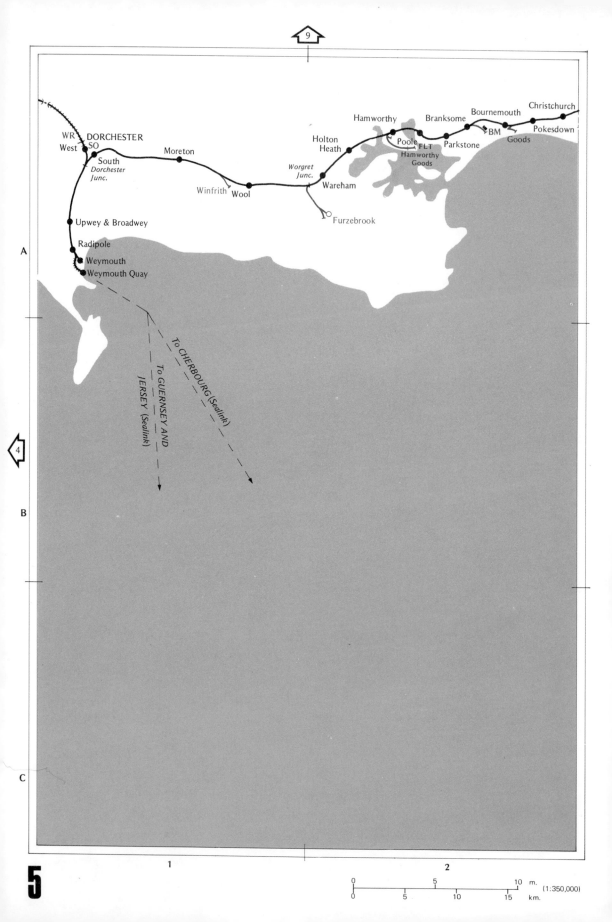

WR
West
DORCHESTER
SO
South
Dorchester Junc.

Moreton

Holton Heath

Hamworthy

Branksome

Bournemouth
Christchurch

Poole
FLT
Parkstone
BM
Goods
Pokesdown

Hamworthy Goods

Worgret Junc.

Winfrith Wool

Wareham

Furzebrook

Upwey & Broadwey

Radipole

Weymouth
Weymouth Quay

To CHERBOURG (Sealink)

To GUERNSEY AND JERSEY (Sealink)

A

4

B

C

5

1

2

0   5   10 m.

0   5   10   15 km.

(1:350,000)

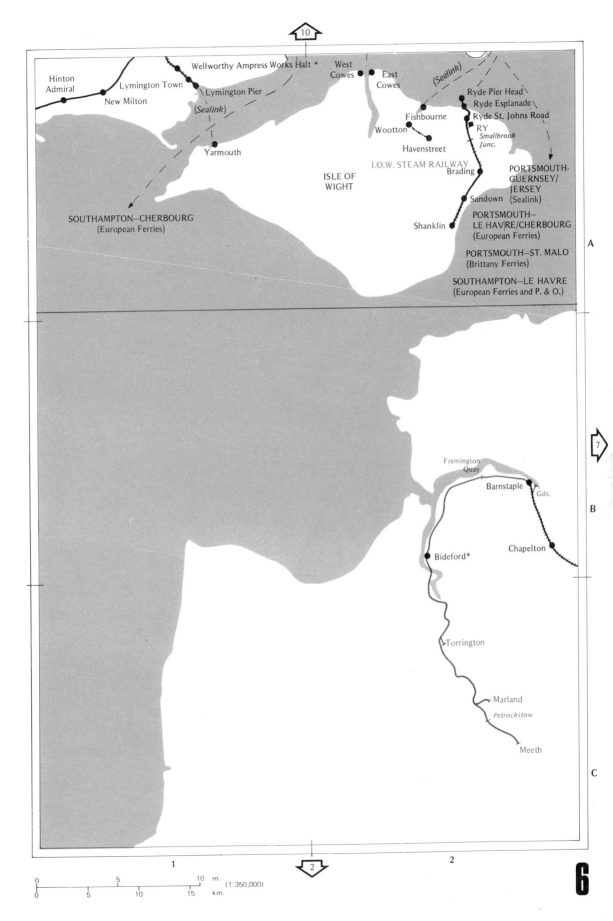

SOUTHAMPTON—CHERBOURG
(European Ferries)

Hinton
Admiral

New Milton

Lymington Town

Wellworthy Ampress Works Halt *

Lymington Pier

(Sealink)

Yarmouth

West
Cowes

East
Cowes

(Sealink)

Fishbourne

Wootton

Havenstreet

ISLE OF
WIGHT

I.O.W. STEAM RAILWAY

Brading

Sandown

Shanklin

Ryde Pier Head

Ryde Esplanade

Ryde St. Johns Road

RY
*Smallbrook
Junc.*

PORTSMOUTH-
GUERNSEY/
JERSEY
(Sealink)

PORTSMOUTH—
LE HAV|RE/CHERBOURG
(European Ferries)

PORTSMOUTH—ST. MALO
(Brittany Ferries)

SOUTHAMPTON—LE HAVRE
(European Ferries and P. & O.)

Fremington
Quay

Barnstaple

Gds.

Bideford*

Chapelton

Torrington

Marland

Petrockstow

Meeth

10

7

2

2

1

2

A

B

C

m.
0   5   10   (1:350,000)
0   5   10   15 km.

6

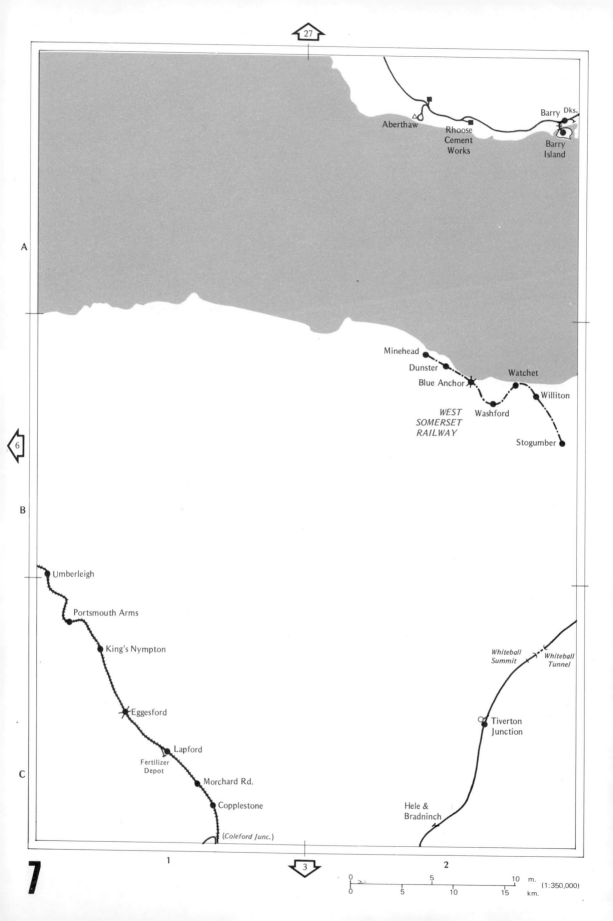

Barry Dks.

Aberthaw
Rhoose
Cement
Works

Barry
Island

Minehead
Dunster
Blue Anchor
Watchet
Williton
Washford

WEST SOMERSET RAILWAY

Stogumber

Umberleigh

Portsmouth Arms

King's Nympton

Whiteball Summit
Whiteball Tunnel

Eggesford

Tiverton
Junction

Lapford

Fertilizer
Depot

Morchard Rd.

Copplestone

Hele &
Bradninch

(Coleford Junc.)

7

1

2

0   5   10   m.
                              (1:350,000)
0   5   10   15   km.

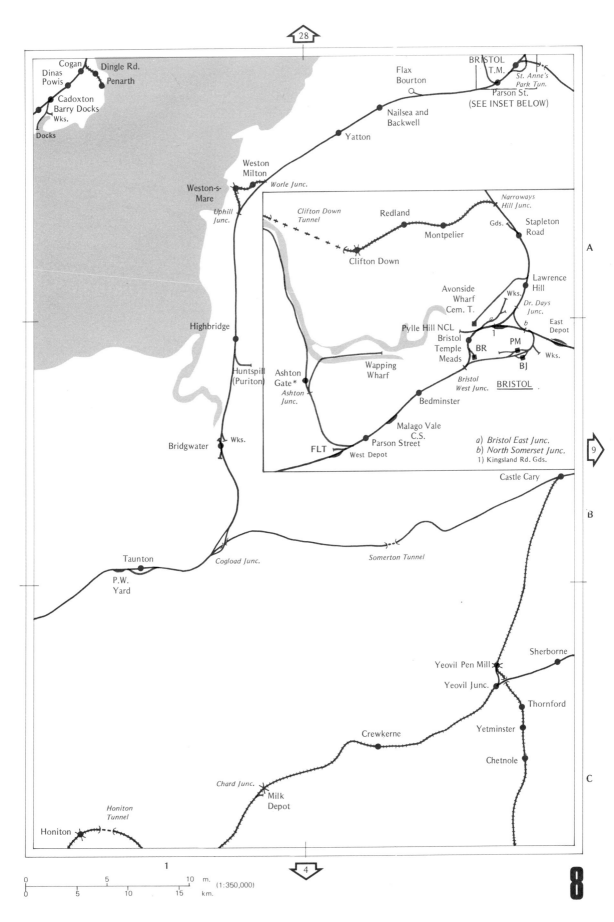

Cogan
Dinas Powis
Dingle Rd.
Penarth
Cadoxton
Barry Docks
Wks.
Docks

BRISTOL T.M.
Flax Bourton
St. Anne's Park Tun.
Parson St.
(SEE INSET BELOW)

Nailsea and Backwell

Yatton

Weston Milton

Weston-s-Mare

Worle Junc.

Uphill Junc.

A

Clifton Down Tunnel
Redland
Montpelier
Narroways Hill Junc.
Gds.
Stapleton Road

Clifton Down

Lawrence Hill

Avonside Wharf Cem. T.
Wks.
Dr. Days Junc.

Highbridge

Pylle Hill NCL
Bristol Temple Meads
BR
PM
1
East Depot
Wks.
BJ

Huntspill (Puriton)

Ashton Gate*
Ashton Junc.

Wapping Wharf

Bristol West Junc.
BRISTOL

Bedminster

Bridgwater
Wks.

Malago Vale C.S.

FLT
West Depot
Parson Street

a) Bristol East Junc.
b) North Somerset Junc.
1) Kingsland Rd. Gds.

Castle Cary

B

Taunton
P.W. Yard

Cogload Junc.
Somerton Tunnel

9

Sherborne

Yeovil Pen Mill
Yeovil Junc.

Thornford

Crewkerne

Yetminster

Chetnole

C

Chard Junc.

Honiton Tunnel
Milk Depot

Honiton

1

0   5   10   m.
0   5   10   15   km.   (1:350,000)

8

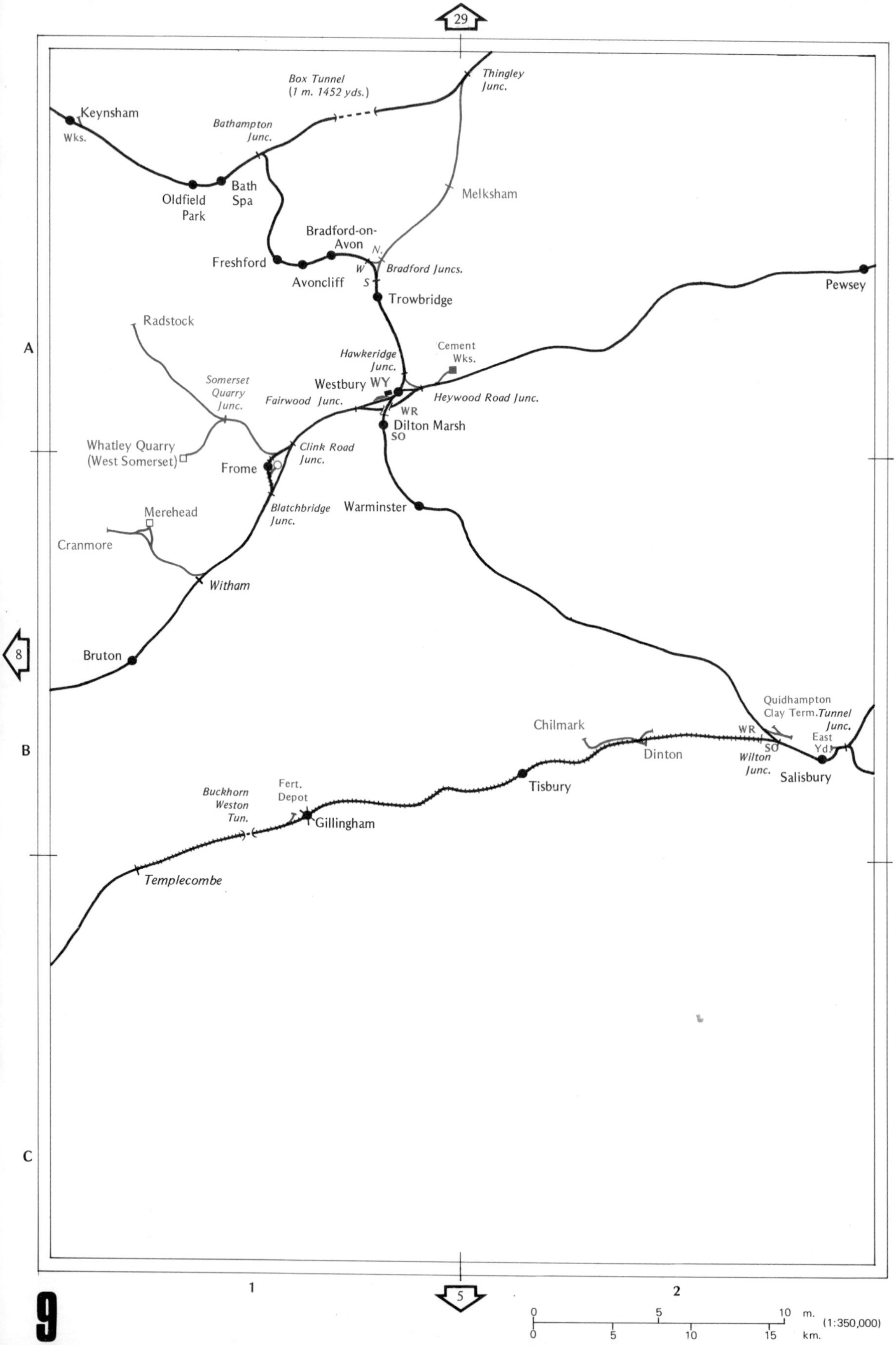

Keynsham

Wks.

Box Tunnel
(1 m. 1452 yds.)

Thingley
Junc.

Bathampton
Junc.

Melksham

Oldfield
Park

Bath
Spa

Bradford-on-
Avon

N.

Freshford

Bradford Juncs.

Avoncliff

W
S

Trowbridge

Pewsey

Radstock

Hawkeridge
Junc.

Cement
Wks.

A

Westbury WY

Somerset
Quarry
Junc.

Fairwood Junc.

Heywood Road Junc.

WR
Dilton Marsh
SO

Whatley Quarry
(West Somerset)

Clink Road
Junc.

Frome

Merehead

Blatchbridge
Junc.

Warminster

Cranmore

Witham

8

Bruton

Chilmark

Quidhampton
Clay Term. *Tunnel
Junc.*

WR
SO

East
Yd.

Dinton

B

Wilton
Junc.

Salisbury

Buckhorn
Weston Tun.

Fert.
Depot

Tisbury

Gillingham

Templecombe

C

2

0		5		10	m.

(1:350,000)

0	5	10	15	km.

9

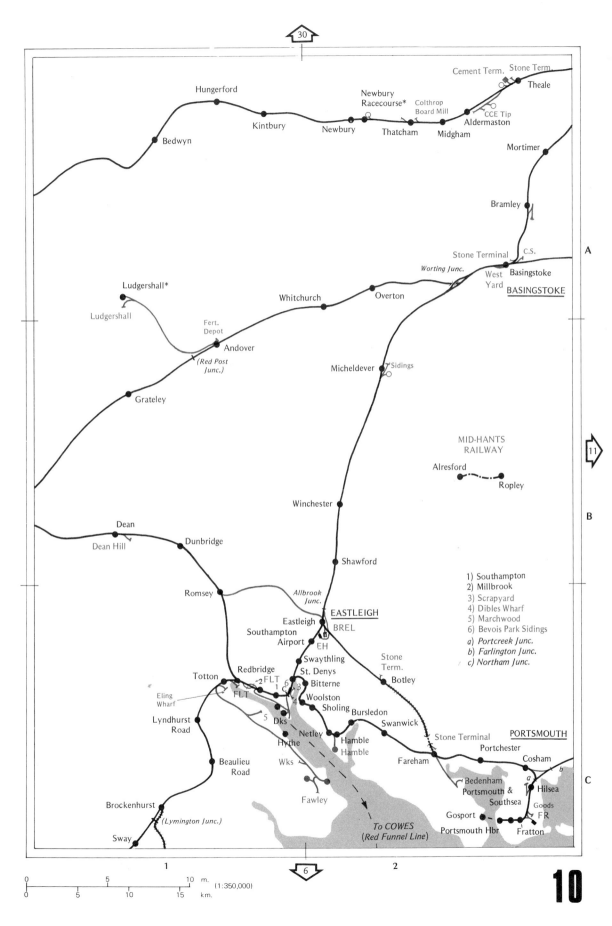

Hungerford

Kintbury

Bedwyn

Newbury

Newbury
Racecourse*

Thatcham

Midgham

Colthrop
Board Mill

Cement Term. Stone Term.

Theale

CCE Tip

Aldermaston

Mortimer

Bramley

Stone Terminal   C.S.

Worting Junc.

West
Yard

Stone Terminal

Basingstoke

BASINGSTOKE

A

Ludgershall*

Ludgershall

Whitchurch

Overton

Fert.
Depot

Andover

(Red Post
Junc.)

Micheldever

Sidings

MID-HANTS
RAILWAY

Alresford

Ropley

11

Grateley

B

Dean

Dean Hill

Dunbridge

Winchester

Romsey

Shawford

Allbrook
Junc.

1) Southampton
2) Millbrook
3) Scrapyard
4) Dibles Wharf
5) Marchwood
6) Bevois Park Sidings

a) *Portcreek Junc.*
b) *Farlington Junc.*
c) *Northam Junc.*

Eastleigh

EASTLEIGH

BREL

Southampton
Airport

EH

Swaythling

St. Denys

Totton

Redbridge

FLT
2

FLT

6
1 C

3

Bitterne

Woolston

Sholing

Stone
Term.

Botley

Eling
Wharf

4

5 Dks

Bursledon

Swanwick

Stone Terminal

PORTSMOUTH

Lyndhurst
Road

Hythe

Netley

Hamble
Hamble

Portchester

Cosham

b

Beaulieu
Road

Wks

Fareham

Bedenham
Portsmouth &
Southsea

a

Hilsea

C

Fawley

Gosport

Goods

FR

Brockenhurst

(Lymington Junc.)

Portsmouth Hbr

Fratton

Sway

To COWES
(Red Funnel Line)

1

2

6

0   5   10 m.
|——————|——————| (1:350,000)
0   5   10   15 km.

10

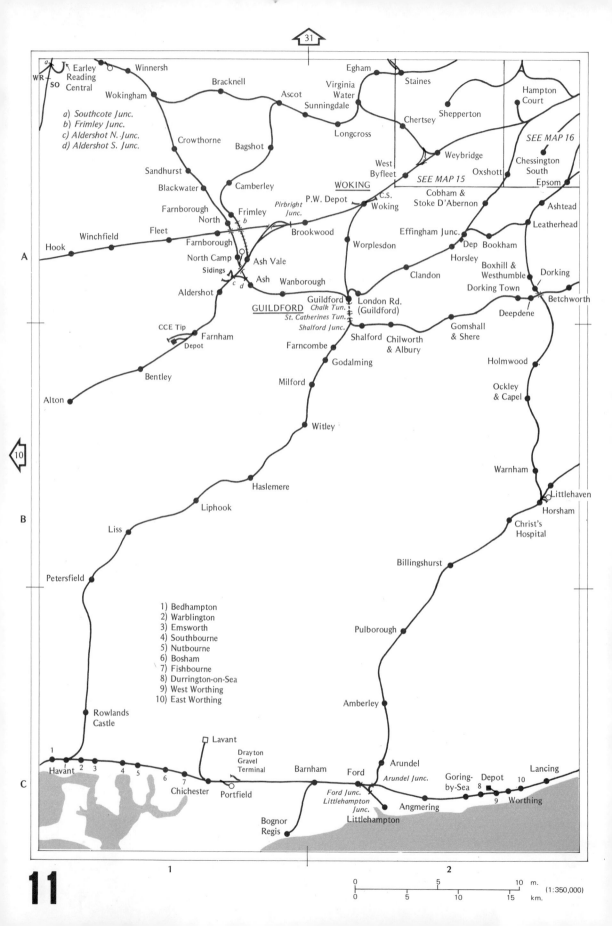

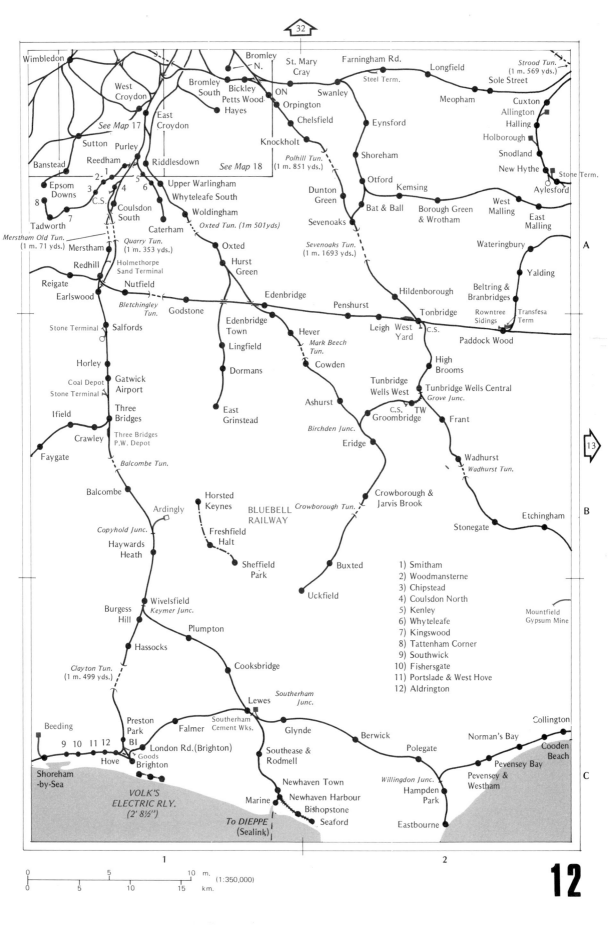

Wimbledon

Bromley N.

St. Mary Cray

Farningham Rd.

Longfield

Sole Street

Strood Tun.
(1 m. 569 yds.)

West Croydon

Bromley South

Bickley

Petts Wood

Hayes

ON

Orpington

Swanley

Steel Term.

Meopham

Cuxton

Allington

See Map 17

East Croydon

Chelsfield

Eynsford

Halling

Holborough

Sutton

Purley

Knockholt

Shoreham

Snodland

Banstead

Reedham

Riddlesdown

See Map 18

Polhill Tun.
(1 m. 851 yds.)

Otford

New Hythe

Stone Term.

2 - 1

Upper Warlingham

Kemsing

Aylesford

Epsom Downs

3

4

5

6

Whyteleafe South

Dunton Green

Bat & Ball

Borough Green & Wrotham

West Malling

8

7

C.S.

Woldingham

Sevenoaks

East Malling

Tadworth

Coulsdon South

Caterham

Oxted Tun. (1m 501yds.)

Merstham Old Tun.
(1 m. 71 yds.)

Merstham

Quarry Tun.
(1 m. 353 yds.)

Oxted

Sevenoaks Tun.
(1 m. 1693 yds.)

Wateringbury

A

Redhill

Holmethorpe
Sand Terminal

Hurst Green

Yalding

Reigate

Nutfield

Edenbridge

Hildenborough

Beltring & Branbridges

Earlswood

Godstone

Penshurst

Tonbridge

Rowntree Sidings

Transfesa Term

Bletchingley Tun.

Edenbridge Town

Leigh

West Yard

C.S.

Stone Terminal

Salfords

Hever

Mark Beech Tun.

Paddock Wood

Horley

Lingfield

Cowden

High Brooms

Coal Depot

Stone Terminal

Gatwick Airport

Dormans

Tunbridge Wells West

Tunbridge Wells Central

Grove Junc.

Ifield

Three Bridges

East Grinstead

Ashurst

C.S.

Groombridge

TW

Frant

Crawley

Three Bridges P.W. Depot

Birchden Junc.

Faygate

Balcombe Tun.

Eridge

Wadhurst

Wadhurst Tun.

13

Balcombe

Horsted Keynes

BLUEBELL RAILWAY

Crowborough Tun.

Crowborough & Jarvis Brook

Stonegate

Etchingham

B

Ardingly

Copyhold Junc.

Freshfield Halt

Haywards Heath

Sheffield Park

Buxted

Stonegate

Mountfield Gypsum Mine

1) Smitham
2) Woodmansterne
3) Chipstead
4) Coulsdon North
5) Kenley
6) Whyteleafe
7) Kingswood
8) Tattenham Corner
9) Southwick
10) Fishersgate
11) Portslade & West Hove
12) Aldrington

Uckfield

Wivelsfield

Keymer Junc.

Burgess Hill

Plumpton

Hassocks

Clayton Tun.
(1 m. 499 yds.)

Cooksbridge

Lewes

Southerham Junc.

Beeding

9 10 11 12

Preston Park

BI

Falmer

Southerham Cement Wks.

Glynde

Berwick

Collington

Norman's Bay

Cooden Beach

London Rd.(Brighton)

Goods

Brighton

Southease & Rodmell

Polegate

Pevensey Bay

Shoreham -by-Sea

Hove

VOLK'S ELECTRIC RLY. (2' 8½")

Newhaven Town

Willingdon Junc.

Pevensey & Westham

Hampden Park

C

Marine

Newhaven Harbour

Bishopstone

Seaford

Eastbourne

To DIEPPE (Sealink)

1

2

0   5   10 m.

(1:350,000)

0   5   10   15 km.

12

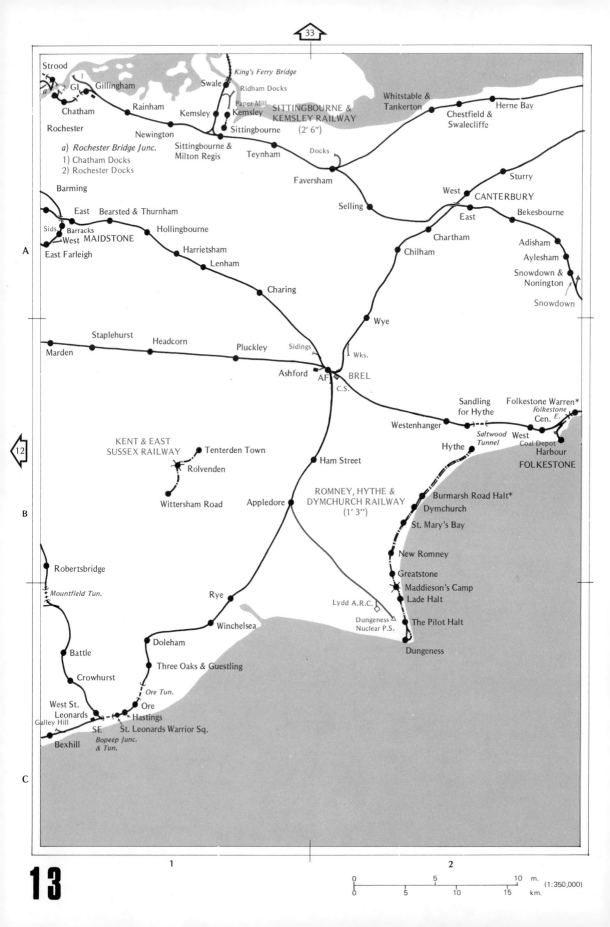

Strood
Gillingham
a)
1
2 Gl
Chatham
Rainham
Kemsley
Paper Mill
Kemsley
Ridham Docks
Swale
King's Ferry Bridge
Rochester
Newington
Sittingbourne
Sittingbourne &
Milton Regis
Teynham
SITTINGBOURNE &
KEMSLEY RAILWAY
(2' 6")
Docks
Whitstable &
Tankerton
Chestfield &
Swalecliffe
Herne Bay

a) Rochester Bridge Junc.
1) Chatham Docks
2) Rochester Docks

Faversham
Selling
West
CANTERBURY
East
Sturry
Bekesbourne
Adisham
Aylesham
Snowdown &
Nonington
Snowdown

Barming
East
Bearsted & Thurnham
Hollingbourne
Sids
Barracks
West MAIDSTONE
East Farleigh
Harrietsham
Lenham
Chartham
Chilham
Wye

A

Marden
Staplehurst
Headcorn
Pluckley
Sidings
Ashford AF
BREL
Wks.
C.S.
Charing

Sandling
for Hythe
Folkestone Warren*
Folkestone
Cen. E.
Westenhanger
Saltwood
Tunnel
West
Coal Depot
Harbour
FOLKESTONE

12

KENT & EAST
SUSSEX RAILWAY
Tenterden Town
Rolvenden
Wittersham Road
Ham Street
Appledore
ROMNEY, HYTHE &
DYMCHURCH RAILWAY
(1' 3")
Hythe
Burmarsh Road Halt*
Dymchurch
St. Mary's Bay
New Romney
Greatstone
Maddieson's Camp
Lade Halt
The Pilot Halt
Dungeness

B

Robertsbridge
Mountfield Tun.
Battle
Crowhurst
West St.
Leonards
Galley Hill
SE
Bexhill
Bopeep Junc.
& Tun.
Ore Tun.
Ore
Hastings
St. Leonards Warrior Sq.
Doleham
Three Oaks & Guestling
Winchelsea
Rye
Lydd A.R.C.
Dungeness
Nuclear P.S.

C

1
2

0   5   10 m.
0   5   10   15 km.
(1:350,000)

13

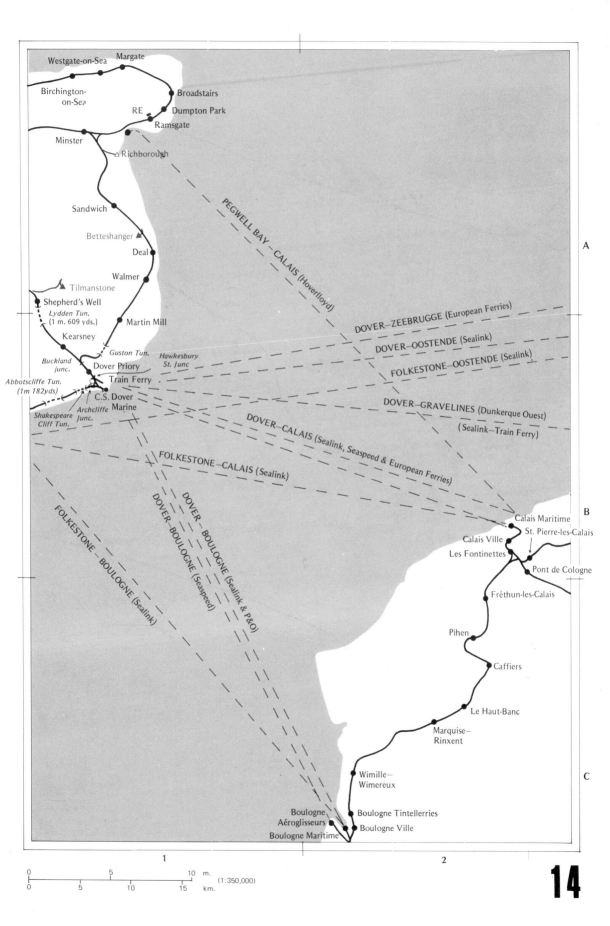

Westgate-on-Sea
Margate
Birchington-
on-Sea
Broadstairs
RE
Dumpton Park
Ramsgate
Minster
△ Richborough
Sandwich
Betteshanger ▲
Deal
Walmer
▲ Tilmanstone
Shepherd's Well
Lydden Tun.
(1 m. 609 yds.)
Martin Mill
Kearsney
Guston Tun.
Hawkesbury
St. Junc
*Buckland
junc.*
Dover Priory
Train Ferry
Abbotscliffe Tun.
(1m 182yds)
C.S. Dover
Marine
*Archcliffe
Junc.*
*Shakespeare
Cliff Tun.*

PEGWELL BAY – CALAIS (Hoverlloyd)

DOVER–ZEEBRUGGE (European Ferries)

DOVER–OOSTENDE (Sealink)

FOLKESTONE–OOSTENDE (Sealink)

DOVER–GRAVELINES (Dunkerque Ouest)

(Sealink–Train Ferry)

DOVER–CALAIS (Sealink, Seaspeed & European Ferries)

FOLKESTONE–CALAIS (Sealink)

Calais Maritime

St. Pierre-les-Calais

Calais Ville

Les Fontinettes

Pont de Cologne

Fréthun-les-Calais

Pihen

Caffiers

Le Haut-Banc

Marquise–
Rinxent

Wimille–
Wimereux

Boulogne
Aéroglisseurs
Boulogne Maritime
Boulogne Tintellerries
Boulogne Ville

DOVER–BOULOGNE (Sealink & P&O)

FOLKESTONE–BOULOGNE (Seaspeed)

DOVER–BOULOGNE

FOLKESTONE–BOULOGNE (Sealink)

A

B

C

1

2

0   5   10 m.
0   5   10   15 km.
(1:350,000)

14

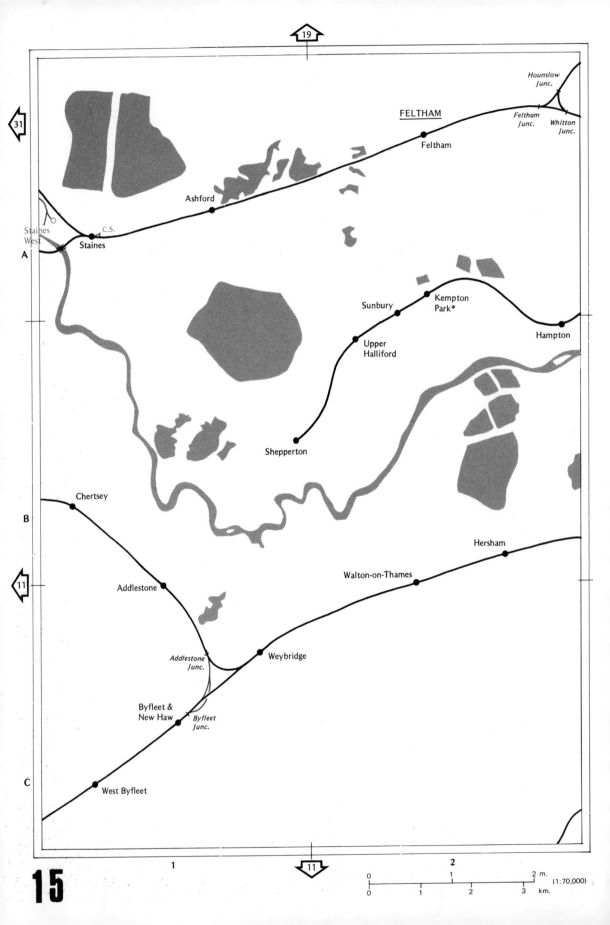

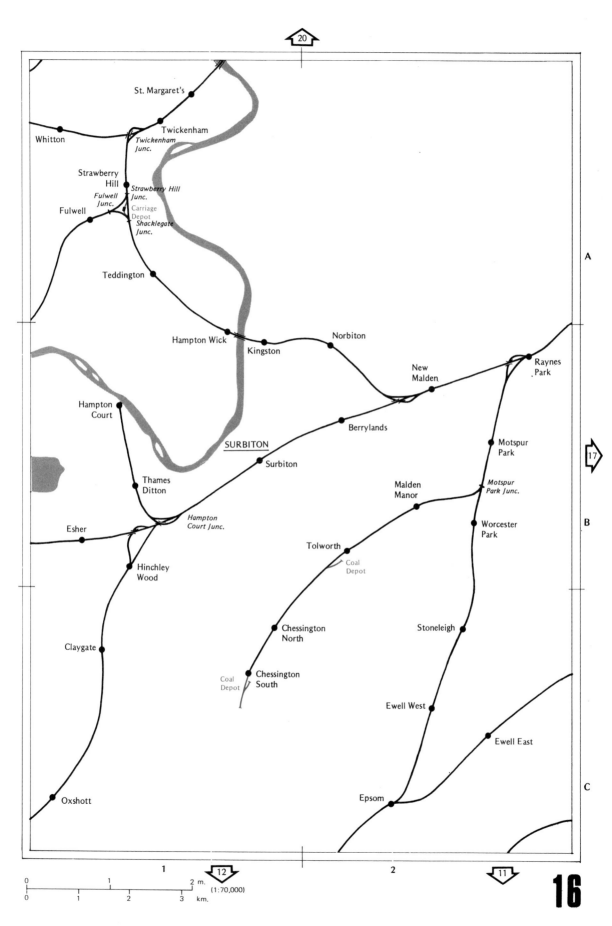

St. Margaret's

Twickenham

Whitton

Twickenham Junc.

Strawberry
Hill

Strawberry Hill Junc.

Fulwell Junc.

Fulwell

Carriage
Depot

Shacklegate Junc.

Teddington

Hampton Wick

Kingston

Norbiton

New
Malden

Raynes
Park

Hampton
Court

Berrylands

SURBITON

Surbiton

Motspur
Park

Esher

Thames
Ditton

Hampton Court Junc.

Malden
Manor

Motspur Park Junc.

Worcester
Park

Hinchley
Wood

Tolworth

Coal
Depot

Claygate

Chessington
North

Stoneleigh

Coal
Depot

Chessington
South

Ewell West

Ewell East

Oxshott

Epsom

A

B

C

0   1   2 m.
(1:70,000)
0   1   2   3   km.

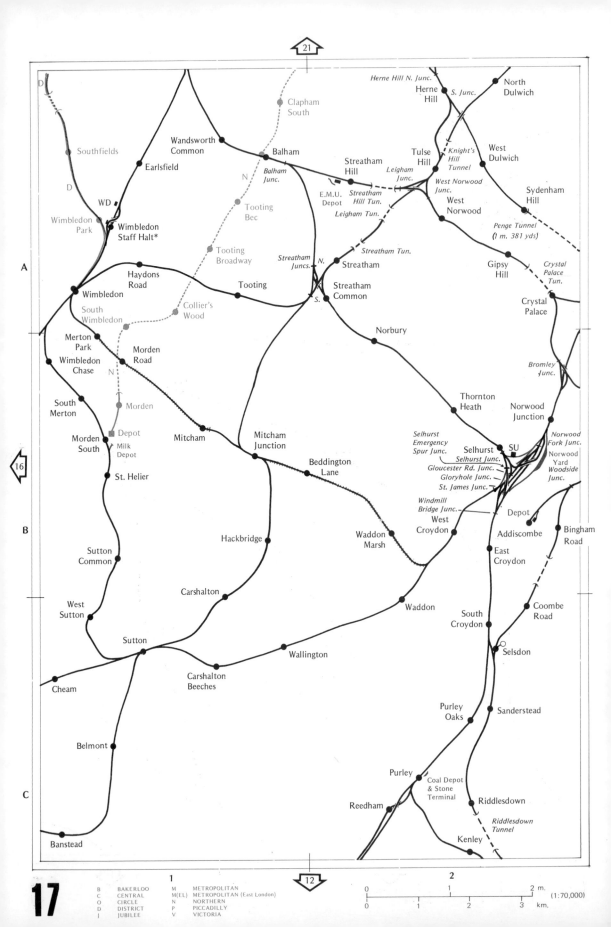

D

Southfields

Wandsworth
Common

Balham

*Clapham
South*

Herne Hill N. Junc.

Herne
Hill

S. Junc.

North
Dulwich

Earlsfield

*Balham
Junc.*

N

Streatham
Hill

Tulse
Hill

*Knight's
Hill
Tunnel*

West
Dulwich

West
Norwood
Junc.

Sydenham
Hill

WD

*Tooting
Bec*

*Leigham
Junc.*

*E.M.U.
Depot*

*Streatham
Hill Tun.*

West
Norwood

Leigham Tun.

Wimbledon
Park

Wimbledon
Staff Halt*

*Tooting
Broadway*

Haydons
Road

*Streatham
Juncs.*

N.

Streatham Tun.

*Penge Tunnel
(1 m. 381 yds)*

A

Tooting

Streatham

Gipsy
Hill

*Crystal
Palace
Tun.*

*Collier's
Wood*

S.

Streatham
Common

Crystal
Palace

*South
Wimbledon*

Wimbledon

Norbury

*Bromley
Junc.*

Merton
Park

Wimbledon
Chase

Morden
Road

N

Thornton
Heath

Norwood
Junction

Morden

Mitcham

Mitcham
Junction

Beddington
Lane

*Selhurst
Emergency
Spur Junc.*

Selhurst

SU

*Norwood
Fork Junc.*

South
Merton

Depot

*Milk
Depot*

Selhurst Junc.

Gloucester Rd. Junc.

Gloryhole Junc.

St. James Junc.

*Norwood
Yard
Woodside
Junc.*

Morden
South

St. Helier

*Windmill
Bridge Junc.*

West
Croydon

Depot

16

B

Hackbridge

Waddon
Marsh

Addiscombe

Bingham
Road

Sutton
Common

East
Croydon

Carshalton

Waddon

South
Croydon

Coombe
Road

West
Sutton

Sutton

Wallington

Selsdon

Sanderstead

Cheam

Carshalton
Beeches

Purley
Oaks

Belmont

C

Purley

*Coal Depot
& Stone
Terminal*

Riddlesdown

Reedham

*Riddlesdown
Tunnel*

Kenley

Banstead

17

B	BAKERLOO		M	METROPOLITAN
C	CENTRAL		M(EL)	METROPOLITAN (East London)
O	CIRCLE		N	NORTHERN
D	DISTRICT		P	PICCADILLY
J	JUBILEE		V	VICTORIA

1

2

0   1   2 m.

0   1   2   3 km.

(1:70,000)

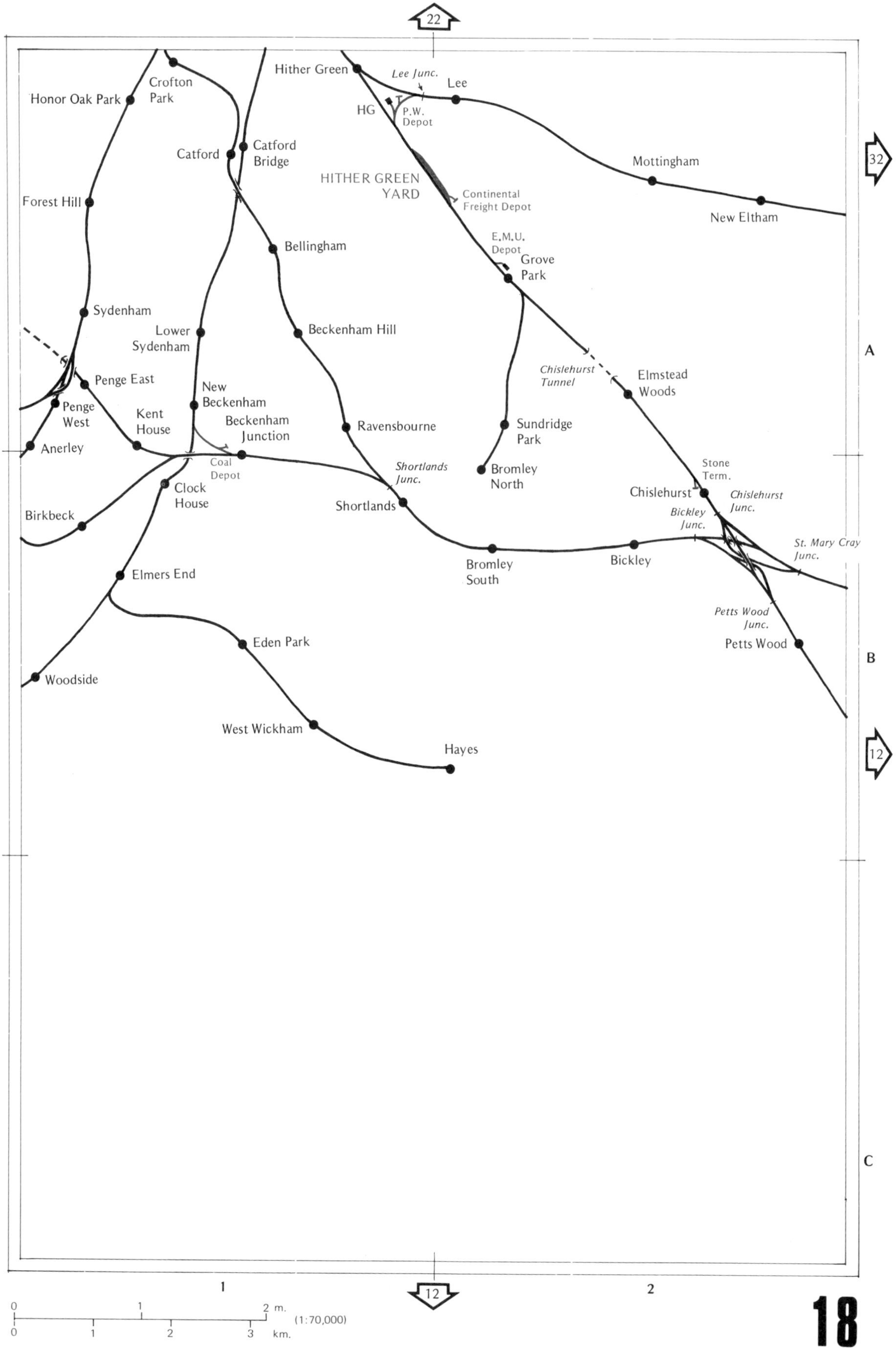

Honor Oak Park

Crofton Park

Hither Green

Lee Junc.

Lee

HG

P.W. Depot

Mottingham

Catford

Catford Bridge

HITHER GREEN YARD

Continental Freight Depot

New Eltham

Forest Hill

Bellingham

E.M.U. Depot

Grove Park

Sydenham

Lower Sydenham

Beckenham Hill

Chislehurst Tunnel

Elmstead Woods

A

Penge East

New Beckenham

Ravensbourne

Sundridge Park

Penge West

Kent House

Beckenham Junction

Stone Term.

Anerley

Coal Depot

Shortlands Junc.

Bromley North

Chislehurst

Chislehurst Junc.

Birkbeck

Clock House

Shortlands

Bickley Junc.

St. Mary Cray Junc.

Bromley South

Bickley

Elmers End

Petts Wood Junc.

Eden Park

Petts Wood

B

Woodside

West Wickham

Hayes

C

1

2

0   1   2 m.

(1:70,000)

0   1   2   3 km.

18

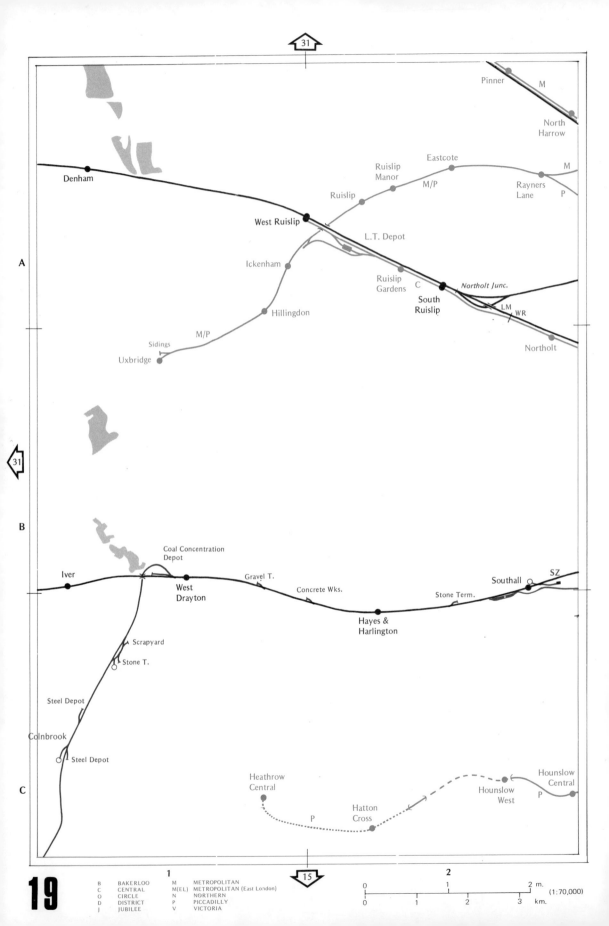

Pinner M

North Harrow

Eastcote

Ruislip Manor

M/P

Ruislip

M

Rayners Lane

P

Denham

West Ruislip

L.T. Depot

Ickenham

Ruislip Gardens C

South Ruislip

Northolt Junc.

LM WR

A

Northolt

Hillingdon

M/P

Sidings

Uxbridge

31

B

Coal Concentration Depot

Iver

West Drayton

Gravel T.

Concrete Wks.

Stone Term.

Southall SZ

Hayes & Harlington

Scrapyard

Stone T.

Steel Depot

Colnbrook

Steel Depot

C

Heathrow Central

Hatton Cross

P

Hounslow West

Hounslow Central

P

19

	1		
B	BAKERLOO	M	METROPOLITAN
C	CENTRAL	M(EL)	METROPOLITAN (East London)
O	CIRCLE	N	NORTHERN
D	DISTRICT	P	PICCADILLY
J	JUBILEE	V	VICTORIA

2

0   1   2 m.

0   1   2   3 km.

(1:70,000)

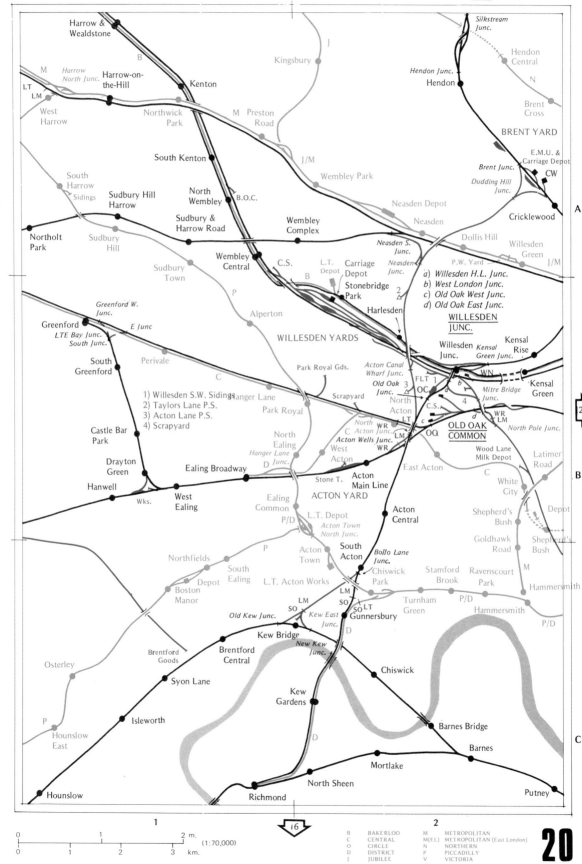

Silkstream Junc.
Hendon Central
Harrow & Wealdstone
Hendon Junc.
Hendon
Brent Cross
BRENT YARD
Kingsbury
J
B
M
Harrow North Junc.
Harrow-on-the-Hill
Kenton
E.M.U. & Carriage Depot
Brent Junc.
CW
LT
LM
West Harrow
Northwick Park
M   Preston Road
Dudding Hill Junc.
South Kenton
J/M
Wembley Park
Cricklewood   A
South Harrow Sidings
North Wembley
B.O.C.
Neasden Depot
Neasden
Dollis Hill
Willesden Green   J/M
Sudbury Hill Harrow
Sudbury & Harrow Road
Wembley Complex
Neasden S. Junc.
P.W. Yard
Northolt Park
Sudbury Hill
Wembley Central
C.S.
L.T. Depot
Carriage Depot
Neasden Junc.
a) Willesden H.L. Junc.
b) West London Junc.
c) Old Oak West Junc.
d) Old Oak East Junc.
WILLESDEN JUNC.
Sudbury Town
B
Stonebridge Park
Harlesden
2
Greenford W. Junc.
Alperton
P
Willesden Junc.
Kensal Green Junc.
Kensal Rise
Greenford
E Junc.
WILLESDEN YARDS
Acton Canal Wharf Junc.
Kensal Green
LTE Bay Junc.
South Junc.
Perivale
C
Park Royal Gds.
Old Oak Junc.
FLT 1
WN
b
South Greenford
Scrapyard
North Acton
OC
3
Mitre Bridge Junc.
4
1) Willesden S.W. Sidings
2) Taylors Lane P.S.
3) Acton Lane P.S.
4) Scrapyard
Hanger Lane
C.S.
WR
LM
Castle Bar Park
Park Royal
North Acton Junc.
Acton Wells Junc.
LT
OQ
d
c
OLD OAK COMMON
North Pole Junc.
Drayton Green
North Ealing
North   C
West Acton
WR
WR
LM
Wood Lane Milk Depot
Latimer Road
Hanwell
Ealing Broadway
D
Hanger Lane Junc.
East Acton
C
White City
B
Wks.
West Ealing
Stone T.
Acton Main Line
ACTON YARD
Shepherd's Bush
Depot
Ealing Common
P/D
Acton Central
Goldhawk Road
Shepherd's Bush
Northfields
South Ealing
L.T. Depot
Acton Town North Junc.
Acton Town
South Acton
Bollo Lane Junc.
Stamford Brook
Ravenscourt Park
M
Hammersmith
Depot
Boston Manor
L.T. Acton Works
Chiswick Park
Turnham Green
P/D
Hammersmith
P/D
LM
SO
LM
SO
SO LT
Gunnersbury
Old Kew Junc.
Kew East Junc.
D
Osterley
Kew Bridge
Chiswick
Brentford Goods
Brentford Central
New Kew Junc.
Syon Lane
Kew Gardens
Barnes Bridge
Isleworth
D
Barnes   C
P
Hounslow East
Mortlake
Hounslow
Richmond
North Sheen
Putney

0   1   2 m.
(1:70,000)
0   1   2   3 km.

B   BAKERLOO   M   METROPOLITAN
C   CENTRAL   M(EL) METROPOLITAN (East London)
O   CIRCLE   N   NORTHERN
D   DISTRICT   P   PICCADILLY
J   JUBILEE   V   VICTORIA

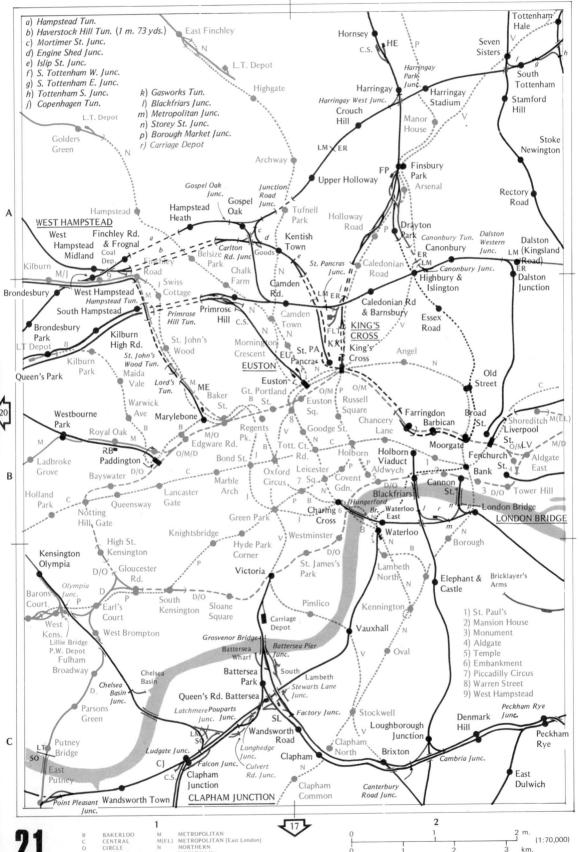

a) Hampstead Tun.
b) Haverstock Hill Tun. (1 m. 73 yds.)
c) Mortimer St. Junc.
d) Engine Shed Junc.
e) Islip St. Junc.
f) S. Tottenham W. Junc.
g) S. Tottenham E. Junc.
h) Tottenham S. Junc.
j) Copenhagen Tun.

k) Gasworks Tun.
l) Blackfriars Junc.
m) Metropolitan Junc.
n) Storey St. Junc.
p) Borough Market Junc.
r) Carriage Depot

1) St. Paul's
2) Mansion House
3) Monument
4) Aldgate
5) Temple
6) Embankment
7) Piccadilly Circus
8) Warren Street
9) West Hampstead

B	BAKERLOO	M	METROPOLITAN
C	CENTRAL	M(EL)	METROPOLITAN (East London)
O	CIRCLE	N	NORTHERN
D	DISTRICT	P	PICCADILLY
J	JUBILEE	V	VICTORIA

(1:70,000)

0   1   2 m.

0   1   2   3 km.

Black Horse Rd.

Wood St.

Barkingside

V   V

St. James Street

Walthamstow Central

Walthamstow Queen's Rd.

Snaresbrook

Newbury Park

C

Copper Mill Junc.

Leyton Midland Road

Wanstead   Redbridge   Gants Hill

Clapton Junc.

Lea Bridge

Leytonstone

Leytonstone High Rd.

IL

TEMPLE MILLS YARD

Clapton

Ilford

C.S.

(G.L.C. DOCKLAND SCHEME PROPOSES A NEW SERVICE FROM N. WOOLWICH TO CAMDEN ROAD WITH NEW STATIONS AT HOMERTON, HACKNEY & DALSTON)

Leyton

Wanstead Park

Forest Gate Junc.

Manor Park

A

Woodgrange Park

Hackney Downs

Homerton

High Meads Junc.

Temple Mills East Junc.

FLT

SF BREL SR

Forest Gate

Hackney (Mare St.)

Lea Junc.

Victoria Park Junc.

LIFT
g

EM

Maryland

London Fields

Channelsea Sidings

a

Stratford

East Ham

Carr. Sids

Thornton Fields C.S.

b
d

M/D

Barking

D

Cambridge Heath

Bow Goods

Stratford Market

Plaistow

Upton Park

Bethnal Green

C

Mile End Sand Term.

Bow Junc.

Chem. Wks.

M/D

Gds.

Bow Rd.

LT ER

West Ham

Plaistow & West Ham

a) Carpenters Rd. N. Junc.
b) Carpenters Rd. S. Junc.
c) Stratford Western Junc.
d) Stratford Southern Junc.
e) Bricklayers Arms Junc.
f) South Bermondsey Junc.
g) Channelsea Junc.

Bethnal Green

M/D

Mile End

Bromley-by-Bow

Abbey Mills Junc.

Stepney Green

Gas Factory Junc.

Canning Town

32

Whitechapel

M(EL)

West Ham Scrapyard

Stepney East

Custom House Victoria Dock

B

Shadwell

Poplar Docks

Wapping

North Woolwich

Rotherhithe

Silvertown Tramway

Silvertown

M(EL)

Southwark Park Junc.

Surrey Docks

Surrey Canal Junc.

B.S.C. Steel Term

Angerstein Wharf

Plumstead

Goods

f

North Kent West Junc.

e

North Kent East Junc.

Westcombe Park

Charlton

Woolwich Dockyard

Woolwich Arsenal

C.S.

South Bermondsey

L.T. Depot

Deptford

Sids.

Angerstein Junc.

New Cross Gate

New Cross

Greenwich

Maze Hill

Queens Road Peckham

Blackheath Tunnel

Nunhead

St. John's

Brockley

Parks Bridge Junc.

Lewisham

Blackheath

Kidbrooke

Falconwood

Courthill Loop Junc. North

C

Ladywell Junc.

Courthill Loop Junc. South

Eltham Well Hall

Ladywell

Eltham Park

1   2

0   1   2 m.

0   1   2   3 km.

(1:70,000)

B	BAKERLOO	M	METROPOLITAN
C	CENTRAL	M(EL)	METROPOLITAN (East London)
O	CIRCLE	N	NORTHERN
D	DISTRICT	P	PICCADILLY
J	JUBILEE	V	VICTORIA

22

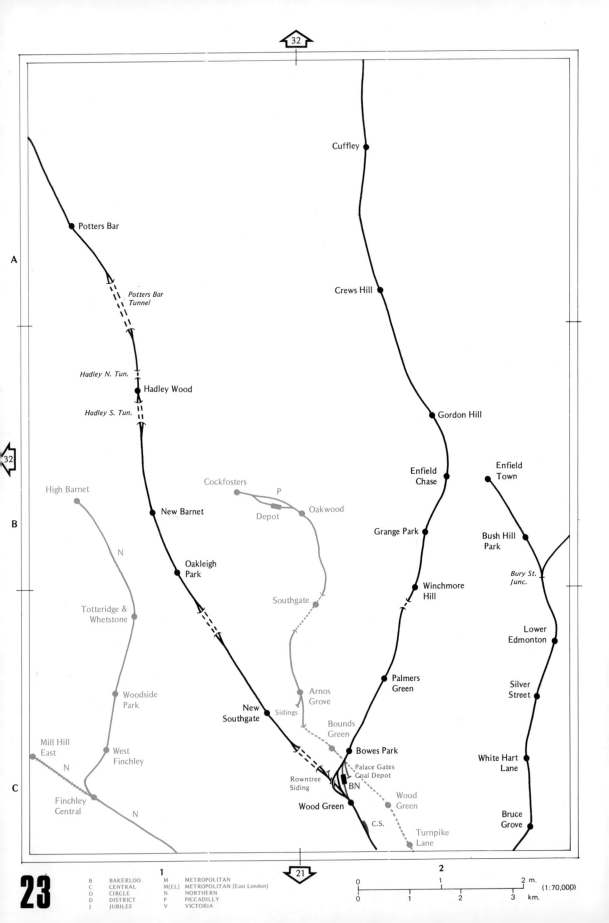

Cuffley

Potters Bar

A

Potters Bar
Tunnel

Crews Hill

Hadley N. Tun.

Hadley Wood

Gordon Hill

Hadley S. Tun.

Enfield
Chase

Enfield
Town

Cockfosters

P

High Barnet

Depot

Oakwood

B

New Barnet

Grange Park

Bush Hill
Park

N

Oakleigh
Park

Winchmore
Hill

Bury St.
Junc.

Totteridge &
Whetstone

Southgate

Lower
Edmonton

Woodside
Park

Arnos
Grove

Palmers
Green

Silver
Street

Mill Hill
East

New
Southgate

Sidings

Bounds
Green

West
Finchley

N

Bowes Park

White Hart
Lane

Palace Gates
Coal Depot

Rowntree
Siding

BN

C

Finchley
Central

N

Wood Green

Wood
Green

Bruce
Grove

C.S.

Turnpike
Lane

23

B	BAKERLOO	M	METROPOLITAN
C	CENTRAL	M(EL)	METROPOLITAN (East London)
O	CIRCLE	N	NORTHERN
D	DISTRICT	P	PICCADILLY
J	JUBILEE	V	VICTORIA

0   1   2 m.

(1:70,000)

0   1   2   3   km.

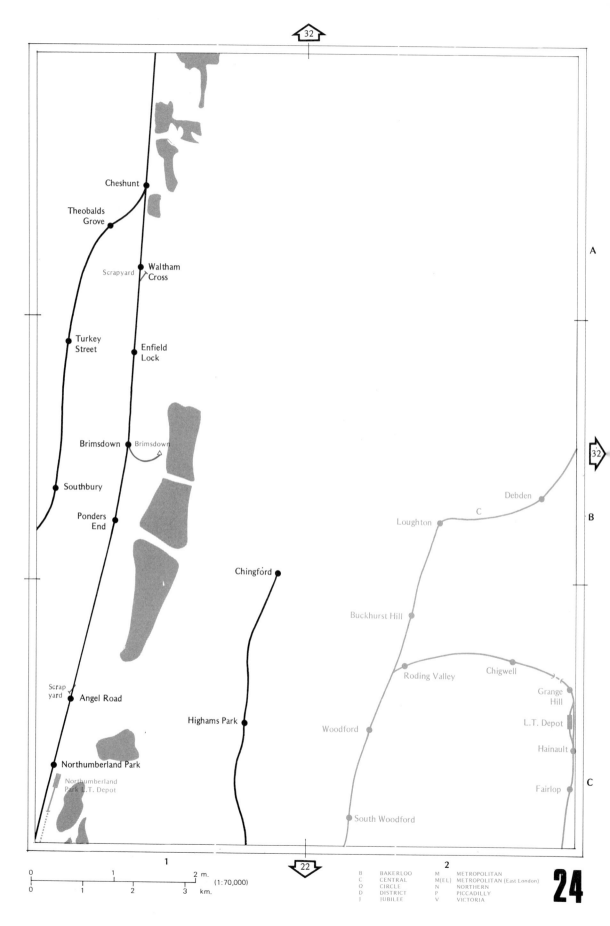

32

Cheshunt

Theobalds
Grove

Waltham
Cross

Scrapyard

Turkey
Street

Enfield
Lock

Brimsdown   Brimsdown

Southbury

Ponders
End

Debden

Loughton   C

B

Chingford

Buckhurst Hill

Roding Valley   Chigwell

Grange
Hill

Scrap
yard   Angel Road

Woodford

L.T. Depot

Highams Park

Hainault

Northumberland Park

Northumberland
Park L.T. Depot

Fairlop   C

South Woodford

22

0   1   2 m.
|————|————|————|————|
0   1   2   3 km.   (1:70,000)

1   2

24

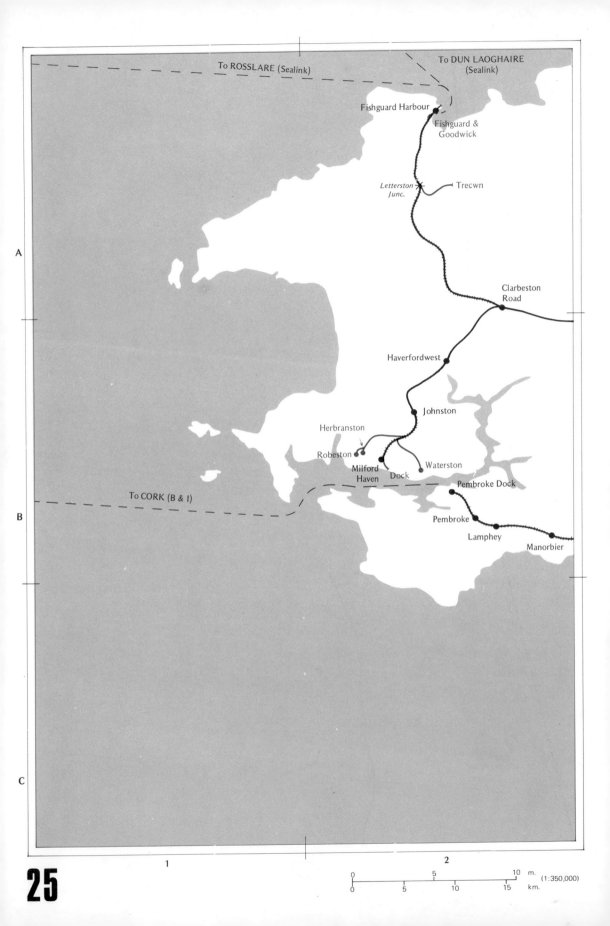

To ROSSLARE (Sealink)

To DUN LAOGHAIRE (Sealink)

Fishguard Harbour

Fishguard & Goodwick

Letterston Junc. — Trecwn

A

Clarbeston Road

Haverfordwest

Johnston

Herbranston

Robeston

Waterston

Milford Haven — Dock

Pembroke Dock

To CORK (B & I)

B

Pembroke

Lamphey

Manorbier

C

1

2

0   5   10 m.   (1:350,000)

0   5   10   15 km.

25

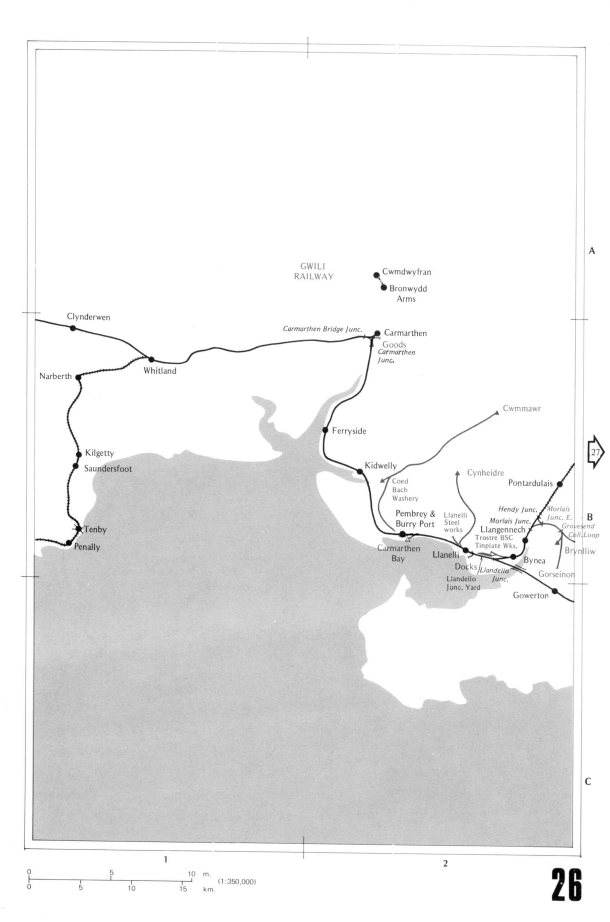

GWILI
RAILWAY

Cwmdwyfran

Bronwydd
Arms

Clynderwen

Carmarthen Bridge Junc.   Carmarthen
Goods
*Carmarthen
Junc.*

Narberth   Whitland

Ferryside

Cwmmawr

Kidwelly

Kilgetty
Saundersfoot

Coed
Bach
Washery

Cynheidre

Pontardulais

27

Pembrey &
Burry Port

Llanelli
Steel
works

Hendy Junc.

*Morlais
Junc. E.*

Morlais Junc.

Llangennech

Trostre BSC
Tinplate Wks.

*Grovesend
Coll. Loop*

B

Tenby
Penally

Carmarthen
Bay

Llanelli

Docks

Bynea

Brynlliw

*Llandeilo
Junc.*

Llandeilo
Junc. Yard

Gorseinon

Gowerton

A

C

1   2

0   5   10 m.   (1:350,000)
0   5   10   15 km.

26

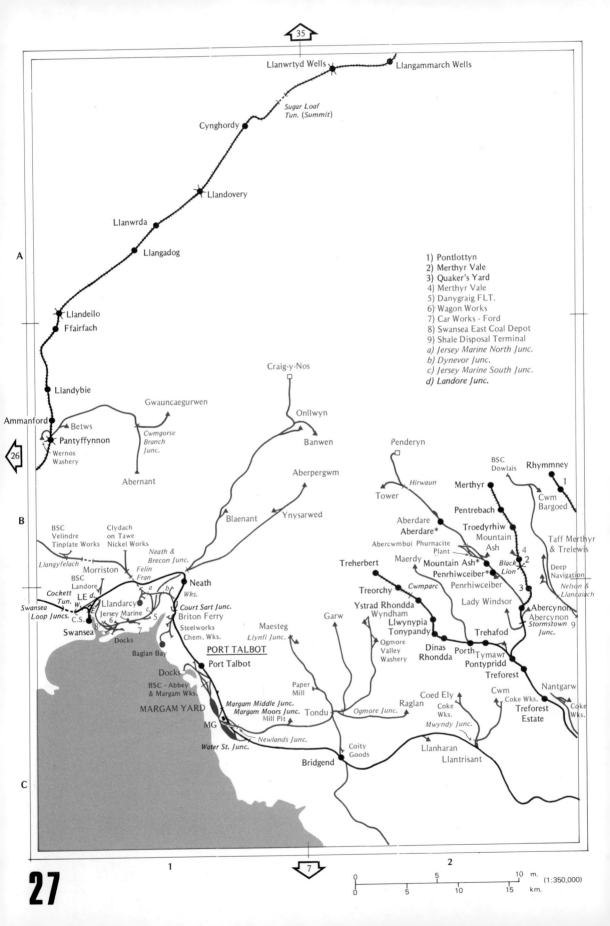

Llanwrtyd Wells
Llangammarch Wells

Sugar Loaf Tun. (Summit)

Cynghordy

Llandovery

Llanwrda

Llangadog

A

Llandeilo
Ffairfach

Llandybie

Gwauncaegurwen

Craig-y-Nos

Ammanford

Betws
Pantyffynnon
Wernos Washery

26

Onllwyn

Banwen

Cwmgorse Branch Junc.

Abernant

Aberpergwm

Penderyn

1) Pontlottyn
2) Merthyr Vale
3) Quaker's Yard
4) Merthyr Vale
5) Danygraig FLT.
6) Wagon Works
7) Car Works - Ford
8) Swansea East Coal Depot
9) Shale Disposal Terminal
a) *Jersey Marine North Junc.*
b) *Dynevor Junc.*
c) *Jersey Marine South Junc.*
d) *Landore Junc.*

BSC Dowlais
Rhymmney

Merthyr
Pentrebach

1

Cwm Bargoed

B

BSC Velindre Tinplate Works
Clydach on Tawe Nickel Works

Llangyfelach

Neath & Brecon Junc.
Morriston
Felin Fran
BSC Landore
Cockett Tun.
LE d.
W.
Swansea Loop Juncs.
C.S.
Swansea
a
b
Neath Wks.
Llandarcy
Jersey Marine
c
5
Court Sart Junc.
Briton Ferry
Steelworks
Chem. Wks.
8
6
7
Docks
Baglan Bay

Blaenant

Ynysarwed

Tower
Hirwaun

Aberdare
Aberdare*
Abercwmboi Phurnacite Plant

Treherbert

Maerdy

Troedyrhiw
Mountain Ash
Mountain Ash*
Black Lion
4
2
Penrhiwceiber*

Treorchy
Cwmparc
Penrhiwceiber
3

Ystrad Rhondda
Wyndham
Llwynypia
Tonypandy
Dinas Rhondda
Garw

Lady Windsor

Trehafod
Porth

Tymawr

Abercynon
Abercynon
Stormstown Junc.

Taff Merthyr & Trelewis

Deep Navigation
Nelson & Llancaiach

9

Maesteg
Llynfi Junc.

Ogmore Valley Washery

PORT TALBOT

Docks
BSC - Abbey & Margam Wks.

MARGAM YARD

MG

Margam Middle Junc.
Margam Moors Junc.
Mill Pit
Water St. Junc.

Port Talbot

Paper Mill

Tondu

Ogmore Junc.

Raglan

Coed Ely
Coke Wks.

Mwyndy Junc.

Pontypridd
Treforest

Cwm
Coke Wks.

Nantgarw

Treforest Estate
Coke Wks.

Newlands Junc.

Coity Goods

Bridgend

Llanharan
Llantrisant

C

27

1

7

2

0   5   10 m.
0   5   10 15 km.
(1:350,000)

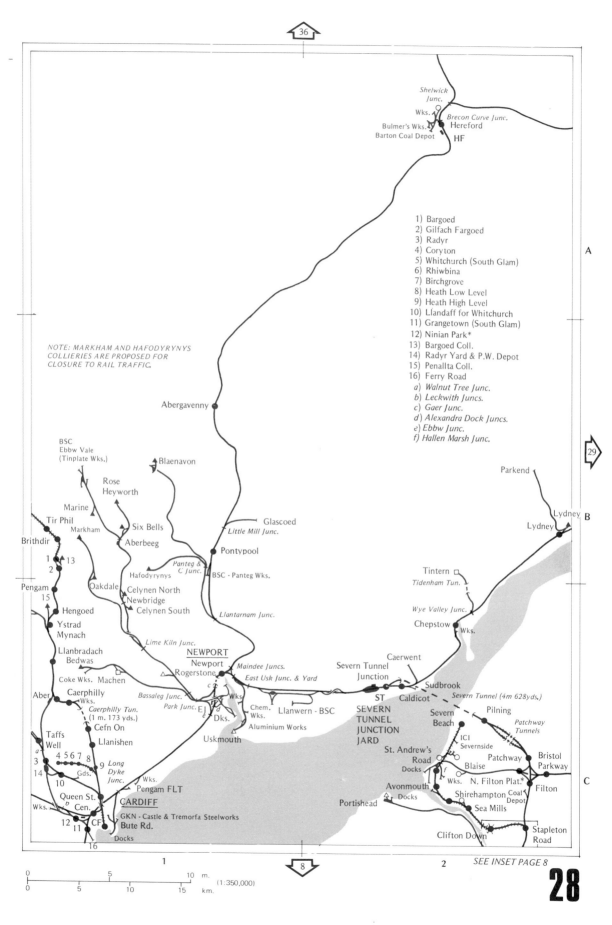

Shelwick Junc.

Wks.
Bulmer's Wks.
Barton Coal Depot
Brecon Curve Junc.
Hereford
HF

A

1) Bargoed
2) Gilfach Fargoed
3) Radyr
4) Coryton
5) Whitchurch (South Glam)
6) Rhiwbina
7) Birchgrove
8) Heath Low Level
9) Heath High Level
10) Llandaff for Whitchurch
11) Grangetown (South Glam)
12) Ninian Park*
13) Bargoed Coll.
14) Radyr Yard & P.W. Depot
15) Penallta Coll.
16) Ferry Road
a) Walnut Tree Junc.
b) Leckwith Juncs.
c) Gaer Junc.
d) Alexandra Dock Juncs.
e) Ebbw Junc.
f) Hallen Marsh Junc.

NOTE: MARKHAM AND HAFODYRYNYS
COLLIERIES ARE PROPOSED FOR
CLOSURE TO RAIL TRAFFIC.

Abergavenny

29

BSC
Ebbw Vale
(Tinplate Wks.)
Blaenavon
Parkend

Rose
Heyworth
Lydney
Marine
Lydney B
Tir Phil
Markham
Six Bells
Glascoed
Brithdir
Aberbeeg
Little Mill Junc.
Pontypool
1 13
Panteg &
C Junc.
Tintern
2
Hafodyrynys
BSC - Panteg Wks.
Tidenham Tun.
Pengam
15
Oakdale
Celynen North
Newbridge
Hengoed
Celynen South
Wye Valley Junc.
Ystrad
Llantarnam Junc.
Chepstow   Wks.
Mynach
Llanbradach
Lime Kiln Junc.
Bedwas
NEWPORT
Coke Wks. Machen
Newport
Maindee Juncs.
Severn Tunnel
Caerwent
Aber
Rogerstone
East Usk Junc. & Yard
Junction
Caerphilly
Bassaleg Junc.
c
Sudbrook
Wks.
Park Junc. E
Wks.
ST
Caldicot
Severn Tunnel (4m 628yds.)
Caerphilly Tun.
d
SEVERN
(1 m. 173 yds.)
Chem.
Llanwern - BSC
TUNNEL
Pilning
Cefn On
e
Dks.
Wks.
JUNCTION
Patchway
Taffs
Llanishen
Aluminium Works
JARD
Severn
Tunnels
Well
Uskmouth
Beach
ICI
a
4 5 6 7
8
St. Andrew's
Severnside
Patchway
Bristol
3
9 Long
Road
Parkway
14
Dyke Junc.
Blaise
10
Gds.
Wks.
Docks
f
Wks. N. Filton Plat.*
Filton
Queen St.
Pengam FLT
Avonmouth
Coal
b
Cen.
Shirehampton
Depot
Wks. 12 11 CF
CARDIFF
GKN - Castle & Tremorfa Steelworks
Docks
Sea Mills
16
Bute Rd.
Portishead
Clifton Down
Stapleton
Docks
Road

0   5   10 m.
0   5   10   15 km.   (1:350,000)

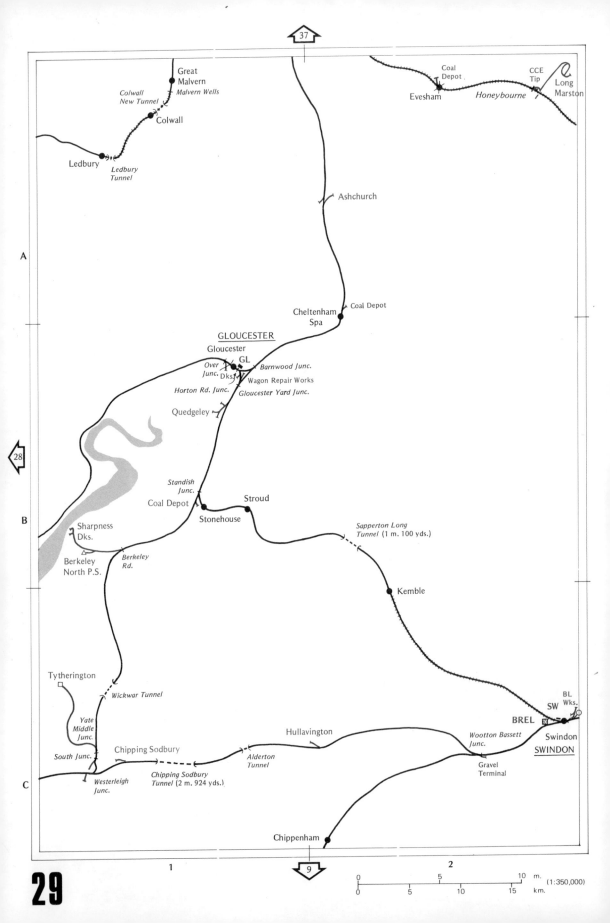

Great
Malvern
*Colwall
New Tunnel*
Malvern Wells
Colwall
Ledbury
*Ledbury
Tunnel*

Coal
Depot
CCE
Tip
Evesham
Honeybourne
Long
Marston

Ashchurch

A

Cheltenham
Spa
Coal Depot

GLOUCESTER
Gloucester
GL
*Over
Junc.*
Dks.
Barnwood Junc.
Wagon Repair Works
Horton Rd. Junc.
Gloucester Yard Junc.
Quedgeley

28

*Standish
Junc.*
Coal Depot
Stroud
Stonehouse
*Sapperton Long
Tunnel (1 m. 100 yds.)*

B

Sharpness
Dks.
Berkeley
North P.S.
*Berkeley
Rd.*

Kemble

Tytherington
Wickwar Tunnel

BL
Wks.
SW
BREL
Swindon
SWINDON

*Yate
Middle
Junc.*
Hullavington
*Wootton Bassett
Junc.*

South Junc.
Chipping Sodbury
*Alderton
Tunnel*
Gravel
Terminal

C
*Westerleigh
Junc.*
*Chipping Sodbury
Tunnel (2 m. 924 yds.)*

Chippenham

0   5   10 m.   (1:350,000)
0   5   10   15 km.

29

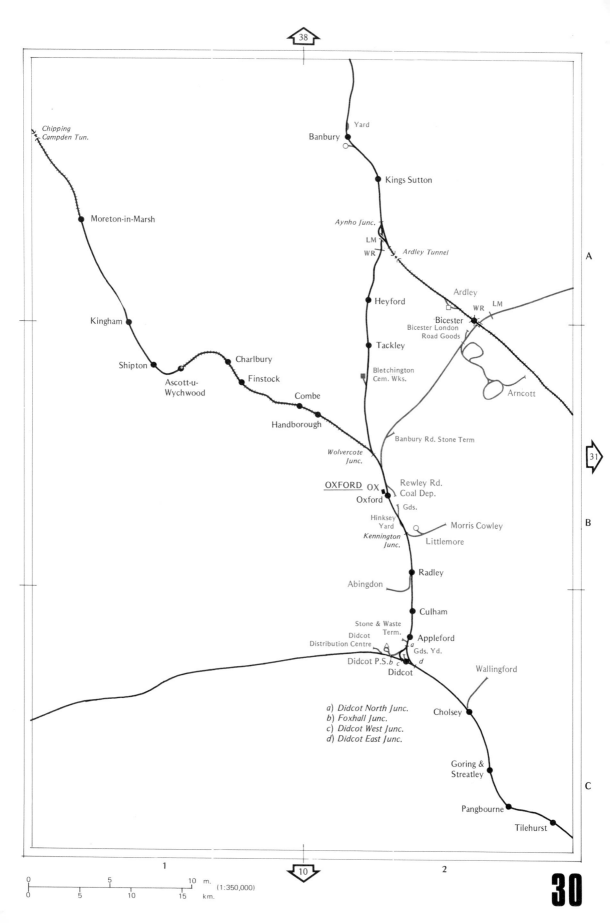

Chipping Campden Tun.

Moreton-in-Marsh

Kingham

Shipton

Ascott-u-Wychwood

Charlbury

Finstock

Combe

Handborough

Banbury

Yard

Kings Sutton

Aynho Junc.

LM

WR

Ardley Tunnel

Heyford

Ardley

WR LM

Bicester

Bicester London Road Goods

Tackley

Bletchington Cem. Wks.

Arncott

Banbury Rd. Stone Term

Wolvercote Junc.

OXFORD OX

Rewley Rd. Coal Dep.

Oxford

Gds.

Hinksey Yard

Kennington Junc.

Morris Cowley

Littlemore

Radley

Abingdon

Culham

Stone & Waste Term.

Didcot Distribution Centre

Appleford

Gds. Yd.

Didcot P.S.

Didcot

Wallingford

Cholsey

a) *Didcot North Junc.*
b) *Foxhall Junc.*
c) *Didcot West Junc.*
d) *Didcot East Junc.*

Goring & Streatley

Pangbourne

Tilehurst

A

B

C

1

2

0   5   10 m.
0   5   10   15   km.
(1:350,000)

30

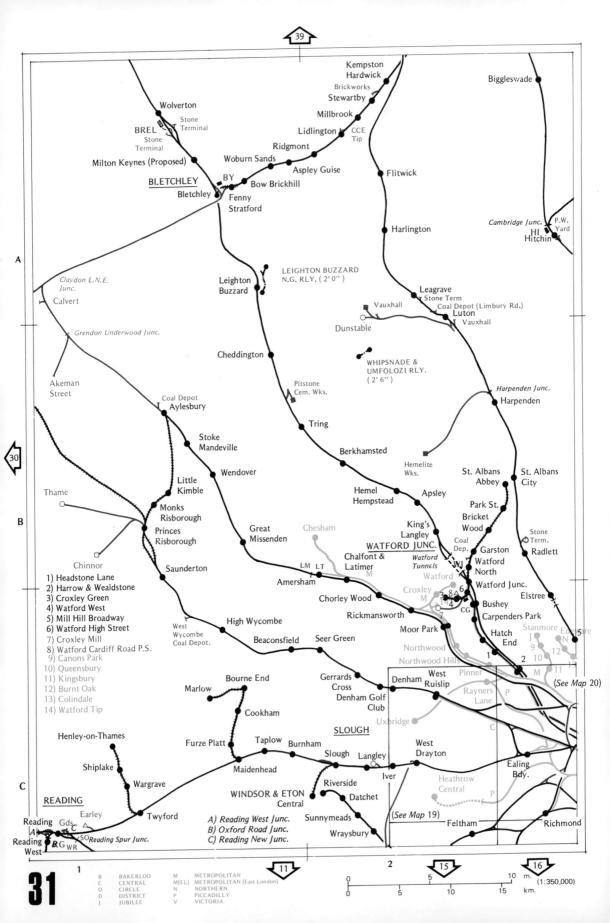

Biggleswade

Kempston
Hardwick
Brickworks
Stewartby
Millbrook
Lidlington
CCE
Tip
Ridgmont
Woburn Sands
Aspley Guise
Bow Brickhill
Flitwick

Wolverton
Stone
Terminal
BREL
Stone
Terminal
Milton Keynes (Proposed)
BLETCHLEY
BY
Bletchley
Fenny
Stratford

Harlington

Cambridge Junc. P.W. Yard
HI
Hitchin

Claydon L.N.E. Junc.
Calvert

LEIGHTON BUZZARD
N.G. RLY. (2' 0")
Leighton
Buzzard

Leagrave
Stone Term
Coal Depot (Limbury Rd.)
Luton
Vauxhall

Vauxhall

Dunstable

Grendon Underwood Junc.

Akeman
Street

Cheddington

Pitstone
Cem. Wks.

WHIPSNADE &
UMFOLOZI RLY.
(2' 6")

Harpenden Junc.
Harpenden

Coal Depot
Aylesbury

Stoke
Mandeville

Wendover

Tring

Berkhamsted

Hemelite
Wks.

St. Albans
Abbey
St. Albans
City

Thame

Little
Kimble

Apsley

Stone
Term.
Radlett

Monks
Risborough
Princes
Risborough

Great
Missenden

Hemel
Hempstead

King's
Langley
WATFORD JUNC.
Coal
Dep.
Watford
Tunnels
WJ

Park St.
Bricket
Wood

Garston
Watford
North

Chinnor

Saunderton

Chesham

Chalfont &
Latimer
LM LT
M
Amersham

Croxley
M

Watford

Watford Junc.
Elstree

1) Headstone Lane
2) Harrow & Wealdstone
3) Croxley Green
4) Watford West
5) Mill Hill Broadway
6) Watford High Street
7) Croxley Mill
8) Watford Cardiff Road P.S.
9) Canons Park
10) Queensbury
11) Kingsbury
12) Burnt Oak
13) Colindale
14) Watford Tip

West
Wycombe
Coal Depot.

High Wycombe

Beaconsfield

Seer Green

Chorley Wood

Rickmansworth

Moor Park

3 8 6
1 4
7
CG

6
Bushey
Carpenders Park

Hatch
End

Stanmore
J
Edgware
N

Northwood
Northwood Hills

1

2
9
M
10 12
11
(See Map 20)

Marlow

Bourne End

Cookham

Gerrards
Cross
Denham Golf
Club

Denham
West
Ruislip
Pinner

Rayners
Lane
P

M

Henley-on-Thames

Furze Platt

Taplow

Burnham

Uxbridge

SLOUGH

West
Drayton

Ealing
Bdy.

Heathrow
Central
P

C

Shiplake

Wargrave

Maidenhead

Slough
Langley
Iver

Twyford

WINDSOR & ETON
Central

Riverside
Datchet

READING
Earley
Gds.
Reading
A
C
Reading
West
B
G
SO
WR
Reading Spur Junc.

A) Reading West Junc.
B) Oxford Road Junc.
C) Reading New Junc.

Sunnymeads

Wraysbury

(See Map 19)
Feltham

Richmond

1

B   BAKERLOO   M   METROPOLITAN
C   CENTRAL   M(EL) METROPOLITAN (East London)
O   CIRCLE   N   NORTHERN
D   DISTRICT   P   PICCADILLY
J   JUBILEE   V   VICTORIA

2

0   5   10 m.
(1:350,000)
0   5   10   15 km.

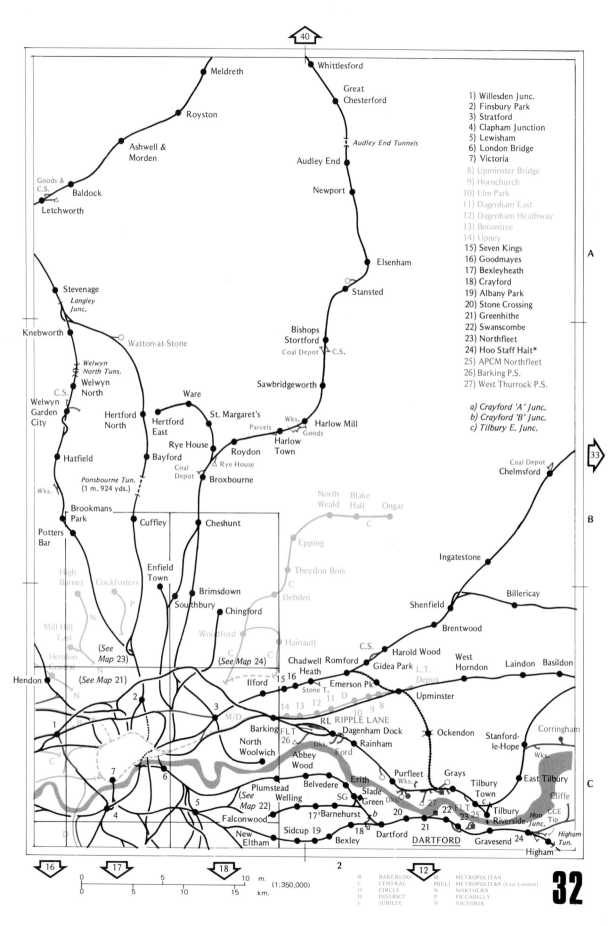

Meldreth

Whittlesford

Great
Chesterford

Royston

Audley End Tunnels

Ashwell &
Morden

Audley End

Goods &
C.S.

Baldock

Newport

Letchworth

1) Willesden Junc.
2) Finsbury Park
3) Stratford
4) Clapham Junction
5) Lewisham
6) London Bridge
7) Victoria
8) Upminster Bridge
9) Hornchurch
10) Elm Park
11) Dagenham East
12) Dagenham Heathway
13) Becontree
14) Upney
15) Seven Kings
16) Goodmayes
17) Bexleyheath
18) Crayford
19) Albany Park
20) Stone Crossing
21) Greenhithe
22) Swanscombe
23) Northfleet
24) Hoo Staff Halt*
25) APCM Northfleet
26) Barking P.S.
27) West Thurrock P.S.

a) Crayford 'A' Junc.
b) Crayford 'B' Junc.
c) Tilbury E. Junc.

Elsenham

Stansted

Stevenage

*Langley
Junc.*

A

Bishops
Stortford
Coal Depot   C.S.

Knebworth

Watton-at-Stone

*Welwyn
North Tuns.*

Sawbridgeworth

Welwyn
North

C.S.

Ware

Welwyn
Garden
City

Hertford
North

Hertford
East

St. Margaret's

Parcels

Wks.

Harlow Mill

Goods

Coal Depot
Chelmsford

Hatfield

Rye House

Roydon

Harlow
Town

33

Wks.

Bayford

Rye House

*Ponsbourne Tun.
(1 m. 924 yds.)*

Coal
Depot

Broxbourne

North
Weald

Blake
Hall

Ongar

B

Brookmans
Park

Cuffley

Cheshunt

C

Potters
Bar

Epping

Ingatestone

Theydon Bois

Enfield
Town

C

Debden

Billericay

High
Barnet

Cockfosters

Brimsdown

Shenfield

P

Southbury

Chingford

Woodford

Brentwood

N

Mill Hill
East

(See Map 23)

C

Hainault

C

C.S.

Harold Wood

West
Horndon

Laindon

Basildon

Hendon
Central

N

(See Map 21)

Chadwell
Heath

Romford

Gidea Park

L.T.
Depot

Hendon

N

Ilford

15 16

Stone T.

Emerson Pk

Upminster

2

14 13 12 11 D

10 9 8

3

M/D

RL RIPPLE LANE

Ockendon

Stanford-
le-Hope

Corringham

1

Barking

FLT
26

Dagenham Dock

Wks.

C

North
Woolwich

Dks.

Rainham

Ford

Purfleet

Grays

East Tilbury

7

6

Abbey
Wood

Belvedere

Erith

Wks.

Tilbury
Town

c

Cliffe

Plumstead

Slade

27

FLT

CCE
Tip

*(See
Map 22)*

Welling

SG

Green

Dks.

20

22

25

Tilbury
Riverside

*Hoo
Junc.*

5

17 Barnehurst

b

23

*Higham
Tun.*

4

Falconwood

a

21

New
Eltham

Sidcup 19

Bexley

18

Dartford

Gravesend 24

DARTFORD

Higham

B   BAKERLOO   M   METROPOLITAN
C   CENTRAL   M(EL) METROPOLITAN (East London)
O   CIRCLE   N   NORTHERN
D   DISTRICT   P   PICCADILLY
J   JUBILEE   V   VICTORIA

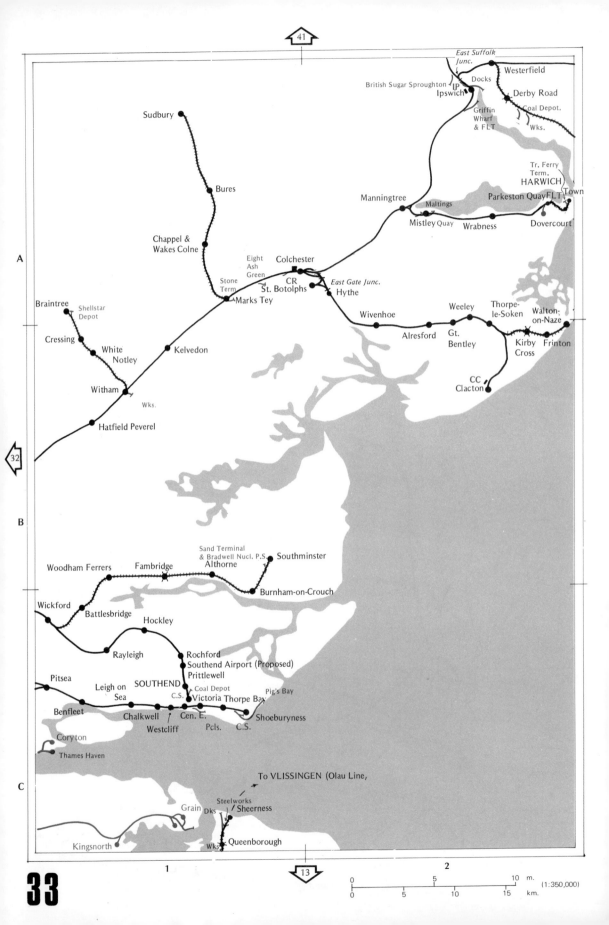

Sudbury

Bures

Chappel &
Wakes Colne

*East Suffolk
Junc.*

British Sugar Sproughton   IP   Docks   Westerfield
Ipswich   Derby Road
                                Coal Depot.
Griffin
Wharf
& FLT   Wks.

Tr. Ferry
Term.
HARWICH

Manningtree   Parkeston Quay FLT   Town

Maltings   Dovercourt
Mistley Quay   Wrabness

Eight
Ash
Green   Colchester

Stone
Term.   CR
                St. Botolphs
A   *East Gate Junc.*
                Hythe
Marks Tey

Weeley   Thorpe-
                le-Soken   Walton-
Wivenhoe   on-Naze

Braintree   Shellstar
            Depot   Alresford   Gt.   Kirby   Frinton
                                          Bentley   Cross
Cressing
          White   CC
          Notley   Kelvedon   Clacton
Witham
            Wks.

Hatfield Peverel

32

B

Sand Terminal
& Bradwell Nucl. P.S.   Southminster
Woodham Ferrers   Fambridge   Althorne

                                Burnham-on-Crouch
Wickford
          Battlesbridge   Hockley

          Rayleigh   Rochford
                        Southend Airport (Proposed)
                        Prittlewell
Pitsea   SOUTHEND
          Leigh on   C.S.   Coal Depot   Pig's Bay
          Sea   Victoria Thorpe Bay
Benfleet   Shoeburyness
          Chalkwell   Cen. E.   C.S.
Coryton   Westcliff   Pcls.

Thames Haven

C   To VLISSINGEN (Olau Line,

                    Steelworks
            Grain Dks Sheerness

Kingsnorth   Wks. Queenborough

33

1   13   2

0   5   10   m.
0   5   10   15   km.

(1:350,000)

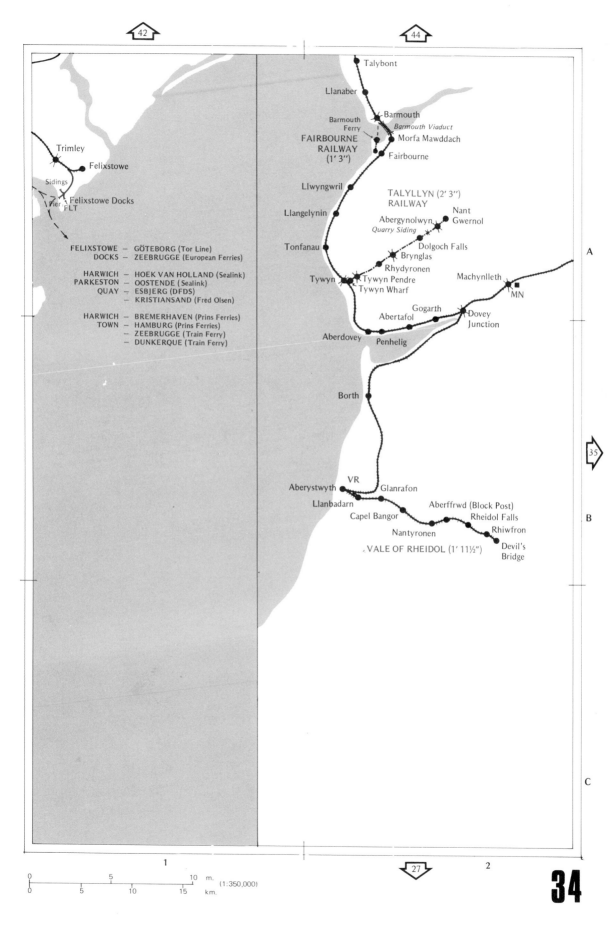

Talybont

Llanaber

Barmouth
Barmouth
Ferry
Barmouth Viaduct
FAIRBOURNE
RAILWAY
(1′ 3″)
Morfa Mawddach

Fairbourne

Llwyngwril

TALYLLYN (2′ 3″)
RAILWAY

Nant
Gwernol
Abergynolwyn
Quarry Siding

Llangelynin

Dolgoch Falls
Tonfanau
Brynglas

Rhydyronen
Machynlleth
Tywyn Pendre
Tywyn
Tywyn Wharf
MN

Gogarth
Abertafol
Dovey
Junction

Aberdovey
Penhelig

Trimley

Felixstowe

Sidings

FLT
Pier
Felixstowe Docks

FELIXSTOWE — GÖTEBORG (Tor Line)
DOCKS — ZEEBRUGGE (European Ferries)

HARWICH — HOEK VAN HOLLAND (Sealink)
PARKESTON — OOSTENDE (Sealink)
QUAY — ESBJERG (DFDS)
— KRISTIANSAND (Fred Olsen)

HARWICH — BREMERHAVEN (Prins Ferries)
TOWN — HAMBURG (Prins Ferries)
— ZEEBRUGGE (Train Ferry)
— DUNKERQUE (Train Ferry)

Borth

VR
Aberystwyth
Glanrafon

Llanbadarn
Aberffrwd (Block Post)
Capel Bangor
Rheidol Falls
Nantyronen
Rhiwfron

VALE OF RHEIDOL (1′ 11½″)
Devil's
Bridge

A

35

B

C

1

2

0   5   10 m.   (1:350,000)
0   5   10   15 km.

34

Barmouth
Barmouth Viaduct
Morfa Mawddach
Fairbourne

TALYLLYN
RAILWAY
(2' 3'')

Nant Gwernol
Dolgoch
Falls
Abergynolwyn
Quarry Siding
Brynglas
Rhydyronen

Heniarth
Llanfair Caereinion

A

Machynlleth
MN

Talerddig

Gogarth
Abertafol
Dovey Junction

Penhelig

Caersws
Newtown

Borth

34

Glanrafon
Aberffrwd
(Block Post)
Rheidol Falls
Capel
Bangor
Rhiwfron
Nantyronen
Devil's Bridge

VALE OF RHEIDOL
(1' 11½'')

B

Penybont

Llandrindod
Wells

C

Builth Road

Garth
Cilmery

1

44

27

2

0   5   10 m.   (1:350,000)
0   5   10   15 km.

35

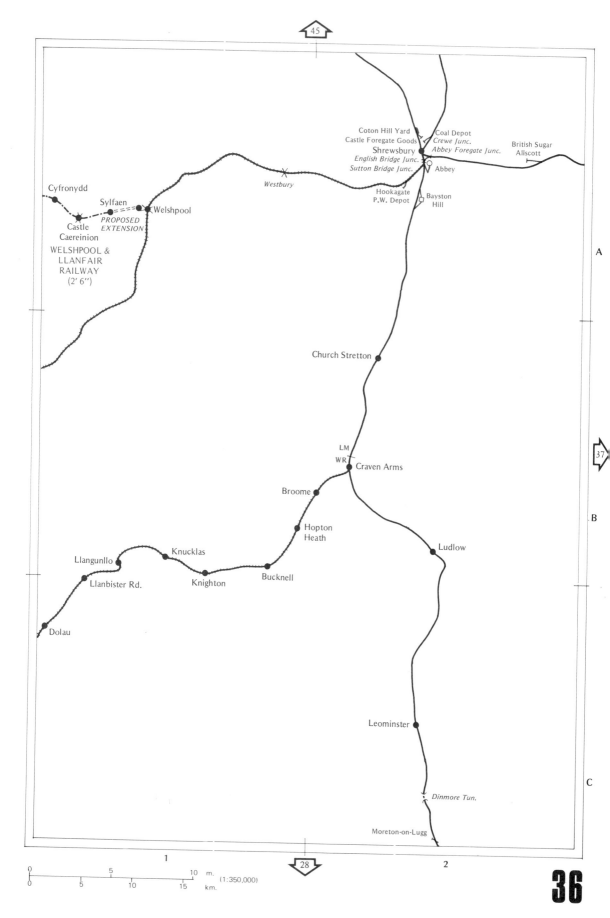

Cyfronydd

Sylfaen
Welshpool
Castle
Caereinion
PROPOSED
EXTENSION

WELSHPOOL &
LLANFAIR
RAILWAY
(2' 6'')

Westbury

Coton Hill Yard
Castle Foregate Goods
Shrewsbury
English Bridge Junc.
Sutton Bridge Junc.

Coal Depot
Crewe Junc.
Abbey Foregate Junc.

British Sugar
Allscott

Abbey

Hookagate
P.W. Depot

Bayston
Hill

A

Church Stretton

37

LM
WR
Craven Arms

Broome

B

Hopton
Heath

Ludlow

Knucklas

Llangunllo

Knighton
Bucknell

Llanbister Rd.

Dolau

Leominster

C

Dinmore Tun.

Moreton-on-Lugg

1   2

0   5   10   m. (1:350,000)
0   5   10   15   km.

36

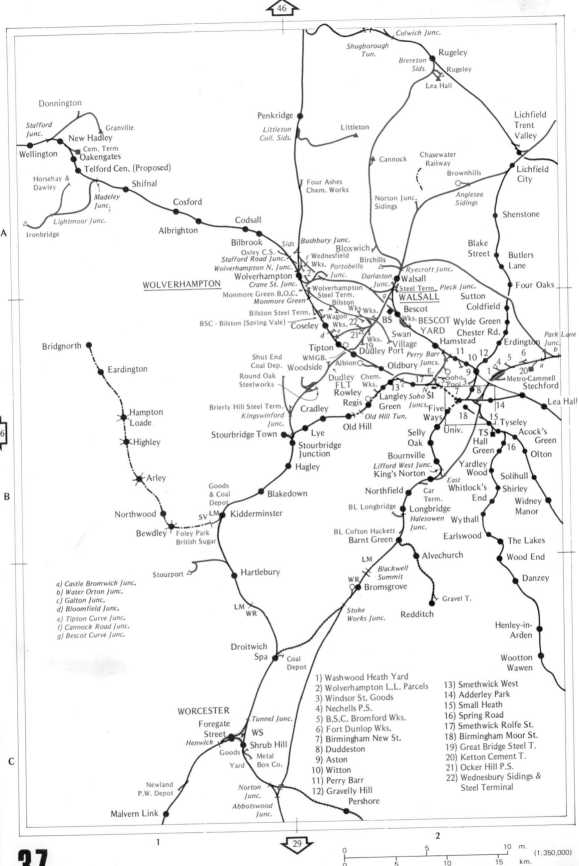

Colwich Junc.
Shugborough Tun.
Rugeley
Brereton Sids.
Rugeley
Lea Hall

Penkridge
Littleton Coll. Sids.
Littleton
Cannock
Chasewater Railway
Brownhills
Lichfield Trent Valley
Lichfield City

Donnington
Stafford Junc.
New Hadley
Granville
Wellington
Cem. Term
Oakengates
Telford Cen. (Proposed)
Horsehay & Dawley
Shifnal
Madeley Junc.
Lightmoor Junc.
Ironbridge
Cosford
Albrighton
Codsall

Four Ashes Chem. Works
Norton Junc. Sidings
Anglesea Sidings
Shenstone
Blake Street
Butlers Lane
Four Oaks

Bilbrook
Sids
Bushbury Junc.
Oxley C.S.
Stafford Road Junc.
Wolverhampton N. Junc.
WOLVERHAMPTON
Wolverhampton
Crane St. Junc.
Monmore Green B.O.C.
Monmore Green
Bilston Steel Term.
BSC - Bilston (Spring Vale)
Coseley
Wednesfield Wks.
Bloxwich
Birchills
Portobello Junc.
Wednesfield
Darlaston Junc.
Wolverhampton Steel Term.
Bilston
Wks Wks.
Wagon Wks.
19
22
21
BS
Walsall
Ryecroft Junc.
Walsall
Steel Term.
Pleck Junc.
WALSALL
Bescot
Wks.
BESCOT YARD
Sutton Coldfield
Wylde Green
Chester Rd.
Hamstead
Erdington
Park Lane Junc.

Bridgnorth
Eardington
Hampton Loade
Highley
Arley
Northwood
Bewdley
Tipton
WMGB.
Shut End Coal Dep.
Woodside
Albion
Dudley Port
Swan Village
Oldbury
Perry Barr Juncs.
E.
Soho Pool
Soho Juncs.
Metro-Cammell
Stechford
11
10 12
9
1 4
5
20
6
a
b

Round Oak Steelworks
Dudley FLT
Rowley Regis
Cradley
Brierly Hill Steel Term.
Kingswinford Junc.
Stourbridge Town
Lye
Stourbridge Junction
Hagley
Blakedown
Goods & Coal Depot
Kidderminster
Foley Park British Sugar
Chem. Wks.
Langley Green
Old Hill
Old Hill Tun.
13
17
N
7
8
14
15
16
Five Ways
Univ.
18
Lea Hall
Tyseley
TS
Acock's Green
Olton

Stourport
Hartlebury
Selly Oak
Bournville
Lifford West Junc.
King's Norton
Northfield
BL Longbridge
Longbridge
Halesowen Junc.
BL Cofton Hackett
Barnt Green
Hall Green
Yardley Wood
East Whitlock's End
Car Term.
Wythall
Earlswood
Solihull
Shirley
Widney Manor
The Lakes
Wood End
Danzey

a) Castle Bromwich Junc.
b) Water Orton Junc.
c) Galton Junc.
d) Bloomfield Junc.
e) Tipton Curve Junc.
f) Cannock Road Junc.
g) Bescot Curve Junc.

Stourport
Blackwell Summit
Alvechurch
LM
WR
Bromsgrove
Gravel T.
Stoke Works Junc.
Redditch
Henley-in-Arden
Wootton Wawen

LM
WR
Droitwich Spa
Coal Depot

WORCESTER
Foregate Street
Henwick
WS
Shrub Hill
Goods Yard
Metal Box Co.
Tunnel Junc.
Newland P.W. Depot
Norton Junc.
Abbotswood Junc.
Malvern Link
Pershore

1) Washwood Heath Yard
2) Wolverhampton L.L. Parcels
3) Windsor St. Goods
4) Nechells P.S.
5) B.S.C. Bromford Wks.
6) Fort Dunlop Wks.
7) Birmingham New St.
8) Duddeston
9) Aston
10) Witton
11) Perry Barr
12) Gravelly Hill

13) Smethwick West
14) Adderley Park
15) Small Heath
16) Spring Road
17) Smethwick Rolfe St.
18) Birmingham Moor St.
19) Great Bridge Steel T.
20) Ketton Cement T.
21) Ocker Hill P.S.
22) Wednesbury Sidings & Steel Terminal

1   2

0   5   10 m.
0   5   10   15 km.
(1:350,000)

37

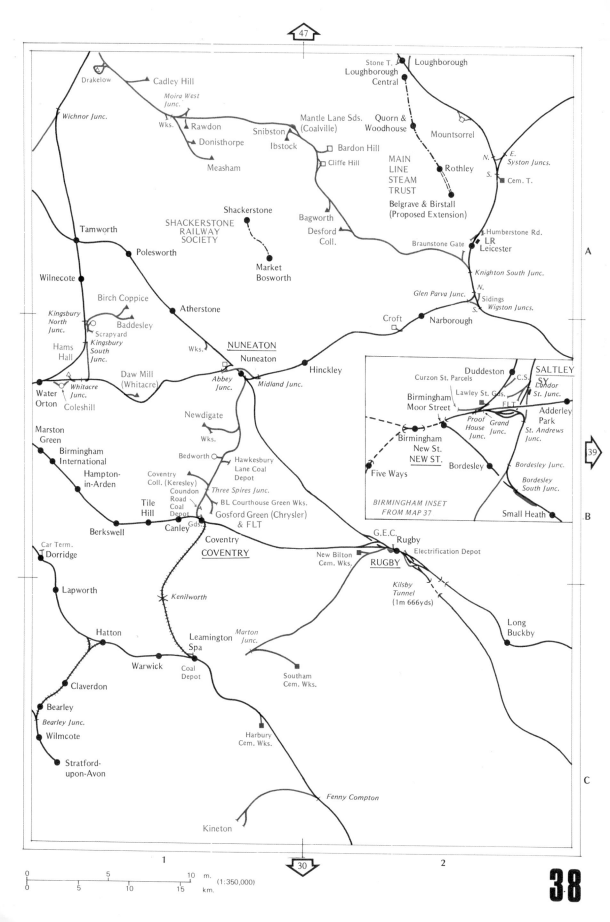

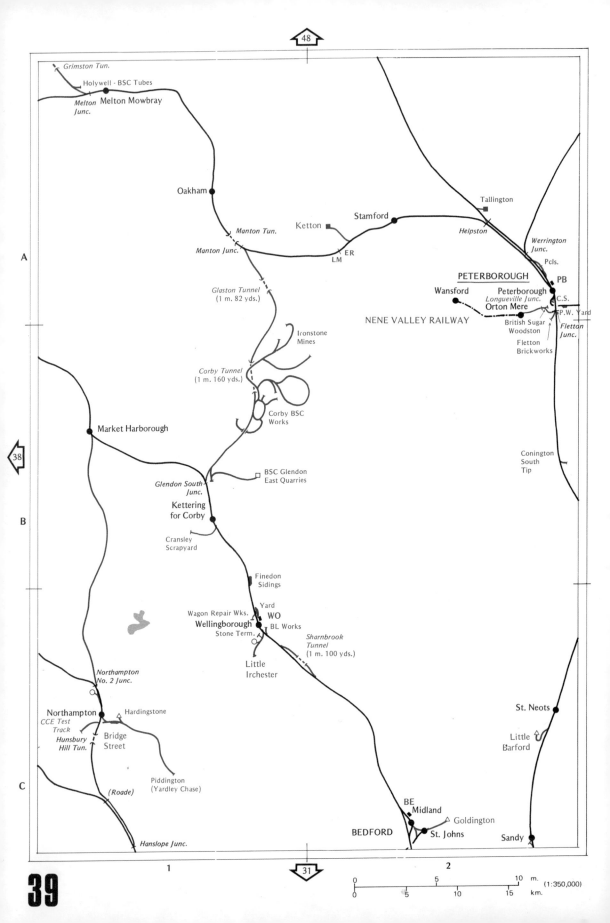

Grimston Tun.
Holywell - BSC Tubes
Melton Melton Mowbray
Junc.

Oakham

Manton Tun.

Ketton   Stamford

Manton Junc.

Tallington

Helpston

Werrington Junc.

Pcls.

PETERBOROUGH   PB

Glaston Tunnel
(1 m. 82 yds.)

Wansford   Peterborough   C.S.
Longueville Junc.   P.W. Yard
Orton Mere

NENE VALLEY RAILWAY

British Sugar
Woodston   *Fletton Junc.*

Fletton
Brickworks

Ironstone
Mines

Corby Tunnel
(1 m. 160 yds.)

Corby BSC
Works

Market Harborough

BSC Glendon
East Quarries

Conington
South
Tip

*Glendon South
Junc.*

Kettering
for Corby

Cransley
Scrapyard

Finedon
Sidings

Yard
Wagon Repair Wks.   WO
Wellingborough   BL Works
Stone Term.

*Sharnbrook
Tunnel*
(1 m. 100 yds.)

Little
Irchester

St. Neots

*Northampton
No. 2 Junc.*

Little
Barford

Northampton   Hardingstone
*CCE Test
Track*
*Hunsbury   Bridge
Hill Tun.*   Street

Piddington
(Yardley Chase)

BE
Midland   Goldington

BEDFORD   St. Johns   Sandy

(Roade)

Hanslope Junc.

0   5   10 m.
(1:350,000)
0   5   10   15   km.

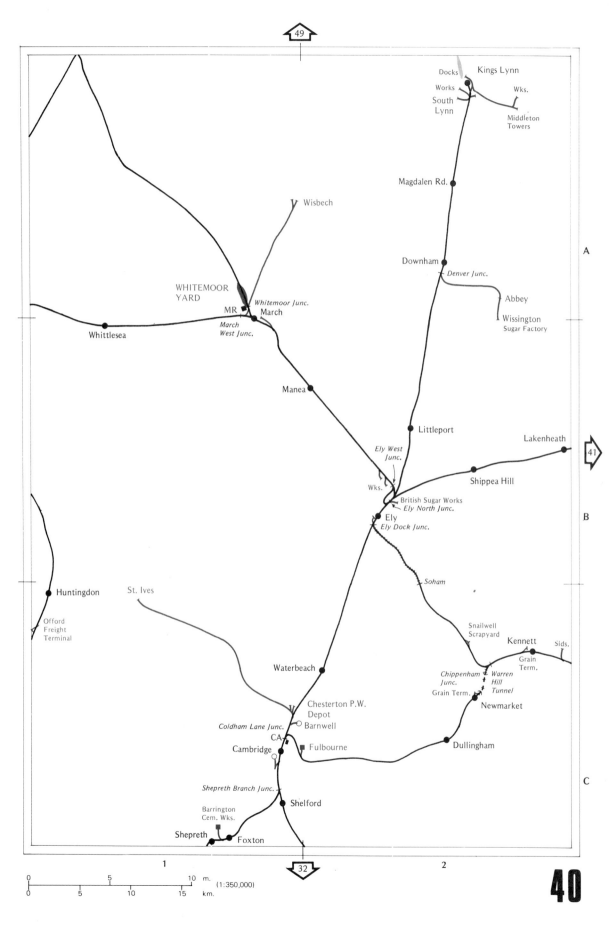

Docks
Kings Lynn
Works
Wks.
South
Lynn
Middleton
Towers

Magdalen Rd.

Downham
Denver Junc.
Abbey
Wissington
Sugar Factory

A

Wisbech

WHITEMOOR
YARD
MR *Whitemoor Junc.*
March
*March
West Junc.*
Whittlesea

Manea

Littleport

Lakenheath

*Ely West
Junc.*
Wks.
Shippea Hill
British Sugar Works
Ely North Junc.
Ely
Ely Dock Junc.

B

St. Ives

Soham

Huntingdon

Offord
Freight
Terminal

Snailwell
Scrapyard
Kennett
Sids.
Grain
Term.

Waterbeach
*Chippenham
Junc.*
*Warren
Hill
Tunnel*
Grain Term.
Newmarket

Chesterton P.W.
Depot
Coldham Lane Junc.
Barnwell
CA
Cambridge
Fulbourne
Dullingham

C

Shepreth Branch Junc.
Shelford

Barrington
Cem. Wks.
Shepreth
Foxton

0   5   10 m.   (1:350,000)
0   5   10   15 km.

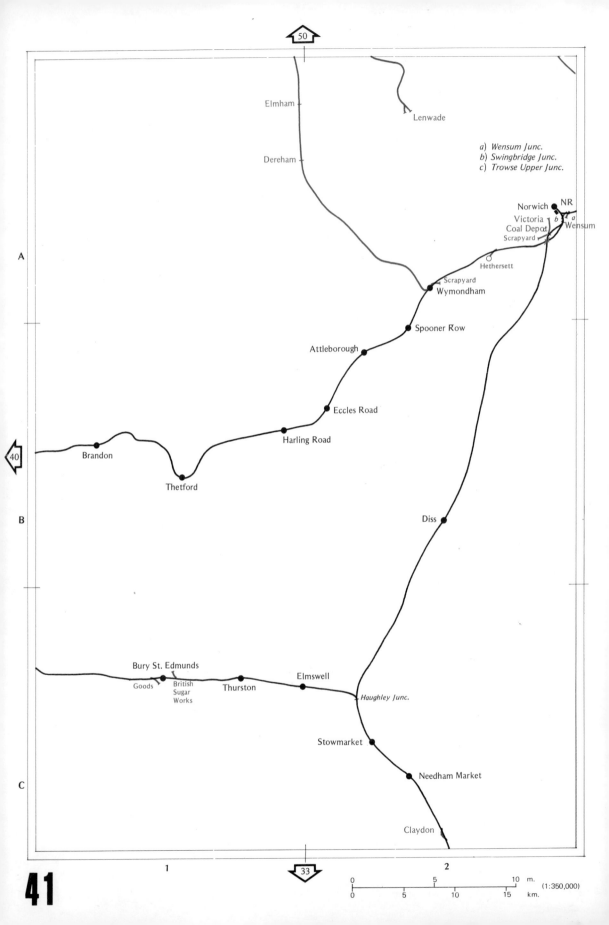

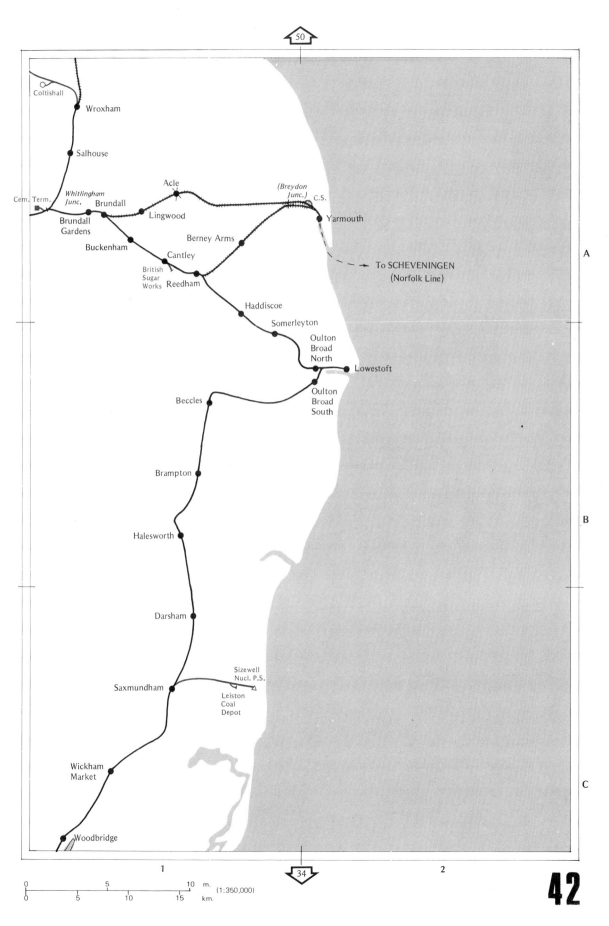

Coltishall

Wroxham

Salhouse

Cem. Term. *Whitlingham Junc.* Brundall

Acle

(Breydon Junc.) C.S.

Brundall Gardens

Lingwood

Yarmouth

Berney Arms

Buckenham

Cantley

To SCHEVENINGEN
(Norfolk Line)

British Sugar Works Reedham

A

Haddiscoe

Somerleyton

Oulton Broad North

Lowestoft

Beccles

Oulton Broad South

Brampton

B

Halesworth

Darsham

Sizewell Nucl. P.S.

Saxmundham

Leiston Coal Depot

C

Wickham Market

Woodbridge

1

2

0   5   10 m.   (1:350,000)
0   5   10   15 km.

42

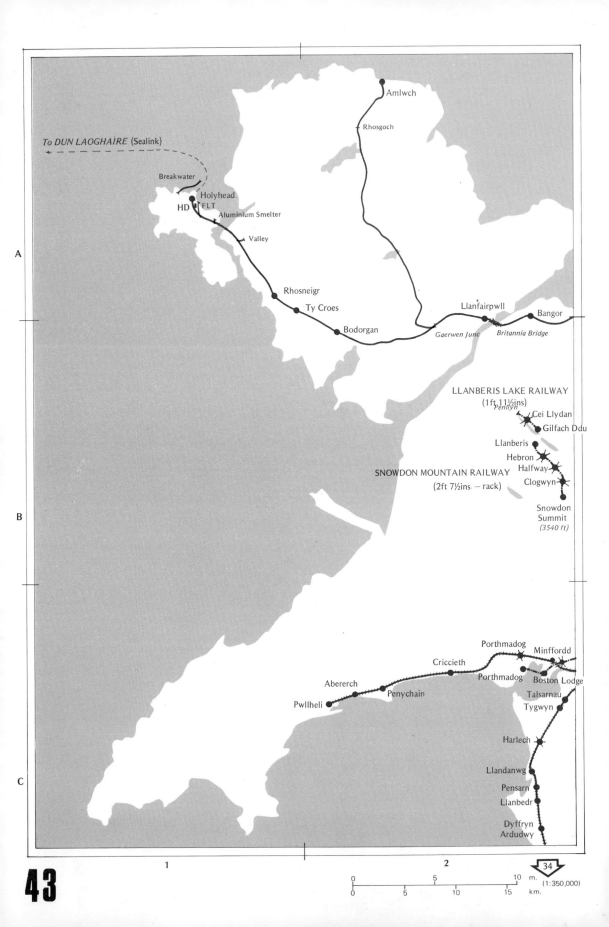

To DUN LAOGHAIRE (Sealink)

Amlwch

Rhosgoch

Breakwater
Holyhead
HD FLT
Aluminium Smelter

Valley

Rhosneigr

Ty Croes

Bodorgan

Llanfairpwll

Gaerwen Junc

Britannia Bridge

Bangor

LLANBERIS LAKE RAILWAY
(1ft 11½ins)

Penllyn

Cei Llydan

Gilfach Ddu

Llanberis

SNOWDON MOUNTAIN RAILWAY

(2ft 7½ins — rack)

Hebron
Halfway
Clogwyn

Snowdon
Summit
(3540 ft)

Porthmadog

Minffordd

Criccieth

Porthmadog

Boston Lodge

Abererch

Penychain

Talsarnau

Tygwyn

Pwllheli

Harlech

Llandanwg

Pensarn

Llanbedr

Dyffryn
Ardudwy

A

B

C

1

2

34

0   5   10 m.
                      (1:350,000)
0   5   10   15 km.

43

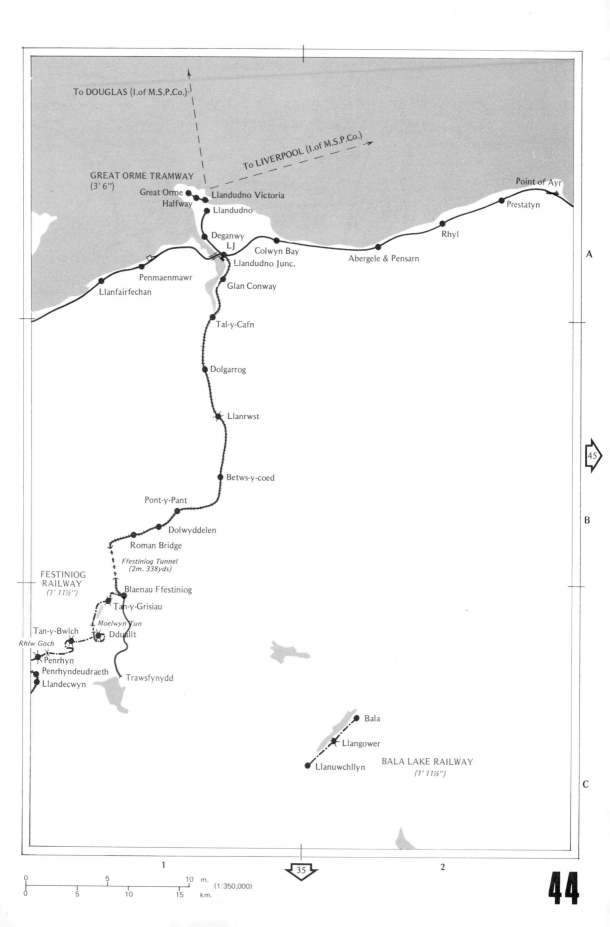

To DOUGLAS (I.of M.S.P.Co.)

To LIVERPOOL (I.of M.S.P.Co.)

Point of Ayr

GREAT ORME TRAMWAY
(3' 6")

Prestatyn

Great Orme
Halfway

Llandudno Victoria

Llandudno

Rhyl

Deganwy

LJ

Colwyn Bay

Abergele & Pensarn

Penmaenmawr

Llandudno Junc.

Llanfairfechan

Glan Conway

A

Tal-y-Cafn

Dolgarrog

Llanrwst

45

Betws-y-coed

B

Pont-y-Pant

Dolwyddelen

Roman Bridge

Ffestiniog Tunnel
(2m. 338yds)

FESTINIOG
RAILWAY
(1' 11½")

Blaenau Ffestiniog

Tan-y-Grisiau

Moelwyn Tun

Tan-y-Bwlch

Dduallt

Rhiw Goch

Penrhyn

Penrhyndeudraeth

Trawsfynydd

Llandecwyn

Bala

Llangower

Llanuwchllyn

BALA LAKE RAILWAY
(1' 11½")

C

1

35

2

0   5   10   m.   (1:350,000)
0   5   10   15   km.

44

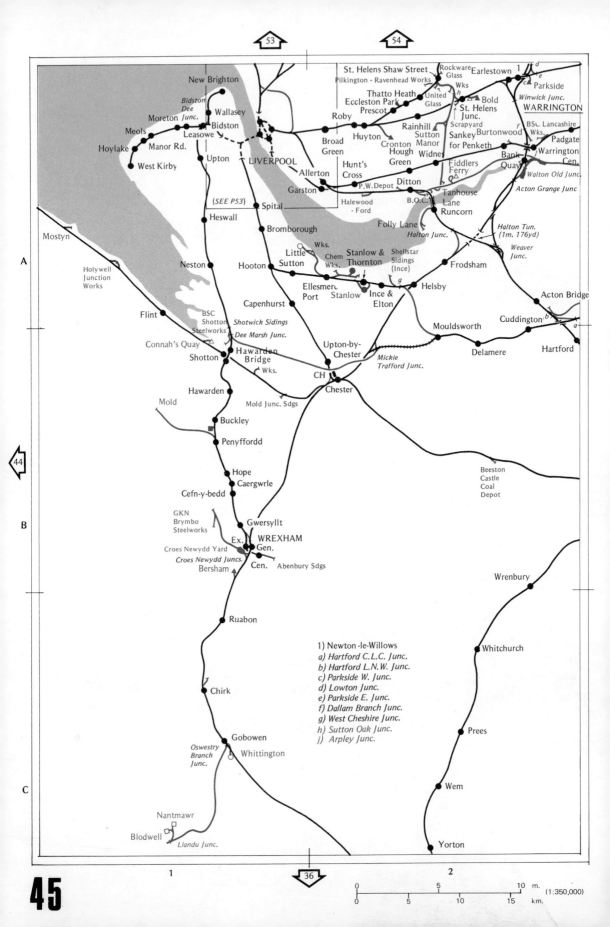

WARRINGTON

St. Helens Shaw Street
Pilkington - Ravenhead Works
Rockware Glass
Earlestown
Parkside
Winwick Junc.
Thatto Heath
Eccleston Park
Prescot
United Glass
Bold
St. Helens Junc.
Scrapyard
BSC Lancashire Wks.
Padgate
Roby
Rainhill
Sutton Manor
Sankey for Penketh
Burtonwood
Warrington Cen.
New Brighton
Bidston Dee Junc.
Wallasey
Moreton Junc.
Bidston
Leasowe
Upton
Broad Green
Huyton
Cronton
Hough Green
Widnes
Fiddlers Ferry
Bank Quay
Walton Old Junc.
Acton Grange Junc.
Meols
Manor Rd.
LIVERPOOL
Hunt's Cross
Ditton
Tanhouse Lane
Runcorn
Hoylake
West Kirby
Allerton
Garston
P.W. Depot
B.O.C.
Folly Lane
Halton Junc.
Halton Tun.
(1m. 176yd)
Weaver Junc.
(SEE P53)
Halewood - Ford
Spital
Heswall
Bromborough
Wks.
Chem Wks.
Stanlow & Thornton
Shellstar Sidings (Ince)
Frodsham
Mostyn
Little Sutton
Ellesmere Port
Stanlow
Ince & Elton
Helsby
Acton Bridge
Holywell Junction Works
Neston
Hooton
Cuddington
Hartford
Flint
Capenhurst
BSC Shotton Steelworks
Shotwick Sidings
Dee Marsh Junc.
Upton-by-Chester
Mouldsworth
Delamere
Connah's Quay
Shotton
Hawarden Bridge
Wks.
Mickle Trafford Junc.
CH
Chester
Hawarden
Mold
Mold Junc. Sdgs
Beeston Castle Coal Depot
Buckley
Penyffordd
Hope
Caergwrle
Cefn-y-bedd
GKN Brymbo Steelworks
Gwersyllt
WREXHAM
Ex.
Gen.
Cen.
Croes Newydd Yard
Croes Newydd Juncs.
Bersham
Abenbury Sdgs
Wrenbury
Ruabon
Whitchurch

1) Newton -le-Willows
a) Hartford C.L.C. Junc.
b) Hartford L.N.W. Junc.
c) Parkside W. Junc.
d) Lowton Junc.
e) Parkside E. Junc.
f) Dallam Branch Junc.
g) West Cheshire Junc.
h) Sutton Oak Junc.
j) Arpley Junc.

Chirk
Prees
Gobowen
Oswestry Branch Junc.
Whittington
Wem
Nantmawr
Blodwell
Llandu Junc.
Yorton

A

B

C

1   2

0   5   10 m.
0   5   10   15 km.
(1:350,000)

45

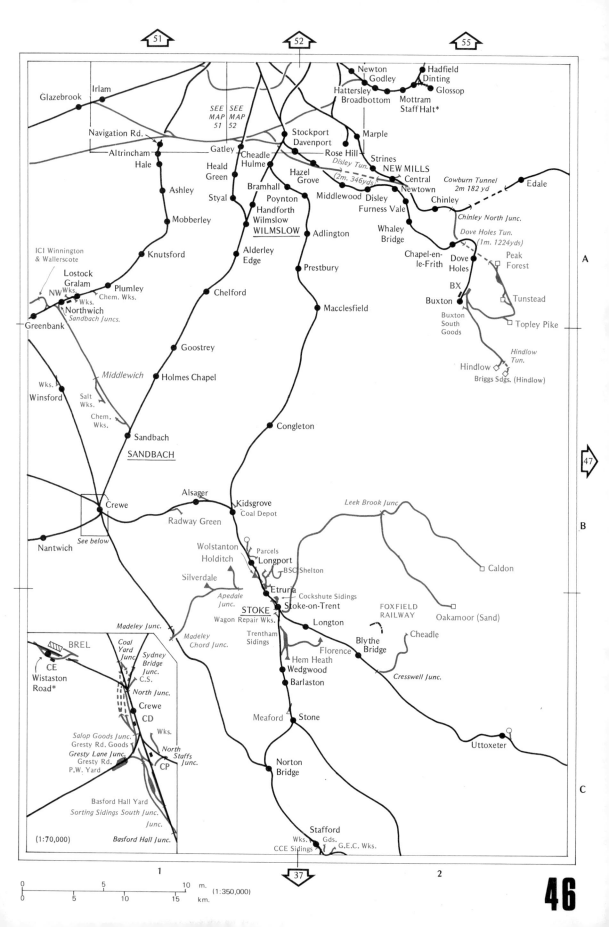

Glazebrook Irlam

Newton Hadfield
Godley Dinting
Hattersley Glossop
Broadbottom Mottram
Staff Halt*

SEE MAP 51 SEE MAP 52

Navigation Rd. Stockport
Davenport

Altrincham Gatley Marple
Hale Cheadle Hulme Rose Hill
Heald Green Strines

Ashley Hazel Grove Disley Tun. NEW MILLS
(2m. 346yds) Central
Styal Bramhall Newtown
Mobberley Poynton Middlewood Disley Cowburn Tunnel
Handforth 2m 182 yd Edale
Wilmslow Furness Vale
ICI Winnington WILMSLOW Adlington Chinley
& Wallerscote Whaley Chinley North Junc.
Alderley Bridge Dove Holes Tun.
Lostock Edge (1m. 1224yds)
Gralam Prestbury Chapel-en- Peak
NW Wks. le-Frith Dove Forest
Plumley Chelford Holes
Knutsford Chem. Wks. BX Tunstead
Northwich Macclesfield Buxton
Greenbank Sandbach Juncs. Topley Pike
Buxton
South
Goods
Goostrey Hindlow
Middlewich Tun.
Winsford Salt Holmes Chapel Hindlow
Wks. Briggs Sdgs. (Hindlow)
Chem.
Wks.
Congleton

Sandbach
SANDBACH

Alsager Leek Brook Junc
Crewe Kidsgrove
Coal Depot
Radway Green
Nantwich Caldon
See below Wolstanton Parcels
Holditch Longport
BSC Shelton
Silverdale FOXFIELD
Etruria RAILWAY
Apedale Cockshute Sidings Oakamoor (Sand)
Junc. STOKE Stoke-on-Trent
Madeley Junc. Wagon Repair Wks. Longton Cheadle
BREL Coal Madeley Trentham Blythe
Yard Chord Junc. Sidings Florence Bridge
CE Junc. Sydney Hem Heath Cresswell Junc.
Wistaston Bridge Wedgwood
Road* Junc. C.S. Barlaston
North Junc. Crewe
CD Meaford Stone
Salop Goods Junc. Wks. Uttoxeter
Gresty Rd. Goods North
Gresty Lane Junc. Staffs
Gresty Rd. Junc. Norton
P.W. Yard CP Bridge
Basford Hall Yard
Sorting Sidings South Junc. Stafford
Junc. Wks. Gds.
(1:70,000) Basford Hall Junc. CCE Sidings G.E.C. Wks.

0 5 10 m.
0 5 10 15 km.
(1:350,000)

1 2

Oughtibridge
Chapeltown
Rotherham
Thrybergh Junc.
Maltby Main
W. E. Firbeck Juncs.
S.
Harworth
Wadsley Bridge*
Brightside
Attercliffe
Sheffield
Darnall
TINSLEY YARD
Thurcroft
Glassworks
Earles Sidings
Hope
Bamford
Hathersage
Dore Station Junc.
Dore
LM
Woodhouse (See Map 50)
Dinnington Station Junc.
Dinnington
Dinnington Colliery Junc.
Kiveton Bridge
Kiveton Park
Brancliffe E. Junc.
Shireoaks Stn. Junc.
Shireoaks
Shireoaks E. Junc.
Worksop
Cem. Wks.
Totley Tun. (3m. 950yds)
Dore S. Junc.
Bradway Tun. (1m. 267yds)
Beighton Junc.
Kiveton Park
Steetley
Woodend Junc.
Manton Wood

A

Grindleford
Dore West Junc.
Renishaw Park
Foxlow Junc.
Westthorpe (Spink Hill)
Hall Lane Junc.
Whitwell
Whitwell Quarry
Elmton & Cresswell Junc.
BH
Seymour Junc.
Seymour
Markham
Bolsover
Cresswell
Welbeck
Scrapyard
Staveley BSC Wks.
Tapton Junc.
Glassworks
Chesterfield
Tube Wks.
ER
LM
Arkwright
Langwith
Warsop Main
Warsop Junc.
Wagon Works
Shirebrook Junc.
Shirebrook
SB
Thoresby
Ollerton
Clipstone Juncs.
Boughton Junc.
Coking Plant
Avenue Carbonisation
Clay Cross Junc.
Welbeck Coll. Junc.
W. E.
W. S.
Mansfield Concentration Sidings
Clay Cross Foundry
Clay Cross Tun. (1m. 24yds)
Pleasley
ER
LM
Clipstone
Bilsthorpe
Teversal
Sherwood
Mansfield
Matlock
High Tor Tuns.
TRAMWAY MUSEUM SOC.
Silverhill
Doe Hill
Mansfield S. Junc.
Mansfield Coll. Junc.
ER
LM
ER
LM
Rufford

46

B

Matlock Bath
Cromford
Tibshelf Branch Junc.
Blackwell Sdgs.
Blackwell Juncs.
WT Wks.
CCE Tip
Sutton
New Hucknall
Sutton in Ashfield
Bentinck
Blidworth
Wirksworth
Cliffe Quarry
Crich
Whatstandwell
Alfreton & Mansfield Parkway
Annesley
Pye Bridge Junc.
Newstead
Linby
Ambergate
Butterley
Pye Hill
Hammersmith
MIDLAND RAILWAY COMPANY
Butterley Works
Denby
Codnor Park Sidings
Hucknall
Calverton
Bestwood Park Junc.
Belper
Heanor Junc.
Moor Green
Lowdham
Duffield
Bennerley
Babbington
Gedling
Burton Joyce
Bennerley Junc.
West Hallam
Trowell Junc.
Radford Junc.
P.W. Depot
Carlton
Netherfield
Little Eaton Junc.
Stanton Ironworks
Cem. T.
Stanton Gate
Nottingham
NM
Lenton Juncs.
Mansfield Junc.
Radcliffe
Mickleover
BREL
Chaddesden Sidings
St Mary's Yard
Spondon
TOTON YARD
TO
FLT
Wks.
North Wilford
Colwick
(Test Track)
DERBY
DY
Peartree
Rly. Tech. Ctre.
Wks.
Spondon
Chilwell
Beeston
Edwalton
Cotgrave
Sinfin N.
Long Eaton
Attenborough
Melbourne Junc.
Sinfin Cen.
Draycott Gravel Pits
Attenborough Junc.
Ruddington
Hilton
Stenson N. Staffs Junc.
Stenson Junc.
Sheet Stores Junc.
TRENT
Trent Juncs.

C

Tutbury
Egginton Junc.
Willington
Worthington Junc.
Castle Donington
Ratcliffe -on- Trent
Hotchley Hill
Stanton Tun.
East Leake
(Test Track)
BU
Leicester Junc.
Burton-on-Trent
Branston Junc.
Birmingham Curve Junc.
Worthington

47

0   5   10 m.
0   5   10   15 km.
(1:350,000)

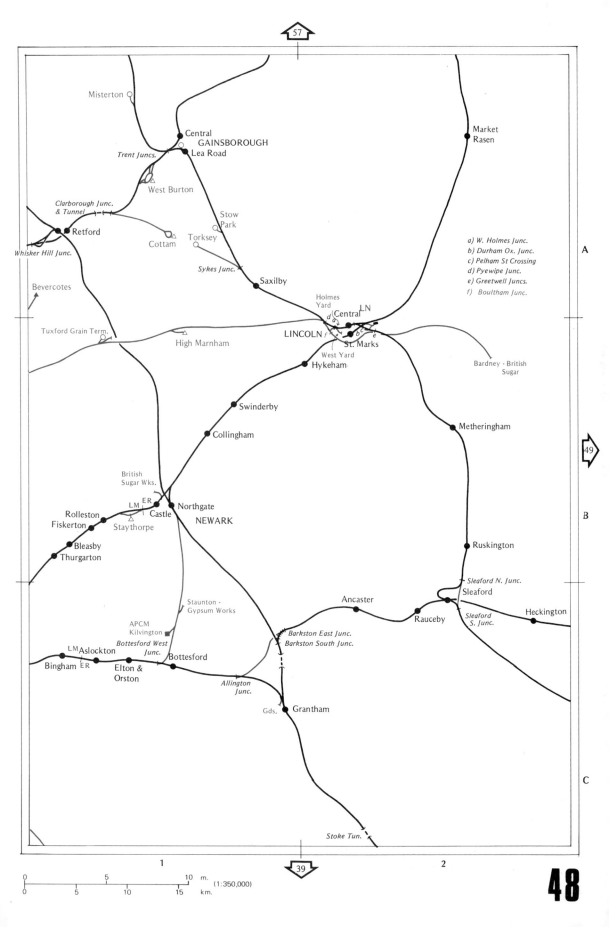

Misterton

Central
GAINSBOROUGH
Lea Road

Trent Juncs.

West Burton

Stow
Park

Clarborough Junc.
& Tunnel

Retford

Cottam

Torksey

Whisker Hill Junc.

Sykes Junc.

Saxilby

Bevercotes

Holmes
Yard

Central
LN

LINCOLN
St. Marks

West Yard

a) W. Holmes Junc.
b) Durham Ox. Junc.
c) Pelham St Crossing
d) Pyewipe Junc.
e) Greetwell Juncs.
f) Boultham Junc.

A

Market
Rasen

Tuxford Grain Term.

High Marnham

Hykeham

Bardney - British
Sugar

Swinderby

Collingham

Metheringham

49

British
Sugar Wks.

LM ER
Castle

Rolleston
Fiskerton

Staythorpe

Northgate

NEWARK

B

Ruskington

Bleasby
Thurgarton

Staunton -
Gypsum Works

Sleaford N. Junc.
Sleaford

Ancaster

Raucaby

Sleaford
S. Junc.

Heckington

APCM
Kilvington

Barkston East Junc.
Barkston South Junc.

LM Aslockton
Bingham ER

Bottesford West
Junc.

Bottesford

Elton &
Orston

*Allington
Junc.*

Gds. Grantham

C

Stoke Tun.

1

2

0   5   10 m.
0   5   10   15 km.   (1:350,000)

48

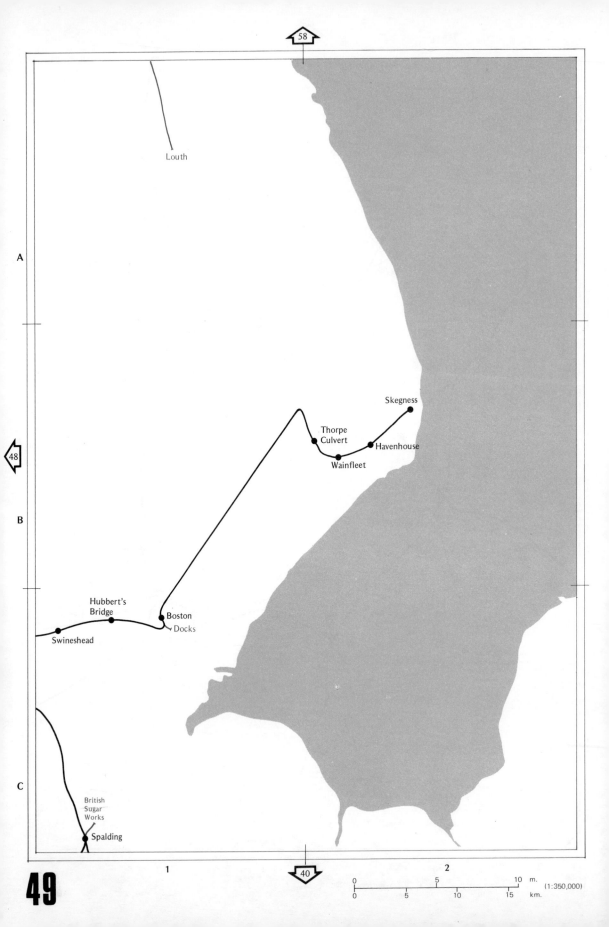

58

Louth

A

48

Skegness

Thorpe
Culvert

Wainfleet

Havenhouse

B

Hubbert's
Bridge

Boston

Docks

Swineshead

C

British
Sugar
Works

Spalding

49

1

40

2

0   5   10   m.

0   5   10   15   km.

(1:350,000)

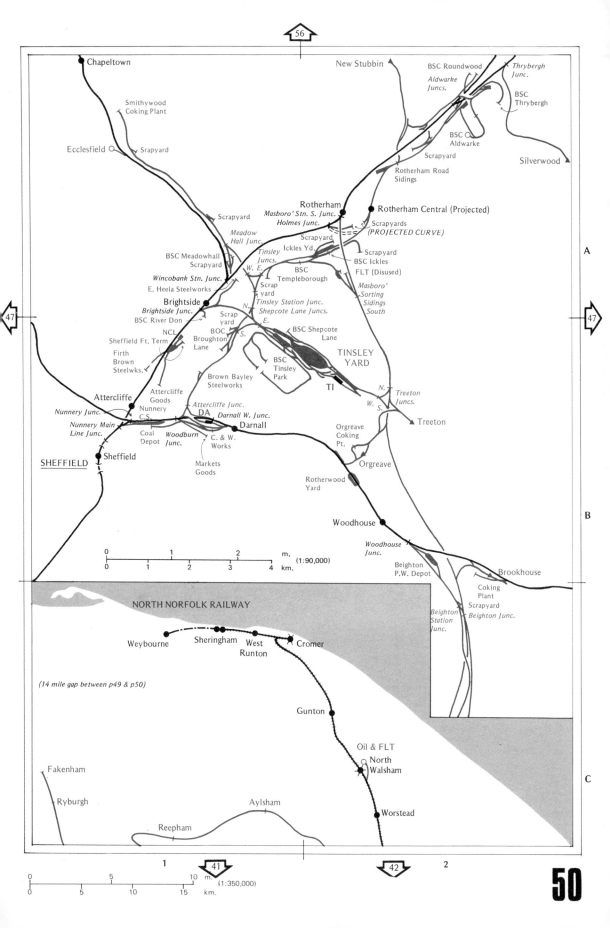

Chapeltown

Smithywood
Coking Plant

Ecclesfield   Scrapyard

New Stubbin

BSC Roundwood
Aldwarke Juncs.   *Thrybergh Junc.*

BSC Thrybergh

BSC Aldwarke

Scrapyard

Silverwood

Rotherham Road Sidings

Scrapyard

Rotherham
Masboro' Stn. S. Junc.   Rotherham Central (Projected)
Holmes Junc.   Scrapyards   *(PROJECTED CURVE)*

Meadow Hall Junc.   Scrapyard

Scrapyard   Ickles Yd.   Scrapyard
BSC Ickles
FLT (Disused)

BSC Meadowhall Scrapyard   *Tinsley Juncs. W. E.*
BSC Templeborough

Wincobank Stn. Junc.   Scrap yard   *Masboro' Sorting Sidings South*
E. Heela Steelworks   *Tinsley Station Junc.*

Brightside   *Shepcote Lane Juncs.*   *N.*
Brightside Junc.   Scrap yard   *E.*   BSC Shepcote Lane
BSC River Don

NCL   BOC
Sheffield Ft. Term   Broughton   *S.*
Lane   TINSLEY YARD
Firth   BSC Tinsley Park
Brown
Steelwks.   TI   *N.*
W.   *Treeton Juncs.*
Brown Bayley   *S.*
Steelworks
Attercliffe   Treeton
Attercliffe
Goods
Attercliffe   Nunnery
Nunnery Junc.   C.S.   *Attercliffe Junc.*
Darnall W. Junc.   Orgreave
*Nunnery Main   DA   Coking
Line Junc.*   Coal   Darnall   Pt.
Depot   *Woodburn
Junc.*   C. & W.
Works   Orgreave
SHEFFIELD   Sheffield   Markets
Goods   Rotherwood
Yard

Woodhouse

B

*Woodhouse
Junc.*
Beighton
P.W. Depot   Brookhouse

Coking
Plant
Scrapyard
*Beighton
Station
Junc.*   *Beighton Junc.*

0   1   2   m. (1:90,000)
0   1   2   3   4   km.

NORTH NORFOLK RAILWAY

Weybourne   Sheringham   West   Cromer
Runton

(14 mile gap between p49 & p50)

Gunton

Oil & FLT

Fakenham   North
Walsham

Ryburgh

Aylsham   Worstead

Reepham

C

1   41   42   2

0   5   10   m. (1:350,000)
0   5   10   15   km.

50

47   47

A

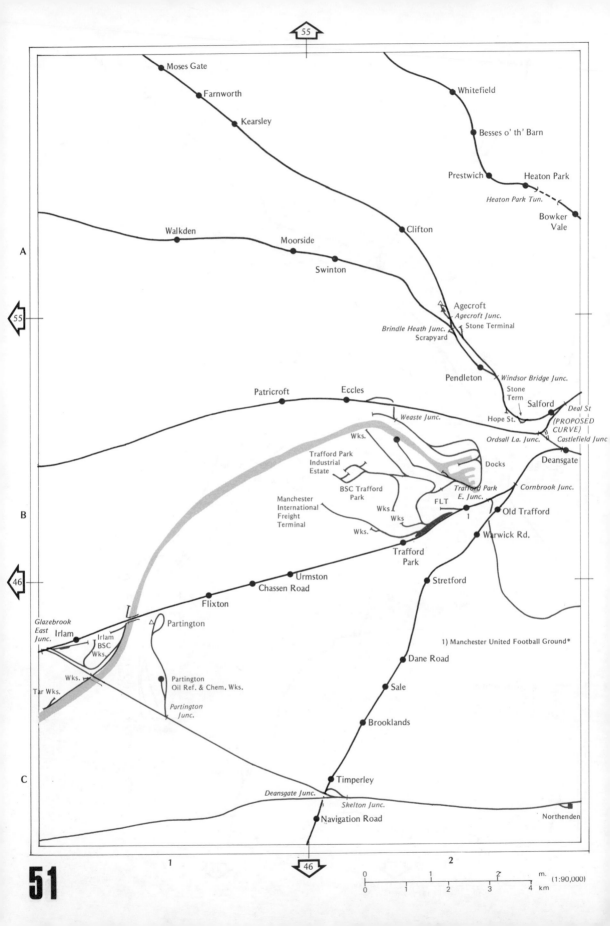

Moses Gate

Farnworth

Kearsley

Whitefield

Besses o' th' Barn

Prestwich   Heaton Park

Heaton Park Tun.

Bowker
Vale

Walkden

Moorside   Clifton

A

Swinton

Agecroft
Agecroft Junc.
Brindle Heath Junc.   Stone Terminal
Scrapyard

Pendleton   *Windsor Bridge Junc.*

Stone
Term

Patricroft   Eccles   *Weaste Junc.*   Salford   *Deal St
(PROPOSED
CURVE)*

Hope St.   *Ordsall La. Junc.*   Castlefield Junc

Wks.   Docks   Deansgate

Trafford Park
Industrial
Estate   *Trafford Park
E. Junc.*   *Cornbrook Junc.*

BSC Trafford
Park   FLT   Old Trafford

B
Manchester
International
Freight
Terminal   Wks   Wks   1   Warwick Rd.

Wks.

Trafford
Park   Stretford

Urmston
Chassen Road

46

Flixton   *Glazebrook
East
Junc.*   Partington   Dane Road   1) Manchester United Football Ground*

Irlam   Irlam
BSC
Wks.   Sale

Wks.   Partington
Oil Ref. & Chem. Wks.   Brooklands

Tar Wks.   *Partington
Junc.*

C   Timperley

Deansgate Junc.
Skelton Junc.   Northenden

Navigation Road

1   2

0   1   2   m.
0   1   2   3   4   km   (1:90,000)

51

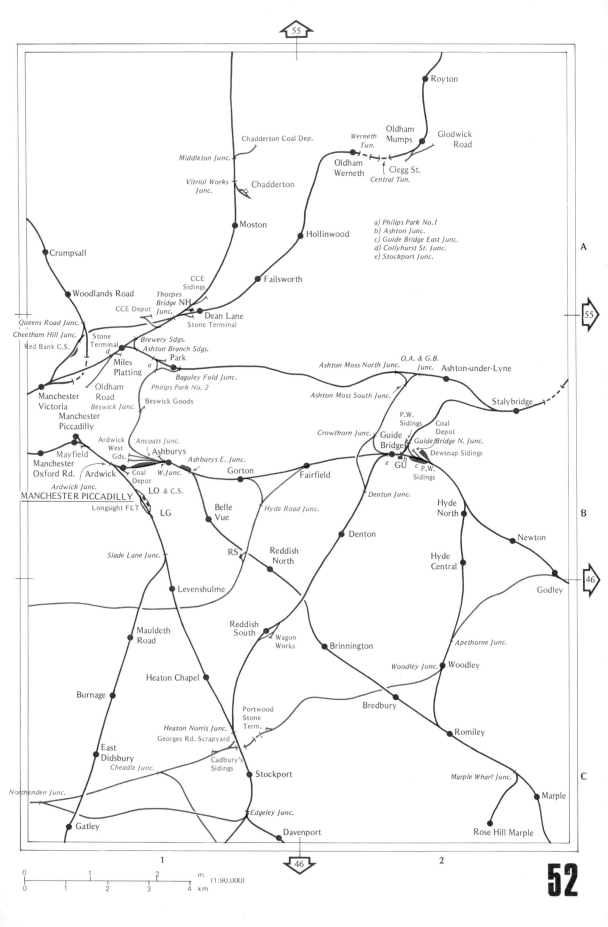

Royton

Oldham
Mumps

Glodwick
Road

Chadderton Coal Dep.

*Werneth
Tun.*

Middleton Junc.

Oldham
Werneth

Clegg St.

*Vitriol Works
Junc.*

Chadderton

Central Tun.

Moston

Hollinwood

a) Philips Park No.1
b) Ashton Junc.
c) Guide Bridge East Junc.
d) Collyhurst St. Junc.
e) Stockport Junc.

Crumpsall

Failsworth

Woodlands Road

CCE
Sidings

*Thorpes
Bridge* NH
Junc.

CCE Depot

Dean Lane
Stone Terminal

Queens Road Junc.
Cheetham Hill Junc.

Red Bank C.S.

Stone
Terminal
d

Brewery Sdgs.
Ashton Branch Sdgs.

Park

Miles
Platting

a

Baguley Fold Junc.

Ashton Moss North Junc.

O.A. & G.B.
Junc.

Ashton-under-Lyne

Manchester
Victoria

Oldham
Road

Beswick Junc.

Philips Park No. 2

Beswick Goods

Ashton Moss South Junc.

Stalybridge

Manchester
Piccadilly

P.W.
Sidings

Coal
Depot

Mayfield

Ancoats Junc.

Ardwick
West
Gds.

Ashburys

Crowthorn Junc.

Guide
Bridge

Guide Bridge N. Junc.

Manchester
Oxford Rd.

Ardwick

Coal
Depot

W.Junc.

Ashburys E. Junc.

Gorton

Fairfield

e

GU

b

c

Dewsnap Sidings

P.W.
Sidings

Ardwick Junc.

LO & C.S.

Longsight FLT

LG

Belle
Vue

Hyde Road Junc.

Denton Junc.

Hyde
North

RS

Reddish
North

Denton

Hyde
Central

Newton

Slade Lane Junc.

Levenshulme

Godley

Mauldeth
Road

Reddish
South

Wagon
Works

Brinnington

Apethorne Junc.

Woodley

Heaton Chapel

Woodley Junc.

Burnage

Bredbury

Romiley

Portwood
Stone
Term.

Heaton Norris Junc.

Georges Rd. Scrapyard

East
Didsbury

Cheadle Junc.

Cadbury's
Sidings

Stockport

Marple Wharf Junc.

Northenden Junc.

Marple

Edgeley Junc.

Gatley

Davenport

Rose Hill Marple

0   1   2   m. (1:90,000)
0   1   2   3   4   km

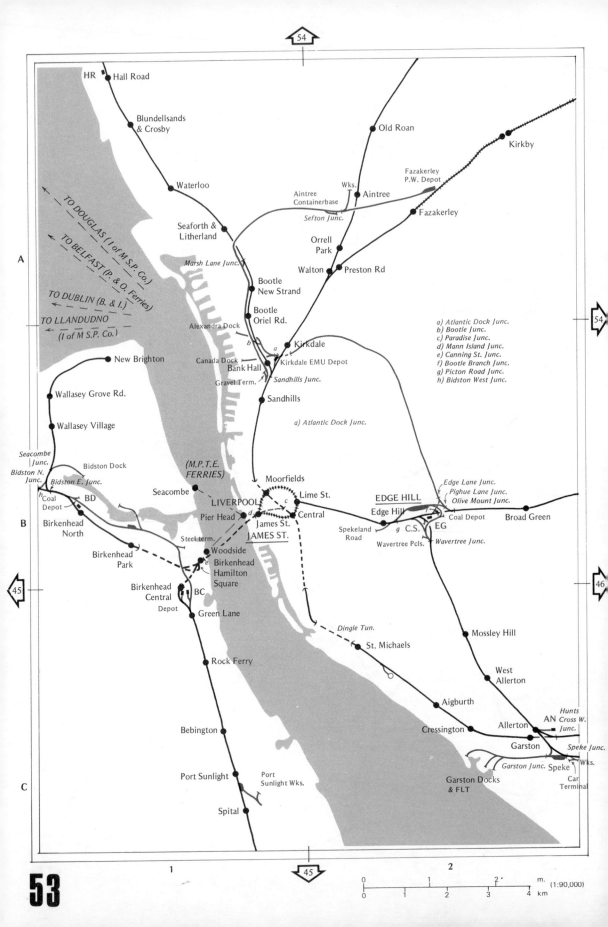

HR Hall Road

Blundellsands
& Crosby

Old Roan

Kirkby

Waterloo

Fazakerley
P.W. Depot

Seaforth &
Litherland

Wks.
Aintree
Aintree
Containerbase

Fazakerley

Sefton Junc.

TO DOUGLAS (I of M S.P. Co.)

Orrell
Park

TO BELFAST (P. & O. Ferries)

A

Marsh Lane Junc.

TO DUBLIN (B. & I.)

Walton
Preston Rd

TO LLANDUDNO
(I of M S.P. Co.)

Bootle
New Strand

a) Atlantic Dock Junc.
b) Bootle Junc.
c) Paradise Junc.
d) Mann Island Junc.
e) Canning St. Junc.
f) Bootle Branch Junc.
g) Picton Road Junc.
h) Bidston West Junc.

Bootle
Oriel Rd.

Alexandra Dock

b

a

Kirkdale

Canada Dock

Bank Hall

Kirkdale EMU Depot

Gravel Term.

Sandhills Junc.

New Brighton

Sandhills

a) Atlantic Dock Junc.

Wallasey Grove Rd.

Wallasey Village

Seacombe
Junc.
Bidston N.
Junc.

Bidston Dock

(M.P.T.E.
FERRIES)

Moorfields

Edge Lane Junc.
Pighue Lane Junc.
Olive Mount Junc.

Bidston E. Junc.

Seacombe

Lime St.

EDGE HILL

h Coal
Depot

BD

LIVERPOOL

d

c

Central

Edge Hill

Coal Depot

Broad Green

B

Pier Head

James St.
JAMES ST.

Spekeland
Road

g

C.S.

EG

Birkenhead
North

Steel term.

Woodside

Wavertree Pcls.

Wavertree Junc.

Birkenhead
Park

e

Birkenhead
Hamilton
Square

Birkenhead
Central
Depot

BC

Green Lane

Dingle Tun.

Mossley Hill

Rock Ferry

St. Michaels

West
Allerton

Aigburth

Hunts
Cross W.
Junc.

Bebington

Cressington

Allerton
AN

Garston

Speke Junc.
Wks.

C

Port Sunlight

Port
Sunlight Wks.

Garston Junc.
Speke

Car
Terminal

Garston Docks
& FLT

Spital

0   1   2   m. (1:90,000)
0   1   2   3   4 km

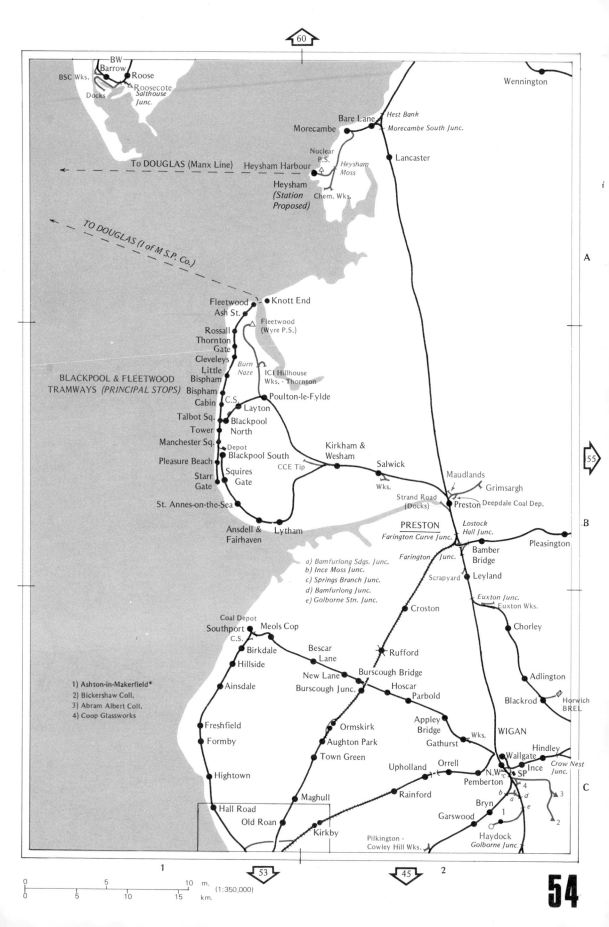

BW
Barrow
Roose
BSC Wks.
Roosecote
Docks
Salthouse Junc.

Wennington

Bare Lane
Hest Bank
Morecambe
Morecambe South Junc.
Lancaster

Nuclear P.S.
To DOUGLAS (Manx Line)
Heysham Harbour
Heysham Moss
Heysham
(Station Proposed)
Chem. Wks.

TO DOUGLAS (I of M S.P. Co.)

A

i

Fleetwood
Knott End
Ash St.
Fleetwood (Wyre P.S.)
Rossall
Thornton Gate
Cleveleys
Little Bispham
Burn Naze
ICI Hillhouse Wks. - Thornton
BLACKPOOL & FLEETWOOD
TRAMWAYS (PRINCIPAL STOPS)
Bispham
Cabin
C.S.
Poulton-le-Fylde
Layton
Talbot Sq.
Blackpool North
Tower
Manchester Sq.
Depot
Pleasure Beach
Blackpool South
Kirkham & Wesham
Salwick
Maudlands
Grimsargh
Starr Gate
Squires Gate
CCE Tip
Wks.
Strand Road (Docks)
Preston
Deepdale Coal Dep.
St. Annes-on-the-Sea

55

B

Ansdell & Fairhaven
Lytham
PRESTON
Farington Curve Junc.
Lostock Hall Junc.
Pleasington

a) Bamfurlong Sdgs. Junc.
b) Ince Moss Junc.
c) Springs Branch Junc.
d) Bamfurlong Junc.
e) Golborne Stn. Junc.
Bamber Bridge
Farington Junc.
Leyland
Scrapyard
Euxton Junc.
Euxton Wks.

Croston
Chorley

Coal Depot
Southport
Meols Cop
C.S.
Birkdale
Bescar Lane
Rufford
Burscough Bridge
Adlington
Hillside
New Lane
Hoscar
Parbold
Blackrod
Horwich BREL
Ainsdale
Burscough Junc.
1) Ashton-in-Makerfield*
2) Bickershaw Coll.
3) Abram Albert Coll.
4) Coop Glassworks
Appley Bridge
Wks.
WIGAN
Freshfield
Ormskirk
Gathurst
Hindley
Formby
Aughton Park
Wallgate
Town Green
Upholland
Orrell
Ince
Crow Nest Junc.
N.W.
SP
Hightown
Pemberton
b
4
d
3
Maghull
Rainford
a
e
Bryn
C
Hall Road
Garswood
1
Old Roan
Kirkby
Pilkington - Cowley Hill Wks.
Haydock
Golborne Junc.
2

1

2

0   5   10 m.
0   5   10   15 km.
(1:350,000)

53

45

54

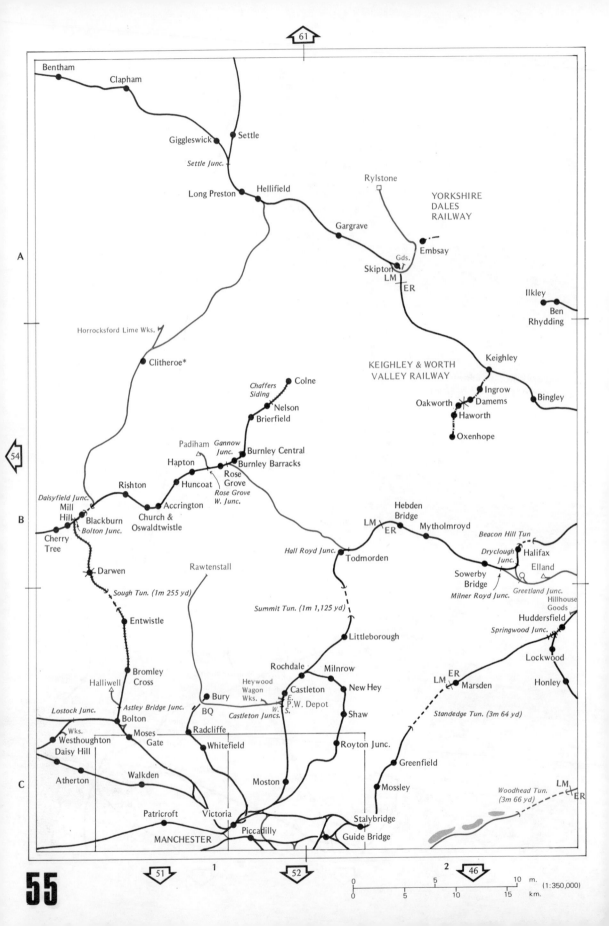

Bentham
Clapham
Giggleswick
Settle
Settle Junc.
Long Preston
Hellifield
Gargrave
Rylstone
YORKSHIRE
DALES
RAILWAY
Gds.
Embsay
Skipton
LM
ER
Ilkley
Ben
Rhydding

A

Horrocksford Lime Wks.
Clitheroe*
KEIGHLEY & WORTH
VALLEY RAILWAY
Keighley
Chaffers Siding
Colne
Ingrow
Bingley
Nelson
Oakworth
Damems
Brierfield
Haworth
Padiham
Gannow Junc.
Burnley Central
Oxenhope
Hapton
Burnley Barracks
Rose
Grove
Rishton
Huncoat
Rose Grove W. Junc.

Hebden
Bridge
Daisyfield Junc.
Mill
Hill
Accrington
LM
Mytholmroyd
Blackburn
Church &
ER
Beacon Hill Tun
B
Oswaldtwistle
Bolton Junc.
Hall Royd Junc.
*Dryclough
Junc.*
Halifax
Cherry
Tree
Todmorden
Elland
Sowerby
Bridge
Greetland Junc.
Darwen
Rawtenstall
Milner Royd Junc.
Hillhouse
Goods
Sough Tun. (1m 255 yd)
Summit Tun. (1m 1,125 yd)
Huddersfield
Springwood Junc.
Entwistle
Littleborough
Lockwood
Rochdale
Bromley
Milnrow
Cross
Standedge Tun. (3m 64 yd)
Halliwell
Heywood
Wagon
Wks.
Castleton
New Hey
LM
ER
Marsden
Honley
Lostock Junc.
Astley Bridge Junc.
Bury
E.
P.W. Depot
Standedge Tun. (3m 64 yd)
BQ
W.
S.
Shaw
Bolton
Castleton Juncs.
Wks.
Moses
Radcliffe
Royton Junc.
Westhoughton
Gate
Daisy Hill
Whitefield
Greenfield
C
Atherton
Walkden
Moston
Mossley
Woodhead Tun.
(3m 66 yd)
LM
ER
Patricroft
Victoria
Stalybridge
MANCHESTER
Piccadilly
Guide Bridge

1
2

m. (1:350,000)
0   5   10
0   5   10   15
km.

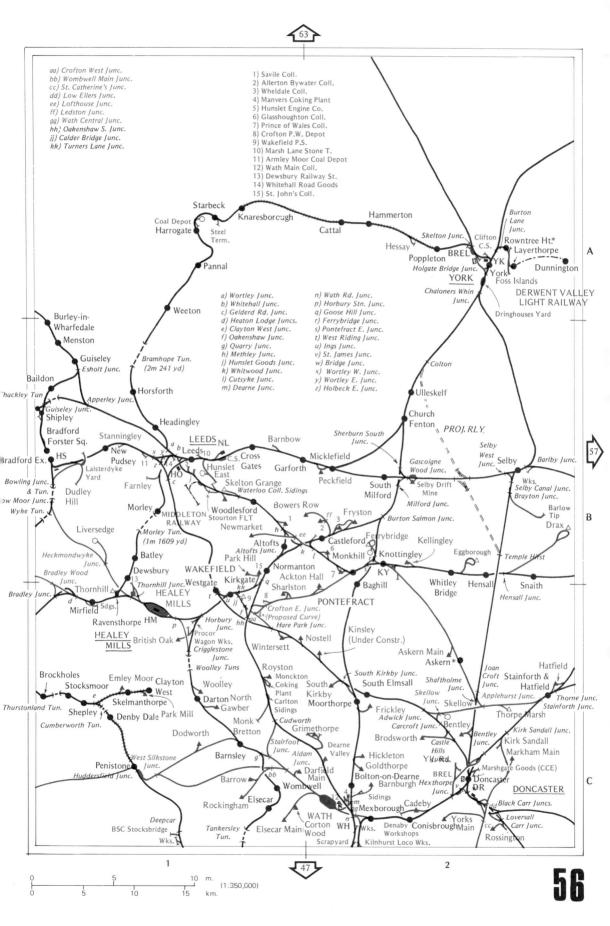

aa) Crofton West Junc.
bb) Wombwell Main Junc.
cc) St. Catherine's Junc.
dd) Low Ellers Junc.
ee) Lofthouse Junc.
ff) Ledston Junc.
gg) Wath Central Junc.
hh) Oakenshaw S. Junc.
jj) Calder Bridge Junc.
kk) Turners Lane Junc.

1) Savile Coll.
2) Allerton Bywater Coll.
3) Wheldale Coll.
4) Manvers Coking Plant
5) Hunslet Engine Co.
6) Glasshoughton Coll.
7) Prince of Wales Coll.
8) Crofton P.W. Depot
9) Wakefield P.S.
10) Marsh Lane Stone T.
11) Armley Moor Coal Depot
12) Wath Main Coll.
13) Dewsbury Railway St.
14) Whitehall Road Goods
15) St. John's Coll.

a) Wortley Junc.
b) Whitehall Junc.
c) Geldred Rd. Junc.
d) Heaton Lodge Juncs.
e) Clayton West Junc.
f) Oakenshaw Junc.
g) Quarry Junc.
h) Methley Junc.
j) Hunslet Goods Junc.
k) Whitwood Junc.
l) Cutsyke Junc.
m) Dearne Junc.
n) Wath Rd. Junc.
p) Horbury Stn. Junc.
q) Goose Hill Junc.
r) Ferrybridge Junc.
s) Pontefract E. Junc.
t) West Riding Junc.
u) Ings Junc.
v) St. James Junc.
w) Bridge Junc.
x) Wortley W. Junc.
y) Wortley E. Junc.
z) Holbeck E. Junc.

0   5   10 m.
0   5   10   15 km.
(1:350,000)

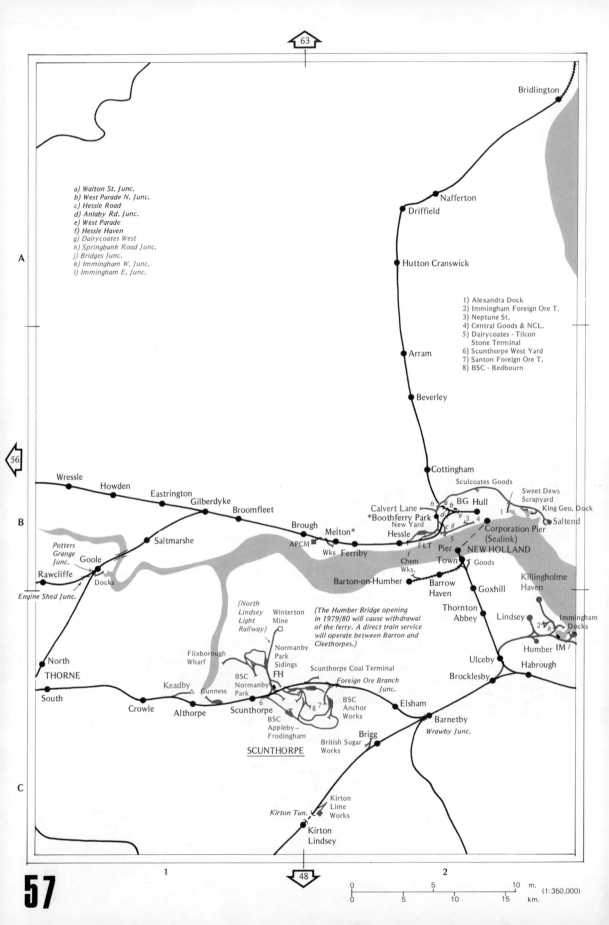

a) Walton St. Junc.
b) West Parade N. Junc.
c) Hessle Road
d) Anlaby Rd. Junc.
e) West Parade
f) Hessle Haven
g) Dairycoates West
h) Springbank Road Junc.
j) Bridges Junc.
k) Immingham W. Junc.
l) Immingham E. Junc.

A

1) Alexandra Dock
2) Immingham Foreign Ore T.
3) Neptune St.
4) Central Goods & NCL.
5) Dairycoates - Tilcon
   Stone Terminal
6) Scunthorpe West Yard
7) Santon Foreign Ore T.
8) BSC - Redbourn

Bridlington

Nafferton
Driffield

Hutton Cranswick

Arram

Beverley

Cottingham

56

Wressle

Howden

Eastrington

Gilberdyke

Broomfleet

Saltmarshe

Potters
Grange
Junc.

Goole

Rawcliffe

Docks

Engine Shed Junc.

Brough

Melton*

APCM

Wks

Ferriby

Sculcoates Goods

Sweet Dews
Scrapyard

Calvert Lane
*Boothferry Park

New Yard

Hessle

FLT

h
a b
d e 3 4
c g
5

BG Hull

King Geo. Dock

1

Saltend

Corporation Pier
(Sealink)

B

Pier
Town

Chem
Wks.

f

Barton-on-Humber

Barrow
Haven

NEW HOLLAND

Goods

Goxhill

Thornton
Abbey

Killingholme
Haven

Lindsey

2
k

Immingham
Docks

Humber IM

Ulceby

Habrough

Brocklesby

North
THORNE

South

Crowle

Keadby

Gunness

Althorpe

(North
Lindsey
Light
Railway)

Winterton
Mine

Flixborough
Wharf

Normanby
Park
Sidings

FH

BSC
Normanby
Park

Scunthorpe

6

(The Humber Bridge opening
in 1979/80 will cause withdrawal
of the ferry. A direct train service
will operate between Barton and
Cleethorpes.)

Scunthorpe Coal Terminal

Foreign Ore Branch
Junc.

8 7

BSC
Appleby-
Frodingham

BSC
Anchor
Works

Elsham

Barnetby

Wrawby Junc.

SCUNTHORPE

Brigg

British Sugar
Works

C

Kirton Tun.

Kirton
Lime
Works

Kirton
Lindsey

57

1

48

2

0   5   10 m.

0   5   10   15 km.

(1:350,000)

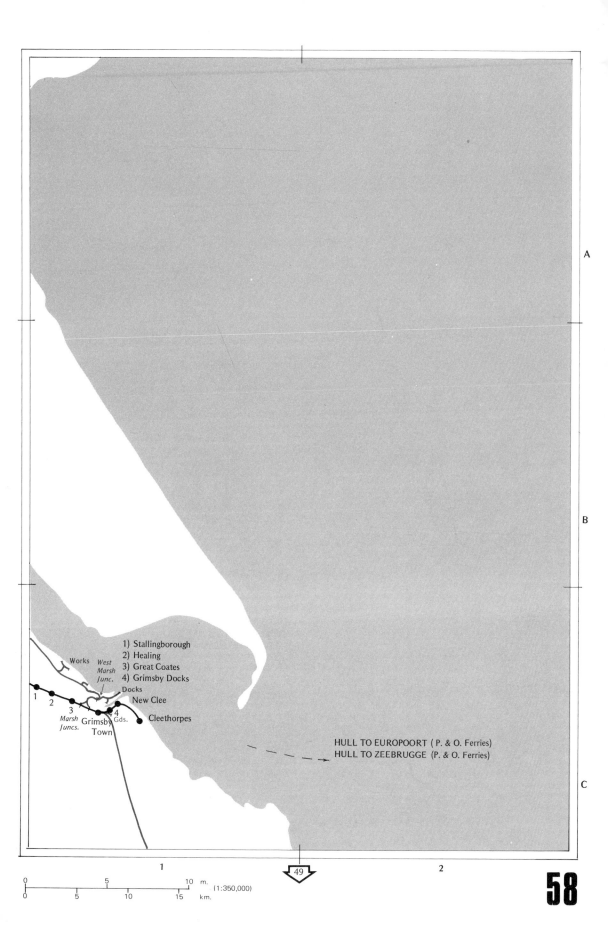

1) Stallingborough
2) Healing
3) Great Coates
4) Grimsby Docks

Works
West Marsh Junc.

Docks
New Clee
Cleethorpes

1
2
3
Marsh Juncs.
Grimsby Town
4
Gds.

HULL TO EUROPOORT (P. & O. Ferries)
HULL TO ZEEBRUGGE (P. & O. Ferries)

A

B

C

1

2

49

0   5   10 m.   (1:350,000)
0   5   10   15   km.

58

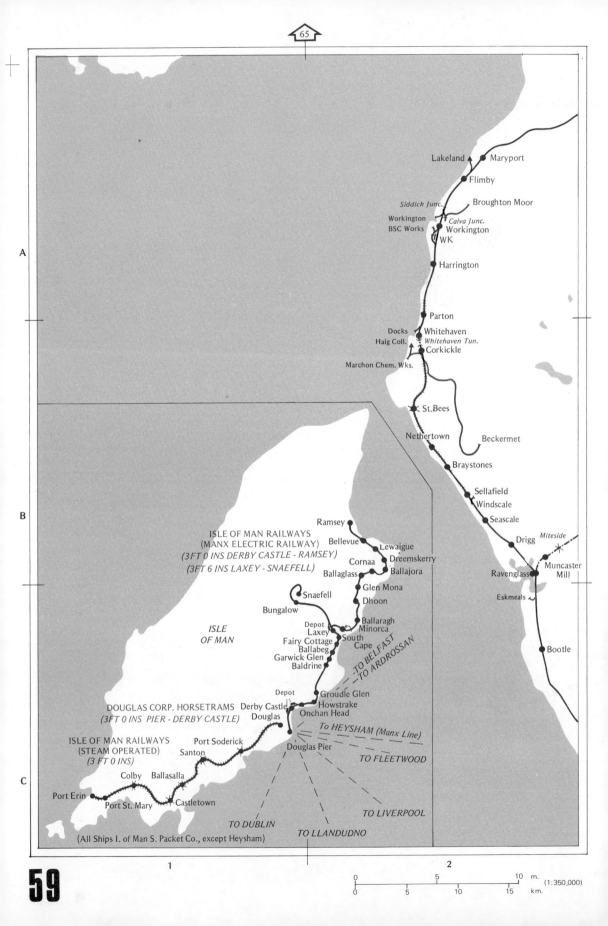

Lakeland
Maryport
Flimby
Broughton Moor
Siddick Junc.
Workington
BSC Works
Calva Junc.
Workington
WK
Harrington
Parton
Docks
Whitehaven
Haig Coll.
Whitehaven Tun.
Corkickle
Marchon Chem. Wks.
St.Bees
Nethertown
Beckermet
Braystones
Sellafield
Windscale
Seascale
Drigg *Miteside*
Muncaster
Mill
Ravenglass
Eskmeals
Bootle

Ramsey
ISLE OF MAN RAILWAYS
(MANX ELECTRIC RAILWAY)
(3FT 0 INS DERBY CASTLE - RAMSEY)
(3FT 6 INS LAXEY - SNAEFELL)
Bellevue
Lewaigue
Dreemskerry
Cornaa
Ballajora
Ballaglass
Glen Mona
Snaefell
Dhoon
Bungalow
Ballaragh
Depot
Minorca
Laxey
South
Cape
ISLE
OF MAN
Fairy Cottage
Ballabeg
Garwick Glen
Baldrine
—TO BELFAST
—TO ARDROSSAN
Depot
Groudle Glen
DOUGLAS CORP. HORSETRAMS
Derby Castle
Howstrake
(3FT 0 INS PIER - DERBY CASTLE)
Douglas
Onchan Head
To HEYSHAM (Manx Line)
ISLE OF MAN RAILWAYS
Port Soderick
(STEAM OPERATED)
Santon
Douglas Pier
TO FLEETWOOD
(3 FT 0 INS)
Colby Ballasalla
Port Erin
Castletown
Port St. Mary
TO LIVERPOOL
TO DUBLIN
TO LLANDUDNO
(All Ships I. of Man S. Packet Co., except Heysham)

0   5   10 m.
|————————————|————————————|
0   5   10   15 km.
(1:350,000)

1   2

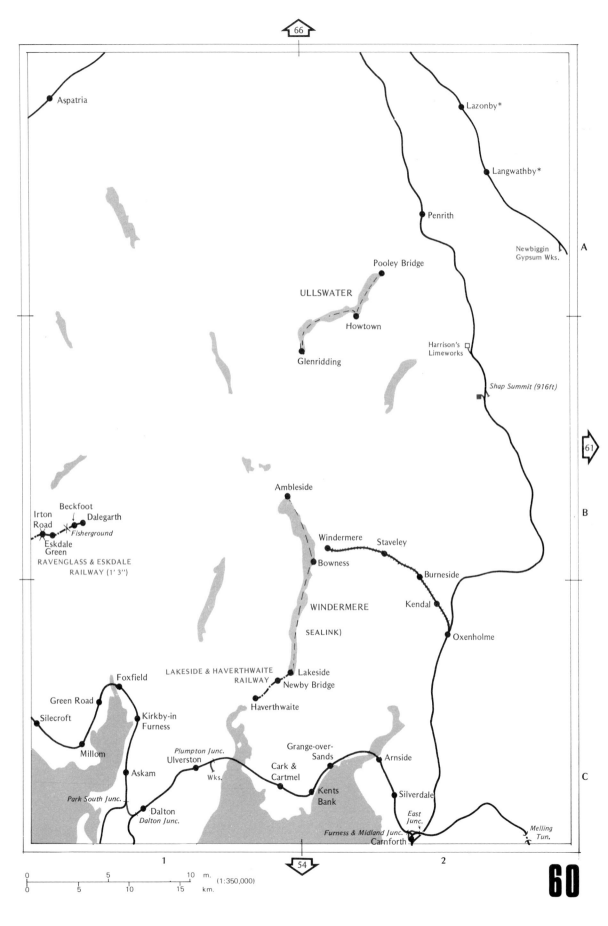

Aspatria

Lazonby*

Langwathby*

Penrith

Newbiggin
Gypsum Wks.

A

Pooley Bridge

ULLSWATER

Howtown

Harrison's
Limeworks

Glenridding

Shap Summit (916ft)

61

Ambleside

Beckfoot
Irton   Dalegarth
Road   Fisherground
Eskdale
Green
RAVENGLASS & ESKDALE
RAILWAY (1' 3'')

Windermere   Staveley

Bowness   Burneside

B

WINDERMERE   Kendal

SEALINK)   Oxenholme

LAKESIDE & HAVERTHWAITE   Lakeside
RAILWAY   Newby Bridge

Haverthwaite

Foxfield

Green Road

Silecroft   Kirkby-in
Furness
Millom

Grange-over-
Sands   Arnside

Plumpton Junc.
Ulverston   Cark &
Wks.   Cartmel
Askam
Kents   Silverdale
Bank
Park South Junc.
East
Dalton   Junc.
Melling
Dalton Junc.   Tun.
Furness & Midland Junc.
Carnforth

C

1

2

0   5   10 m.   (1:350,000)
0   5   10   15 km.

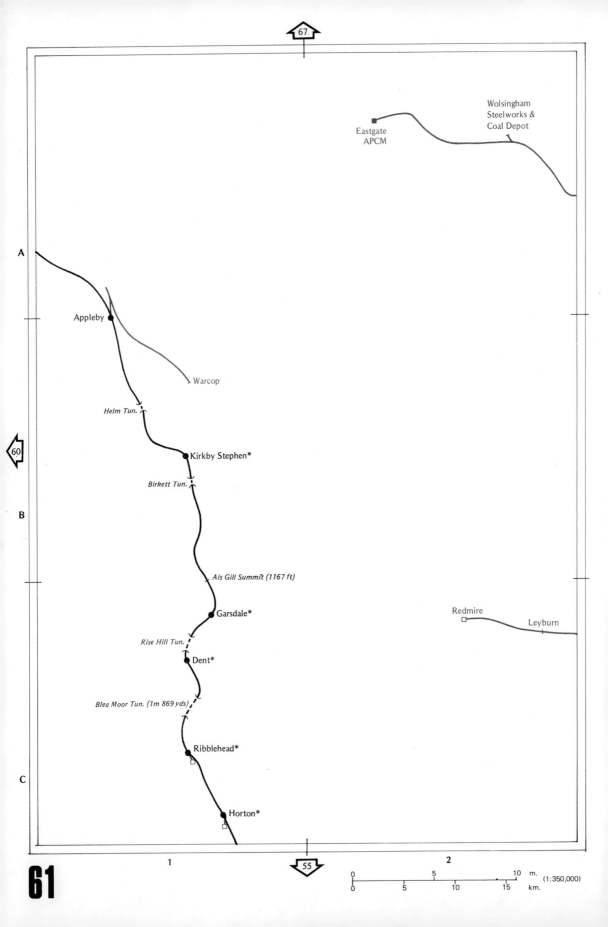

Wolsingham
Steelworks &
Coal Depot

Eastgate
APCM

A

Appleby

Warcop

Helm Tun.

Kirkby Stephen*

Birkett Tun.

B

Ais Gill Summit (1167 ft)

Redmire

Leyburn

Garsdale*

Rise Hill Tun.

Dent*

Blea Moor Tun. (1m 869 yds)

Ribblehead*

C

Horton*

60

61

0   5   10   m.   (1:350,000)

0   5   10   15   km.

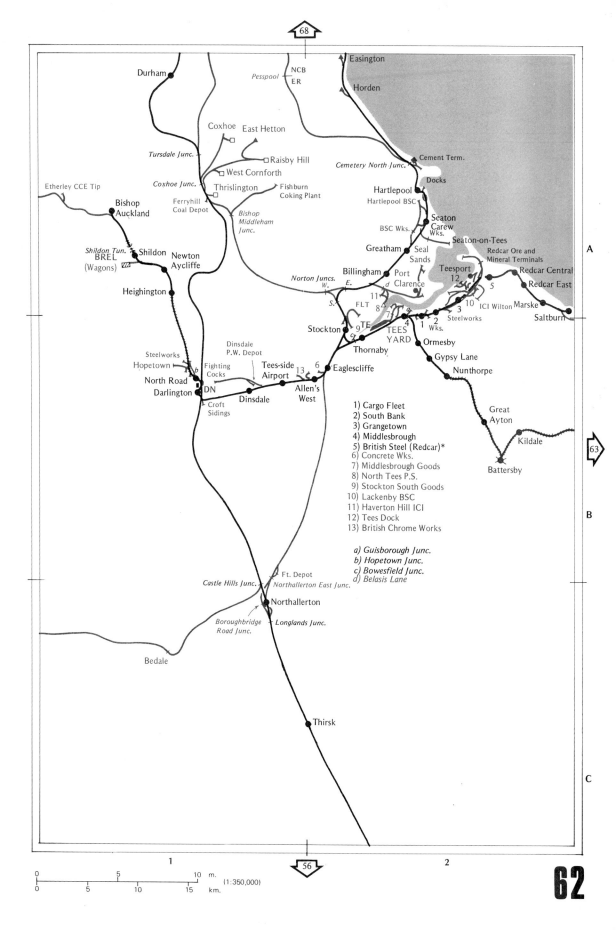

Durham

Pesspool
NCB
ER

Coxhoe   East Hetton

Tursdale Junc.

Raisby Hill

Cemetery North Junc.

Cement Term.

Coxhoe Junc.
West Cornforth

Docks

Etherley CCE Tip
Thrislington
Fishburn
Coking Plant

Bishop
Auckland
Ferryhill
Coal Depot

Hartlepool

Hartlepool BSC

Shildon Tun.   Shildon
BREL
(Wagons)   Newton
Aycliffe

Bishop
Middleham
Junc.

Seaton
Carew
BSC Wks.
Wks.

Seaton-on-Tees

Greatham   Seal
Sands

Redcar Ore and
Mineral Terminals

Heighington

Norton Juncs.
W.

Billingham   Port
Clarence

Teesport
12

Redcar Central

Redcar East

A

d

E.

11   10   ICI Wilton   Marske

Saltburn

S.   FLT   8   3
Steelworks

Steelworks
Hopetown

Dinsdale
P.W. Depot

7   4
9 TE   2
TEES   Wks.
YARD

Stockton   1

North Road
Darlington   DN

Fighting
Cocks

b

Tees-side
Airport

Thornaby

Ormesby

Gypsy Lane

Nunthorpe

Allen's
West

Dinsdale

13   6   Eaglescliffe

Croft
Sidings

Great
Ayton

1) Cargo Fleet
2) South Bank
3) Grangetown
4) Middlesbrough
5) British Steel (Redcar)*
6) Concrete Wks.
7) Middlesbrough Goods
8) North Tees P.S.
9) Stockton South Goods
10) Lackenby BSC
11) Haverton Hill ICI
12) Tees Dock
13) British Chrome Works

Kildale

Battersby

a) Guisborough Junc.
b) Hopetown Junc.
c) Bowesfield Junc.
d) Belasis Lane

B

Ft. Depot
Castle Hills Junc.   Northallerton East Junc.

Northallerton

Boroughbridge
Road Junc.   Longlands Junc.

Bedale

Easington

Horden

Thirsk

C

0   5   10 m.
0   5   10   15   km.
(1:350,000)

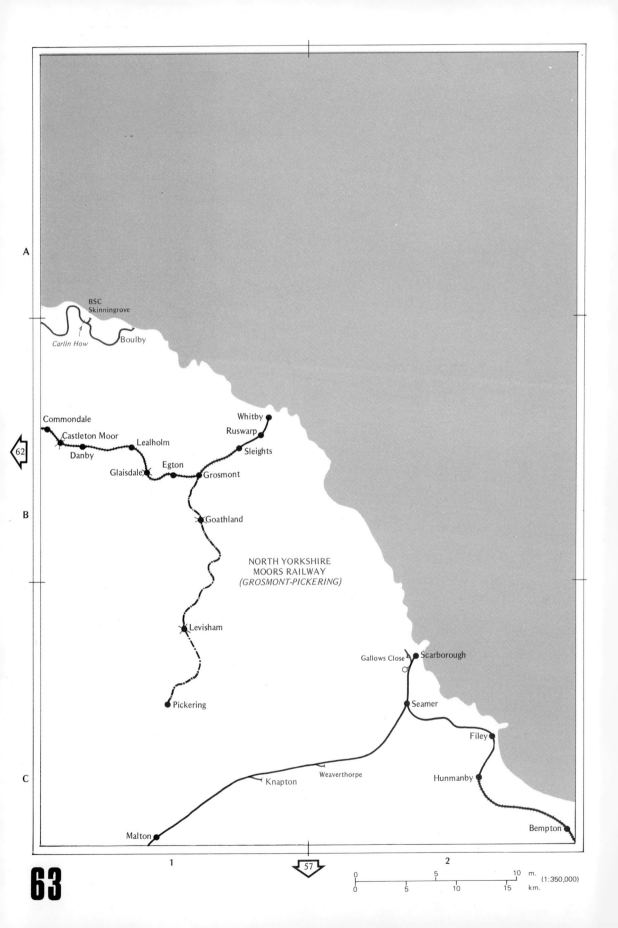

A

BSC
Skinningrove

Carlin How Boulby

Commondale
Castleton Moor
Danby Lealholm

62

Glaisdale Egton

Whitby
Ruswarp
Sleights

Grosmont

B

Goathland

NORTH YORKSHIRE
MOORS RAILWAY
(GROSMONT-PICKERING)

Levisham

Gallows Close Scarborough

Pickering

Seamer

Filey

C

Weaverthorpe
Knapton Hunmanby

Malton

Bempton

1

57

2

0   5   10 m. (1:350,000)
0   5   10   15 km.

63

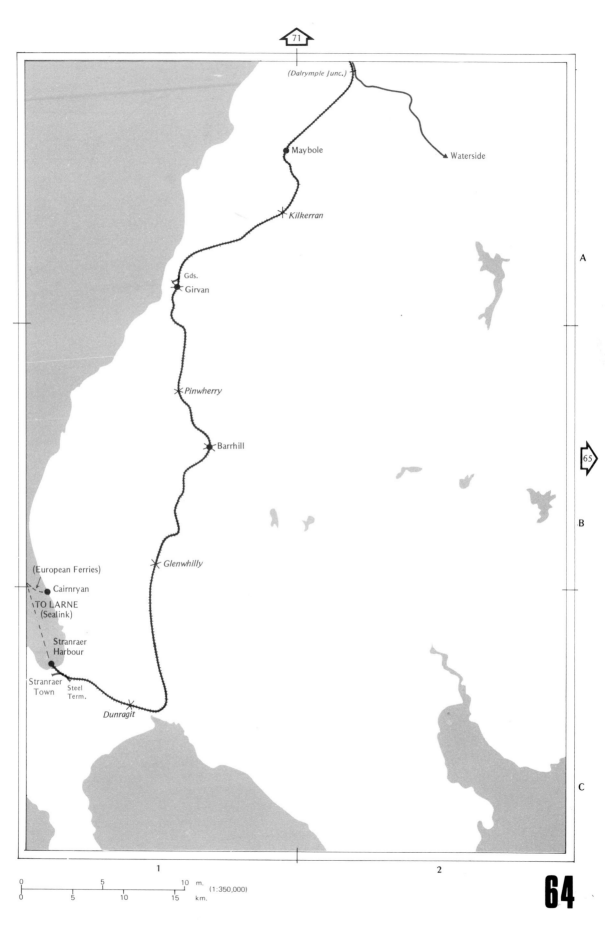

(Dalrymple Junc.)

▲ Waterside

● Maybole

✕ *Kilkerran*

A

✕ Gds.
● *Girvan*

✕ *Pinwherry*

✕ Barrhill

65

B

✕ *Glenwhilly*

(European Ferries)
● Cairnryan
↘ TO LARNE
(Sealink)

● Stranraer
Harbour

Stranraer   Steel
Town   Term.

✕ *Dunragit*

C

0   5   10 m.   (1:350,000)
0   5   10   15 km.

1   2

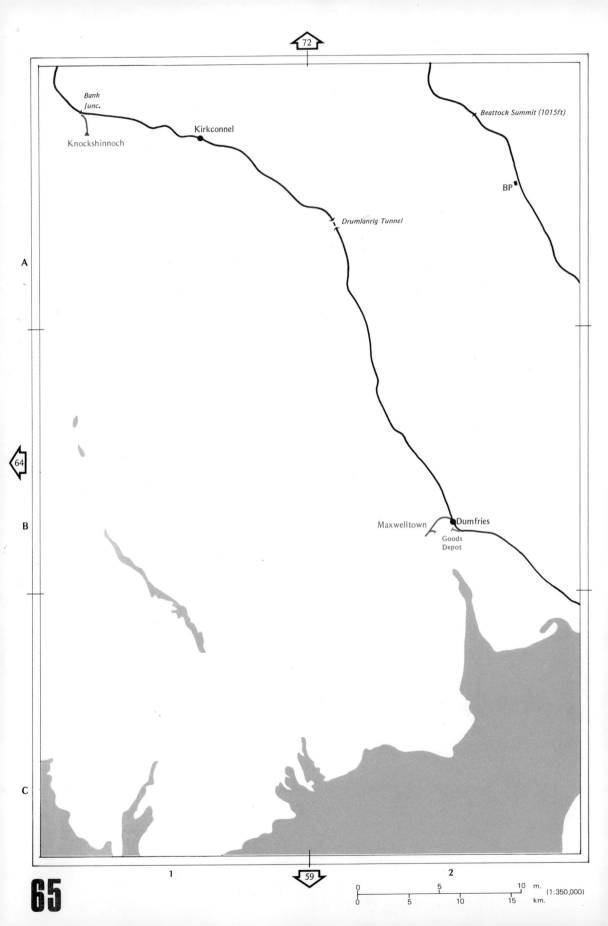

Bank
Junc.

Knockshinnoch

Kirkconnel

Beattock Summit (1015ft)

BP

Drumlanrig Tunnel

A

64

B

Maxwelltown   Dumfries
              Goods
              Depot

C

1

2

65

0   5   10 m. (1:350,000)
0   5   10   15 km.

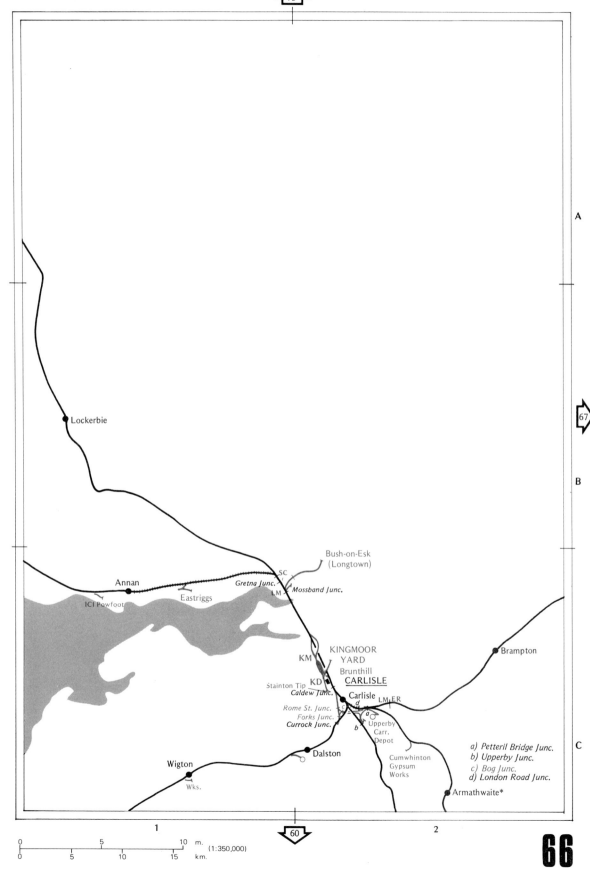

73

67

A

B

Lockerbie

Bush-on-Esk
(Longtown)

SC
Gretna Junc.
Mossband Junc.
LM

Annan

Eastriggs

ICI Powfoot

KINGMOOR
YARD
KM
Brunthill
KD
Stainton Tip
Caldew Junc.
CARLISLE
Carlisle
LM-ER

Brampton

Rome St. Junc.
Forks Junc.
Currock Junc.
d
c
a
b
Upperby
Carr.
Depot

Dalston

Wigton

Wks.

Cumwhinton
Gypsum
Works

a) Petteril Bridge Junc.
b) Upperby Junc.
c) Bog Junc.
d) London Road Junc.

C

Armathwaite*

1

2

60

0   5   10 m.   (1:350,000)
0   5   10   15
km.

66

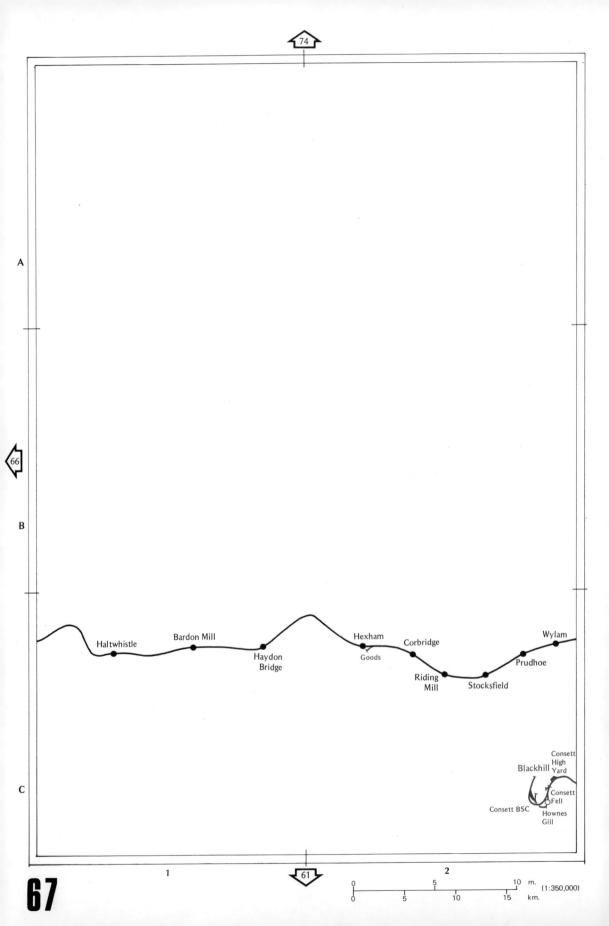

66

A

B

C

Haltwhistle

Bardon Mill

Haydon
Bridge

Hexham
Goods

Corbridge

Riding
Mill

Stocksfield

Prudhoe

Wylam

Consett
High
Yard

Blackhill

Consett
Fell

Consett BSC

Hownes
Gill

1

2

0   5   10 m. (1:350,000)

0   5   10   15
km.

67

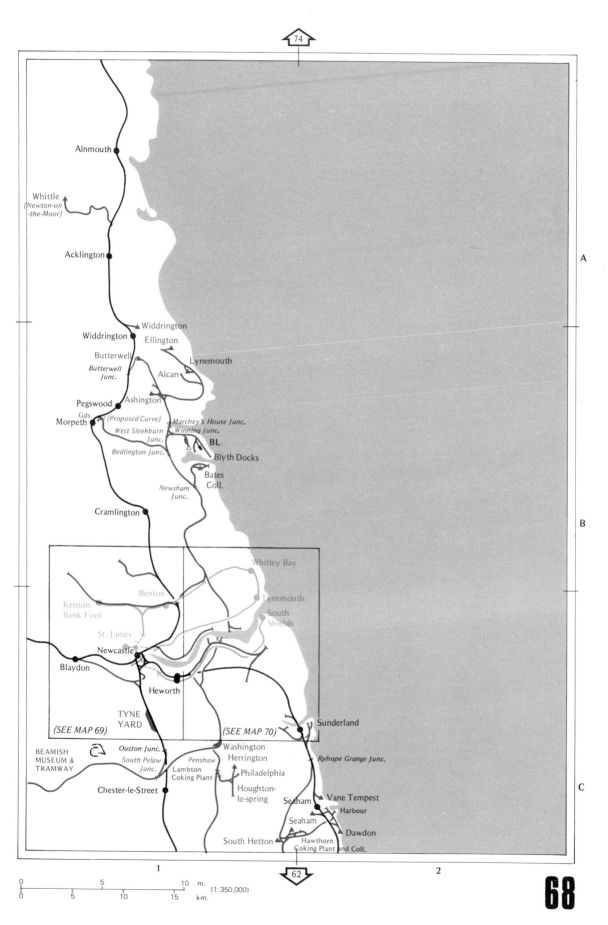

Alnmouth

Whittle
*(Newton-on
-the-Moor)*

Acklington

A

Widdrington
Widdrington
Ellington
Butterwell
*Butterwell
Junc.*
Lynemouth
Alcan
Pegswood
Ashington
Gds.
(Proposed Curve)
Morpeth
Marchey's House Junc.
West Sleekburn
Junc.
Winning Junc.
Bedlington Junc.
BL
Blyth Docks
Bates
Coll.
*Newsham
Junc.*

Cramlington

B

Whitley Bay
Benton
Tynemouth
Kenton
Bank Foot
South
Shields
St. James
Newcastle
Blaydon
Heworth
TYNE
YARD
Sunderland
(SEE MAP 69)
(SEE MAP 70)
BEAMISH
MUSEUM &
TRAMWAY
Ouston Junc.
Washington
Herrington
Ryhope Grange Junc.
South Pelaw
Junc.
Penshaw
Philadelphia
Lambton
Coking Plant
Houghton-
le-spring
C
Chester-le-Street
Seaham
Vane Tempest
Harbour
Seaham
South Hetton
Dawdon
Hawthorn
Coking Plant and Coll.

0   5   10 m.   (1:350,000)
0 5 10 15 km.

68

1   2

Brenkley
Drift

Weetslade
Coal
Depot

Burradon

Killingworth

Callerton
ICI

A

Coxlodge
Fawdon
Wansbeck Road
Regent Centre
Coxlodge-
Rowntrees
Depot

Benton

*Benton
Quarry
Junc.*

Kenton
Bank
Foot

South
Gosforth

Longbenton

Four
Lane
Ends

SOUTH GOSFORTH
METRO CONTROL CENTRE

Ilford
Road

West
Jesmond

*(Section retained
for Empty Stock
movements only)*

Heaton
C.S.

Cement
Term.

Heaton

Walkergate

HT

Chillingham
Road

Jesmond

*Riverside
Junc.*

Byker

Haymarket

Stella
North

Stella
South

St. James

Monument

St. Peters
Scrapyard

Newcastle
Cen.

Manors

Gateshead

f

Forth Goods
Railway St.

e

b

g

c

d

Tyneside Central
Freight Depot

Blaydon

Swalwell

Dunston

Dunston
Staithes

a

h

GD
Gateshead

Eldon St.

B

Derwenthaugh
Coking Plant

Norwood Junc.
Allerdene Junc.

i

j

k

Old
Fold

Felling

Heworth

CCE Depot
Low Fell Yard
Low Fell Junc.

Norwood
Coking Plant

a) *King Edward Bridge West*
b) *King Edward Bridge North*
c) *Greensfield Junc.*
d) *High Street Junc.*
e) *King Edward Bridge*
f) *High Level Bridge*
g) *Park Lane Junc.*
h) *King Edward Bridge East*
j) *Bensham Curve Junc.*
k) *Low Fell Sidings Junc.*

*Springwell
Incline*

TANFIELD
RAILWAY

TYNE
YARD

TY

C

Birtley

0   1   2   m. (1:90,000)
0   1   2   3   4   km

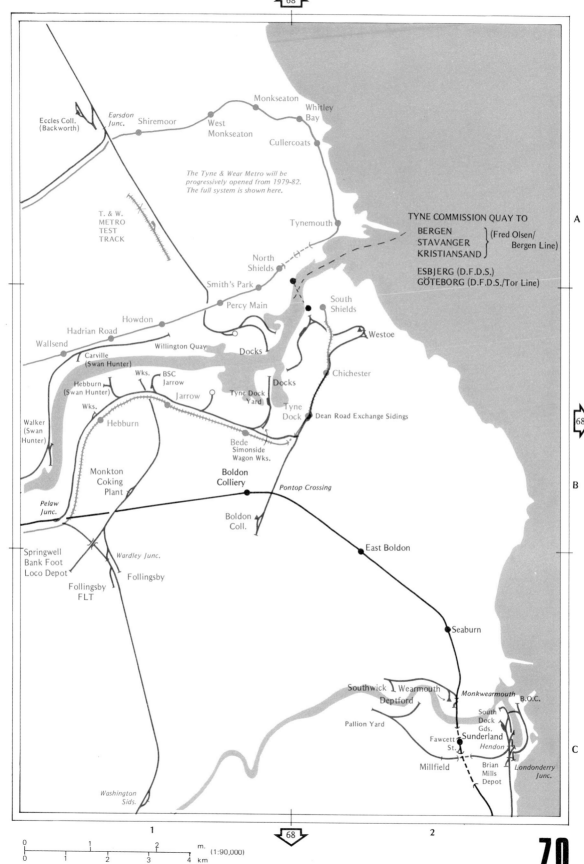

Eccles Coll.
(Backworth)

Earsdon Junc. Shiremoor

West Monkseaton

Monkseaton

Whitley Bay

Cullercoats

T. & W.
METRO
TEST
TRACK

*The Tyne & Wear Metro will be
progressively opened from 1979-82.
The full system is shown here.*

Tynemouth

North Shields

TYNE COMMISSION QUAY TO
BERGEN
STAVANGER } (Fred Olsen/
KRISTIANSAND } Bergen Line)

ESBJERG (D.F.D.S.)
GÖTEBORG (D.F.D.S./Tor Line)

Smith's Park

Percy Main

South Shields

Howdon

Hadrian Road

Willington Quay

Docks

Westoe

Wallsend

Carville
(Swan Hunter)

Wks.

BSC
Jarrow

Chichester

Hebburn
(Swan Hunter)

Jarrow

Docks

Wks.

Tyne Dock
Yard

Hebburn

Tyne
Dock

Dean Road Exchange Sidings

Walker
(Swan
Hunter)

Bede
Simonside
Wagon Wks.

68

Monkton
Coking
Plant

**Boldon
Colliery**

Pontop Crossing

B

*Pelaw
Junc.*

Boldon
Coll.

Springwell
Bank Foot
Loco Depot

East Boldon

Wardley Junc.

Follingsby

Follingsby
FLT

Seaburn

Southwick

Wearmouth

Deptford

Monkwearmouth

B.O.C.

Pallion Yard

South
Dock
Gds.

Sunderland

Fawcett
St.

Hendon

C

Millfield

Brian
Mills
Depot

*Londonderry
Junc.*

*Washington
Sids.*

0   1   2   m. (1:90,000)
0   1   2   3   4 km

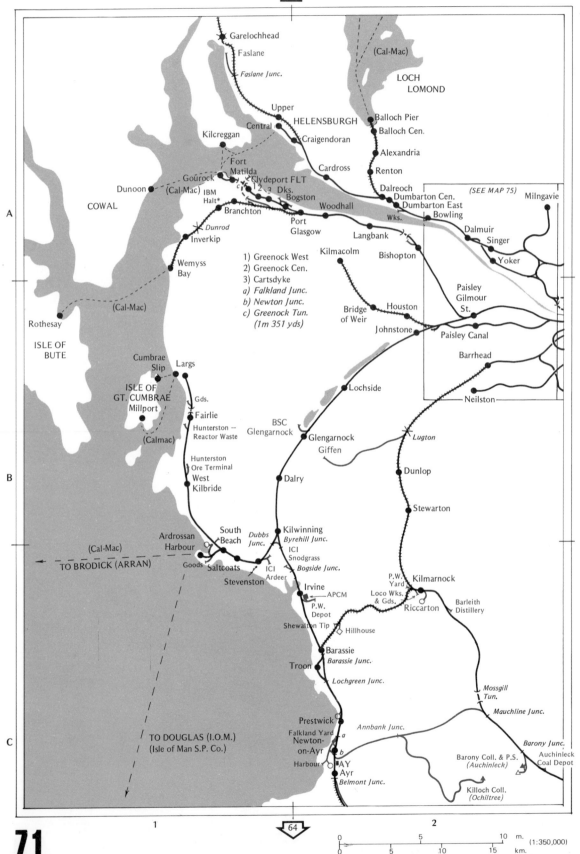

Garelochhead
Faslane
Faslane Junc.

(Cal-Mac)

LOCH
LOMOND

Upper
Central
HELENSBURGH
Craigendoran

Balloch Pier
Balloch Cen.

Kilcreggan
Alexandria

Fort
Matilda
Gourock
Clydeport FLT
c 1 2 3 Dks.
Bogston
Branchton
Port
Glasgow
Woodhall

Cardross
Renton
Dalreoch
Dumbarton Cen.
Dumbarton East
Bowling

Dunoon
(Cal-Mac)
IBM
Halt*

Langbank
Wks.

(SEE MAP 75)
Milngavie

Dalmuir
Singer
Yoker

COWAL

Dunrod
Inverkip

Kilmacolm
Bishopton

Paisley
Gilmour
St.

Wemyss
Bay

1) Greenock West
2) Greenock Cen.
3) Cartsdyke
a) *Falkland Junc.*
b) *Newton Junc.*
c) *Greenock Tun.*
(1m 351 yds)

Houston

Bridge
of Weir
Johnstone

Paisley Canal

(Cal-Mac)

Rothesay

Barrhead

ISLE OF
BUTE

Lochside

Neilston

Cumbrae
Slip
Largs

ISLE OF
GT. CUMBRAE
Millport
Gds.

BSC
Glengarnock

Glengarnock
Giffen

Lugton

Fairlie
Hunterston –
Reactor Waste

(Calmac)

Dunlop

Hunterston
Ore Terminal
West
Kilbride

Dalry

Stewarton

Ardrossan
Harbour

South
Beach

*Dubbs
Junc.*
Kilwinning
Byrehill Junc.
ICI Snodgrass

(Cal-Mac)
TO BRODICK (ARRAN)

Goods
Saltcoats
Stevenston
ICI
Ardeer
Bogside Junc.

P.W.
Yard
Kilmarnock

Irvine
APCM
Loco Wks.
& Gds.
Riccarton

Barleith
Distillery

P.W.
Depot
Shewalton Tip
Hillhouse

Barassie
Barassie Junc.

Troon

Lochgreen Junc.

*Mossgill
Tun.*

Mauchline Junc.

TO DOUGLAS (I.O.M.)
(Isle of Man S.P. Co.)

Prestwick
Annbank Junc.

Falkland Yard
Newton-
on-Ayr
a
b

Barony Junc.
Barony Coll. & P.S.
(*Auchinleck*)
Auchinleck
Coal Depot

Harbour
AY
Ayr
Belmont Junc.

Killoch Coll.
(*Ochiltree*)

1
2

0   5   10 m.
(1:350,000)
0   5   10   15 km.

71

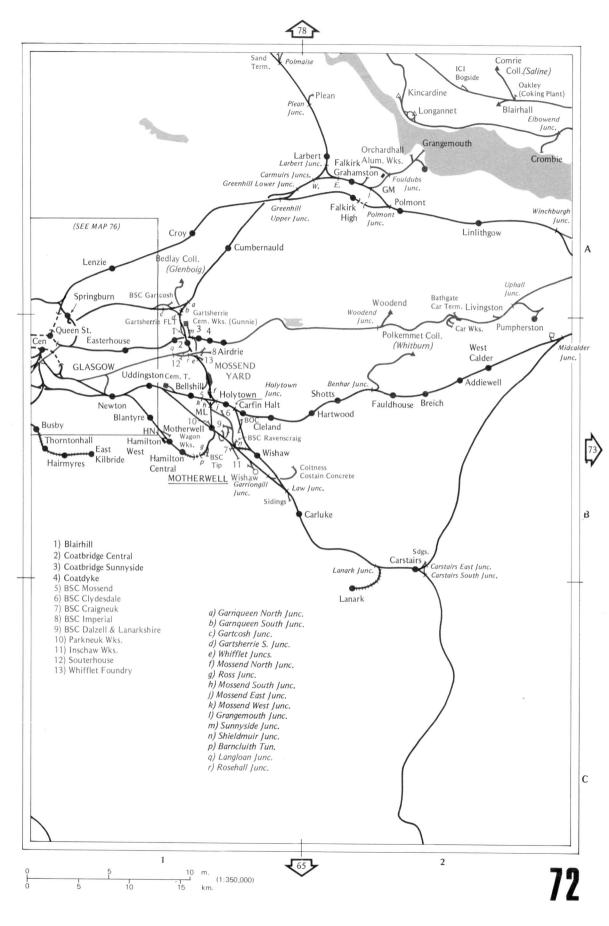

Sand Term.
Polmaise
ICI Bogside
Comrie Coll. *(Saline)*
Oakley (Coking Plant)
Plean
Kincardine
Blairhall
Plean Junc.
Longannet
Elbowend Junc.
Grangemouth
Larbert
Orchardhall Alum. Wks.
Crombie
Larbert Junc.
Falkirk Grahamston
Carmuirs Juncs.
Fouldubs Junc.
Greenhill Lower Junc.
GM
W. *E.*
l
Polmont
Greenhill Upper Junc.
Falkirk High
Polmont Junc.
Linlithgow
Winchburgh Junc.
Croy
Cumbernauld

(SEE MAP 76)

Lenzie
Bedlay Coll. *(Glenboig)*
Woodend
Bathgate Car Term. Livingston
Uphall Junc.
Springburn
BSC Gartcosh
a
Woodend Junc.
Car Wks.
Pumpherston
Gartsherrie FLT
b
Gartsherrie Cem. Wks. (Gunnie)
Queen St.
c
1 *m* *3* *4*
Polkemmet Coll. *(Whitburn)*
West Calder
Midcalder Junc.
Cen
Easterhouse
q *2*
8 Airdrie
Addiewell
GLASGOW
12 *r* *e* *13*
MOSSEND YARD
Uddingston Cem. T.
Holytown Junc.
Busby
Newton
Bellshill
f
Holytown
Shotts
Benhar Junc.
Thorntonhall
Blantyre
5
k *h* *j*
Carfin Halt
Fauldhouse
Breich
Hairmyres
East Kilbride
ML
6
BOC
Hartwood
HN
10
9
Cleland
Motherwell
BSC Ravenscraig
Hamilton West
Wagon Wks.
g
n
Wishaw
Hamilton Central
7
BSC Tip
11
Coltness Costain Concrete
MOTHERWELL
p
Wishaw Garriongill Junc.
Law Junc.
Sidings
Carluke

Sdgs.
Carstairs
Lanark Junc.
Carstairs East Junc.
Carstairs South Junc.
Lanark

1) Blairhill
2) Coatbridge Central
3) Coatbridge Sunnyside
4) Coatdyke
5) BSC Mossend
6) BSC Clydesdale
7) BSC Craigneuk
8) BSC Imperial
9) BSC Dalzell & Lanarkshire
10) Parkneuk Wks.
11) Inschaw Wks.
12) Souterhouse
13) Whifflet Foundry

a) *Garnqueen North Junc.*
b) *Garnqueen South Junc.*
c) *Gartcosh Junc.*
d) *Gartsherrie S. Junc.*
e) *Whifflet Juncs.*
f) *Mossend North Junc.*
g) *Ross Junc.*
h) *Mossend South Junc.*
j) *Mossend East Junc.*
k) *Mossend West Junc.*
l) *Grangemouth Junc.*
m) *Sunnyside Junc.*
n) *Shieldmuir Junc.*
p) *Barncluith Tun.*
q) *Langloan Junc.*
r) *Rosehall Junc.*

A

73

B

C

1
2

0   5   10 m.
0   5   10   15 km.
(1:350,000)

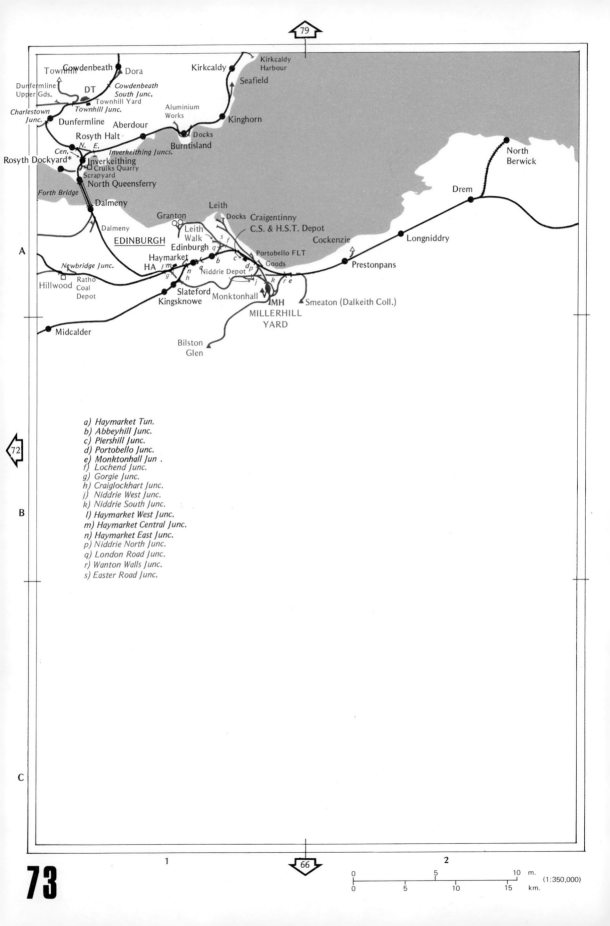

Townhill
Cowdenbeath
Dora
Kirkcaldy
Kirkcaldy Harbour
Seafield
Dunfermline Upper Gds.
DT
Cowdenbeath South Junc.
Townhill Yard
Charlestown Junc.
Townhill Junc.
Aluminium Works
Kinghorn
Dunfermline
Aberdour
Rosyth Halt
N. E.
Docks
Burntisland
Cen.
Inverkeithing Juncs.
Rosyth Dockyard*
Inverkeithing
Cruiks Quarry
North Berwick
Scrapyard
North Queensferry
Forth Bridge
Drem
Dalmeny
Granton
Leith
Dalmeny
Docks
Craigentinny
Leith Walk
C.S. & H.S.T. Depot
EDINBURGH
Cockenzie
Edinburgh
Longniddry
A
Newbridge Junc.
Haymarket
HA
Portobello FLT
Goods
Prestonpans
Hillwood
Ratho Coal Depot
Niddrie Depot
Slateford
Monktonhall
Smeaton (Dalkeith Coll.)
Kingsknowe
Midcalder
MH
MILLERHILL YARD
Bilston Glen

a) Haymarket Tun.
b) Abbeyhill Junc.
c) Piershill Junc.
d) Portobello Junc.
e) Monktonhall Jun .
f) Lochend Junc.
g) Gorgie Junc.
h) Craiglockhart Junc.
j) Niddrie West Junc.
k) Niddrie South Junc.
l) Haymarket West Junc.
m) Haymarket Central Junc.
n) Haymarket East Junc.
p) Niddrie North Junc.
q) London Road Junc.
r) Wanton Walls Junc.
s) Easter Road Junc.

A

B

C

1

2

0 ___ 5 ___ 10 m.
0 ___ 5 ___ 10 ___ 15 km.
(1:350,000)

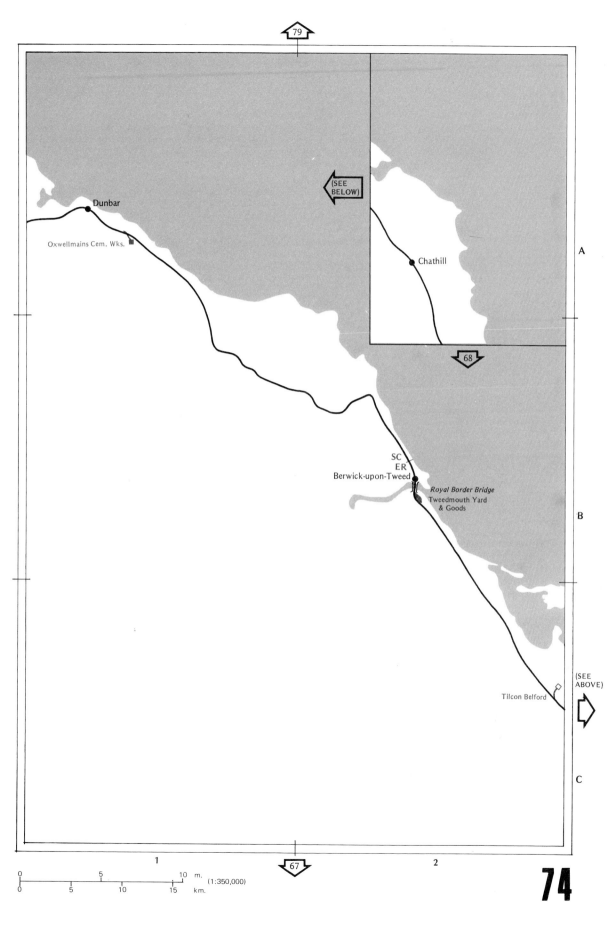

Dunbar

Oxwellmains Cem. Wks.

(SEE BELOW)

Chathill

A

68

SC
ER
Berwick-upon-Tweed

Royal Border Bridge
Tweedmouth Yard
& Goods

B

(SEE ABOVE)

Tilcon Belford

C

1

2

0   5   10 m. (1:350,000)
0   5   10   15 km.

74

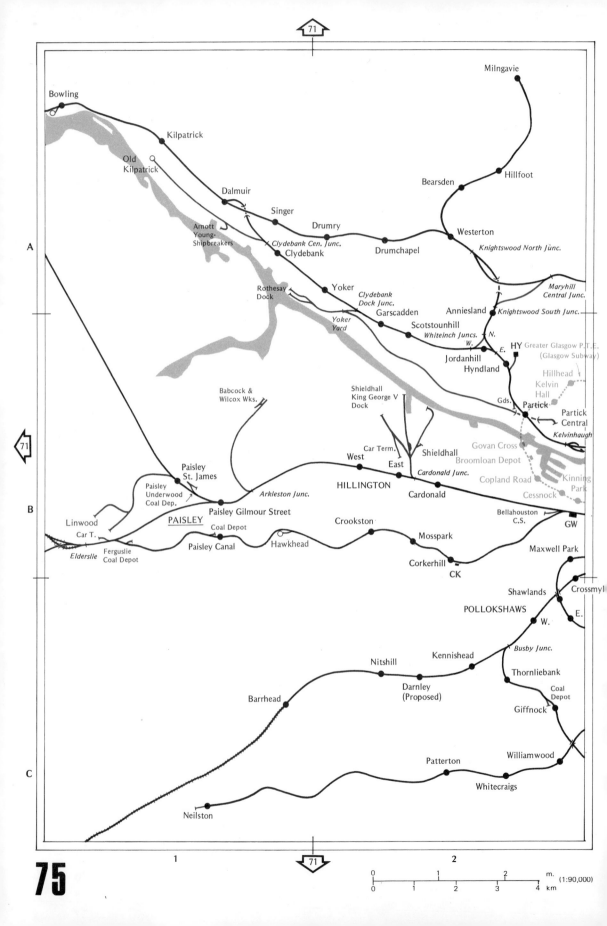

Milngavie

Bowling

Kilpatrick

Old
Kilpatrick

Dalmuir

Singer

Arnott
Young-
Shipbreakers

Clydebank Cen. Junc.
Clydebank

Drumry

Drumchapel

Bearsden

Hillfoot

Westerton

Knightswood North Junc.

A

Rothesay
Dock

Yoker

*Clydebank
Dock Junc.*
Garscadden

*Yoker
Yard*

Scotstounhill

Whiteinch Juncs. N.

W.

Anniesland

*Maryhill
Central Junc.*

Knightswood South Junc.

E.

HY Greater Glasgow P.T.E.
(Glasgow Subway)

Jordanhill
Hyndland

Hillhead

Kelvin
Hall

Gds.

Partick

Partick
Central

Kelvinhaugh

Babcock &
Wilcox Wks.

Shieldhall
King George V
Dock

Car Term.

Shieldhall

Govan Cross

Broomloan Depot

Copland Road

Kinning
Park

Cessnock

West

East

Cardonald Junc.

HILLINGTON

Cardonald

Bellahouston
C.S.

GW

Paisley
St. James

Paisley
Underwood
Coal Dep.

Arkleston Junc.

Paisley Gilmour Street

Crookston

Mosspark

Maxwell Park

Linwood
Car T.

Elderslie

Ferguslie
Coal Depot

PAISLEY

Coal Depot

Paisley Canal

Hawkhead

Corkerhill

CK

Crossmyl

Shawlands

POLLOKSHAWS

E.

W.

Busby Junc.

Nitshill

Kennishead

Thornliebank

Coal
Depot

Barrhead

Darnley
(Proposed)

Giffnock

Williamwood

Patterton

Whitecraigs

Neilston

C

75

1

2

0   1   2   m.   (1:90,000)
0   1   2   3   4   km

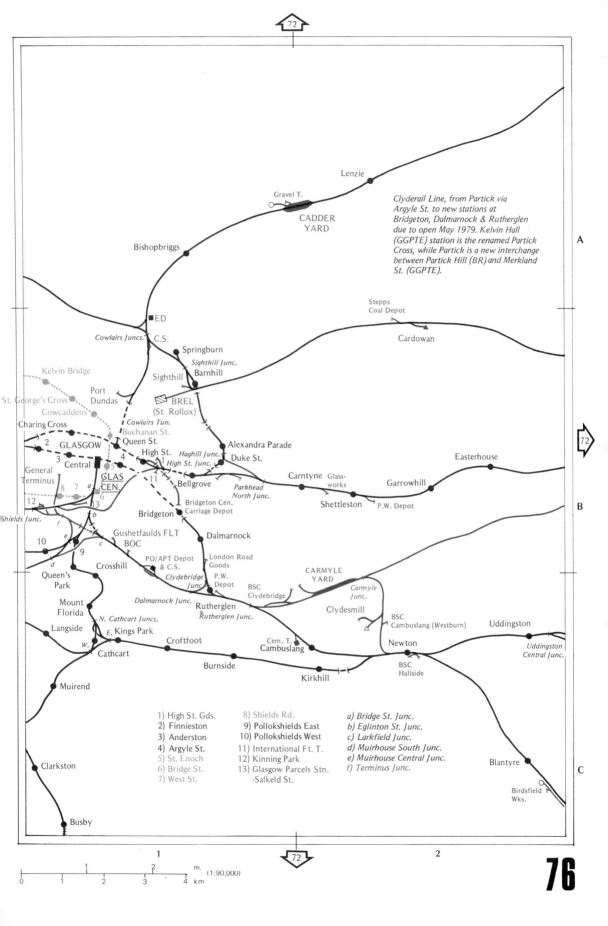

Gravel T.

CADDER
YARD

Lenzie

*Clyderail Line, from Partick via
Argyle St. to new stations at
Bridgeton, Dalmarnock & Rutherglen
due to open May 1979. Kelvin Hall
(GGPTE) station is the renamed Partick
Cross, while Partick is a new interchange
between Partick Hill (BR) and Merkland
St. (GGPTE).*

A

Bishopbriggs

Stepps
Coal Depot

ED

Cowlairs Juncs.   C.S.   Cardowan

Springburn

Sighthill Junc.

Kelvin Bridge   Sighthill   Barnhill

St. George's Cross   Port
Cowcaddens   Dundas

Charing Cross   BREL
                                (St. Rollox)

Cowlairs Tun.
Buchanan St.

2 GLASGOW   Queen St.   Easterhouse

3 Central   High St.   Alexandra Parade
                    4 High St. Junc. Duke St.
General   Haghill Junc.
Terminus   GLAS   11   Carntyne Glass-   Garrowhill
         8 7 a CEN.   Bellgrove   works
12   6   Parkhead   Shettleston
         13   North Junc.   P.W. Depot   B
Shields Junc.   b   Bridgeton
              f   Bridgeton Cen.
          e   Carriage Depot
10   c   Gushetfaulds FLT   Dalmarnock
    9 d BOC   CARMYLE
                                            YARD
Queen's Park   Crosshill   PO/APT Depot   London Road
                           & C.S.   Goods
Mount   Clydebridge   P.W.   Carmyle
Florida   Junc.   Depot   BSC   Junc.
                 N. Cathcart Juncs. Dalmarnock Junc. Clydebridge
Langside   E. Kings Park   Rutherglen   Clydesmill
         W.   Rutherglen Junc.   BSC   Uddingston
    Cathcart   Croftfoot   Cambuslang (Westburn)
                                      Cem. T.   Newton   Uddingston
Muirend   Burnside   Cambuslang   Central Junc.
                                   Kirkhill   BSC
                                                   Hallside
                                              BSC
Clarkston   Blantyre   C

                                                                    Birdsfield
                                                                    Wks.
Busby

1) High St. Gds.   8) Shields Rd.   a) Bridge St. Junc.
2) Finnieston   9) Pollokshields East   b) Eglinton St. Junc.
3) Anderston   10) Pollokshields West   c) Larkfield Junc.
4) Argyle St.   11) International Ft. T. d) Muirhouse South Junc.
5) St. Enoch   12) Kinning Park   e) Muirhouse Central Junc.
6) Bridge St.   13) Glasgow Parcels Stn. f) Terminus Junc.
7) West St.   -Salkeld St.

1   2

72

m. (1:90,000)

0 1 2 3 4 km

76

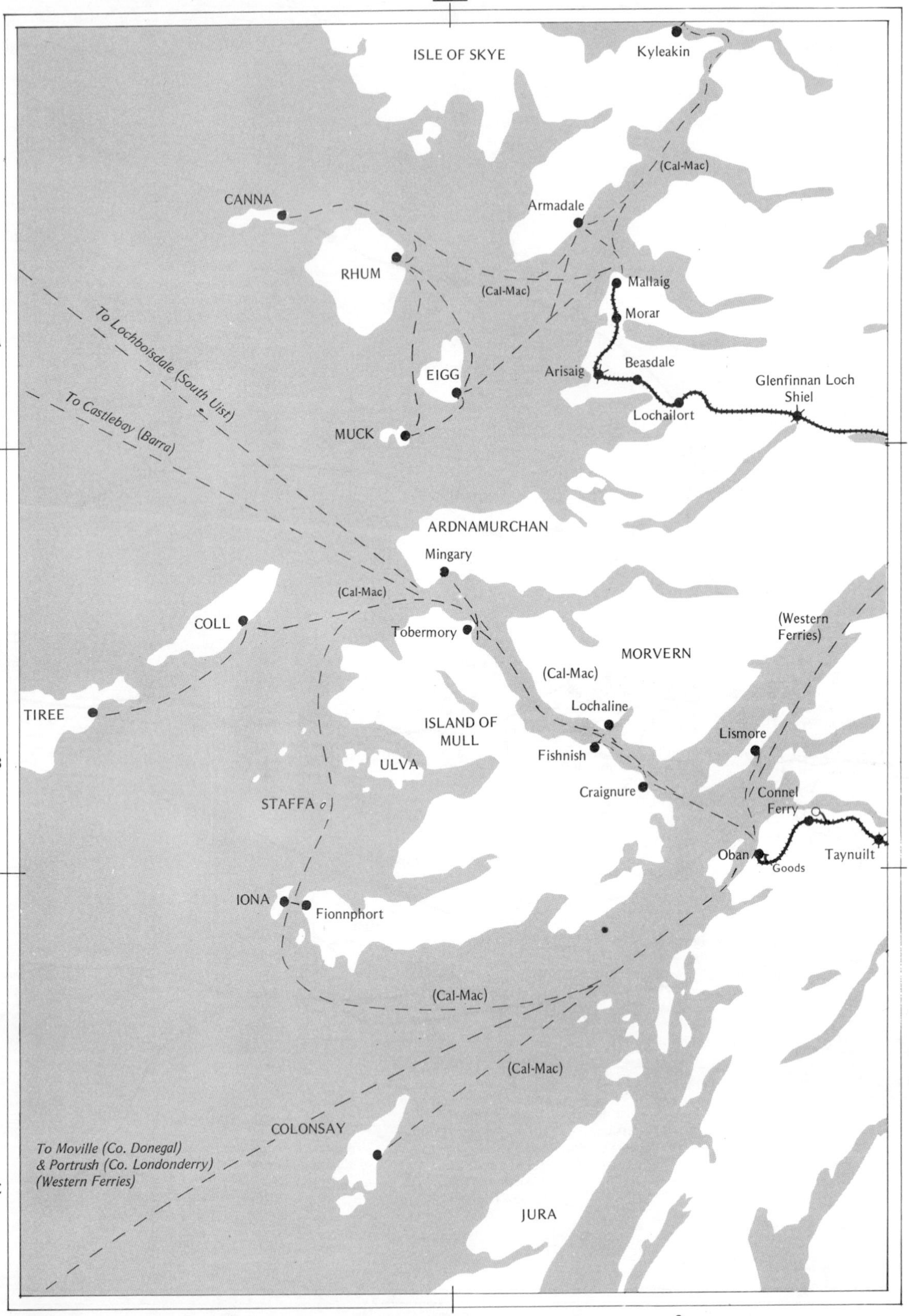

ISLE OF SKYE

Kyleakin

(Cal-Mac)

CANNA

Armadale

RHUM

Mallaig

Morar

EIGG

Beasdale

Arisaig

Glenfinnan Loch
Shiel

MUCK

Lochailort

(Cal-Mac)

To Lochboisdale (South Uist)

To Castlebay (Barra)

A

ARDNAMURCHAN

Mingary

(Cal-Mac)

(Western
Ferries)

COLL

Tobermory

MORVERN

(Cal-Mac)

Lochaline

Lismore

TIREE

Fishnish

ISLAND OF
MULL

B

ULVA

Craignure

Connel
Ferry

STAFFA

IONA

Oban

Taynuilt

Fionnphort

Goods

(Cal-Mac)

(Cal-Mac)

COLONSAY

To Moville (Co. Donegal)
& Portrush (Co. Londonderry)
(Western Ferries)

C

JURA

1

2

0   10   20 m.

(1:700,000)

0   10   20   30 km.

77

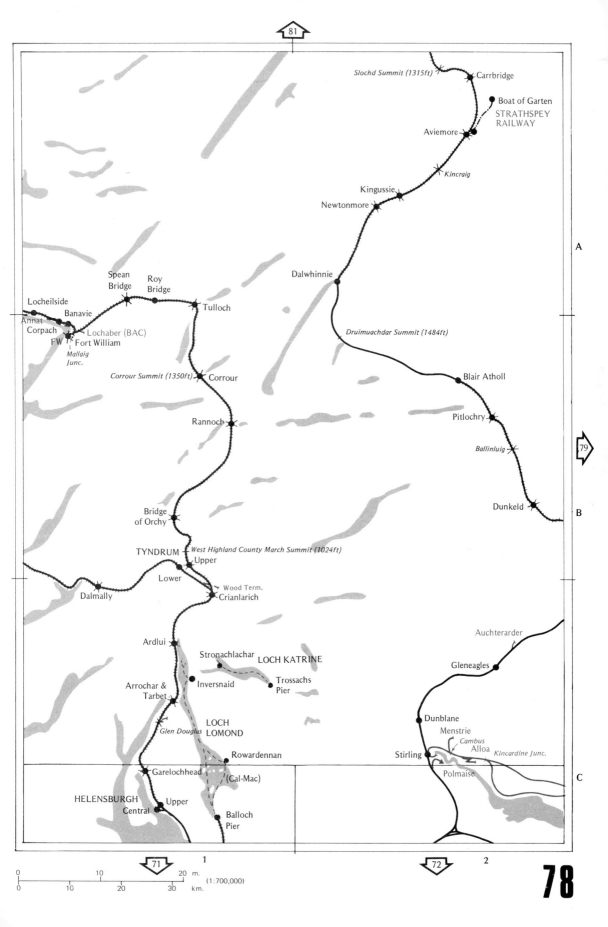

Slochd Summit (1315ft) Carrbridge

Boat of Garten
STRATHSPEY
RAILWAY

Aviemore

Kincraig

Kingussie
Newtonmore

Dalwhinnie

A

Spean
Bridge
Roy
Bridge
Locheilside
Banavie Tulloch
Annat
Corpach
FW
Lochaber (BAC)
Fort William
*Mallaig
Junc.*

Druimuachdar Summit (1484ft)

Blair Atholl

Corrour Summit (1350ft) Corrour

Pitlochry

Ballinluig

Rannoch

79

Dunkeld
B

Bridge
of Orchy

West Highland County March Summit (1024ft)
TYNDRUM
Upper
Lower
Dalmally
↗ Wood Term.
Crianlarich

Ardlui

Stronachlachar LOCH KATRINE

Arrochar &
Tarbet
Inversnaid
Trossachs
Pier
Auchterarder

Gleneagles

Glen Douglas
LOCH
LOMOND
Dunblane
Menstrie
Cambus
Alloa
Kincardine Junc.
Rowardennan
Stirling
HELENSBURGH
Garelochhead
(Cal-Mac)
Polmaise
C
Central
Upper
Balloch
Pier

0   10   20 m.
0   10   20   30 km.
(1:700,000)

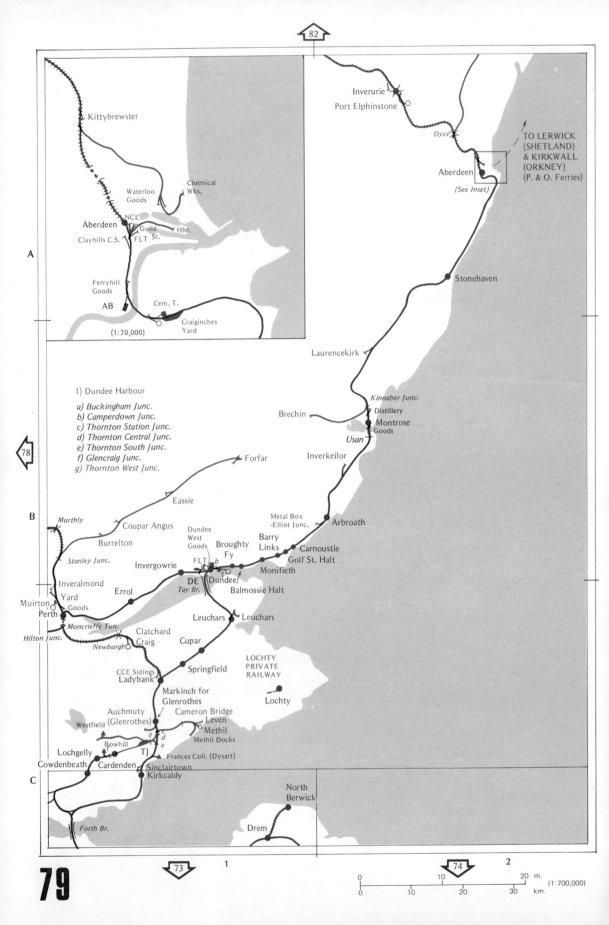

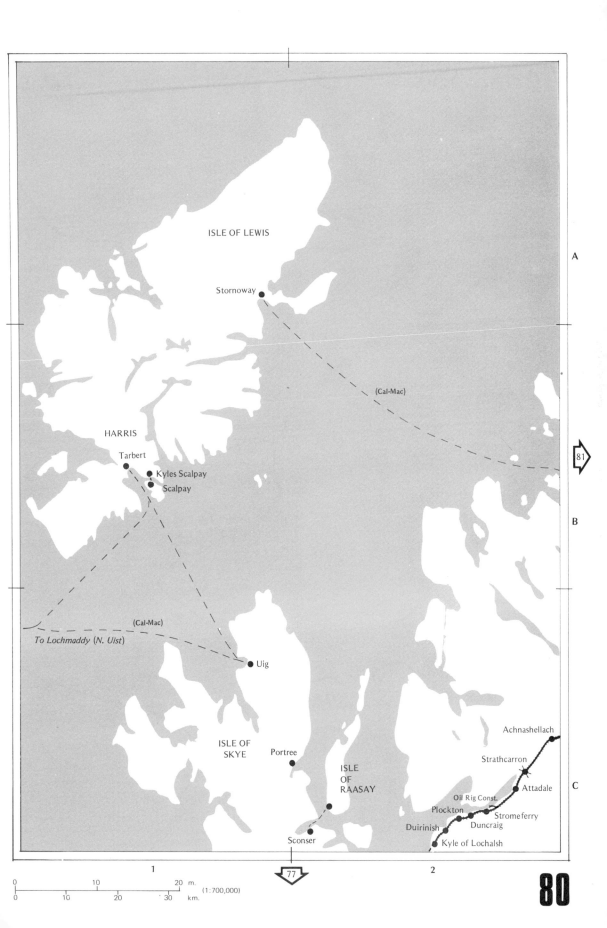

ISLE OF LEWIS

Stornoway

(Cal-Mac)

HARRIS

Tarbert
Kyles Scalpay
Scalpay

(Cal-Mac)

To Lochmaddy (N. Uist)

Uig

Achnashellach

Strathcarron

ISLE OF
SKYE

Portree

Attadale

ISLE
OF
RAASAY

Oil Rig Const.

Plockton

Stromeferry

Duirinish
Duncraig

Sconser

Kyle of Lochalsh

A

81

B

C

1

77

2

0   10   20 m.
0   10   20   30 km.
(1:700,000)

80

Altnabreac

Forsinard

County March
Summit (708 ft)

Kinbrace

Kildonan

Helmsdale

Lairg

Brora

Rogart

Golspie

Invershin

Culrain

Ullapool

Ardgay

Tain

Fearn

Aluminium Wks.

Alness

Pipes
Invergordon

Gds.

Lochluichart

Evanton

Achanalt

Garve

Forres

Achnasheen

Dingwall

Ravens Rock
Summit (458 ft)

Nairn

Luib Summit
(646 ft)

Muir of Ord

Grain

Gds.

IS

Bitumen Sid.
Culloden Moor

Lentran
Welsh's
Bridge
Junc.

Inverness

Millburn
Junc.

Rose
St.

Moy

Tomatin

A

80

B

C

1

78

2

0   10   20 m.
0   10   20   30 km.

(1:700,000)

81

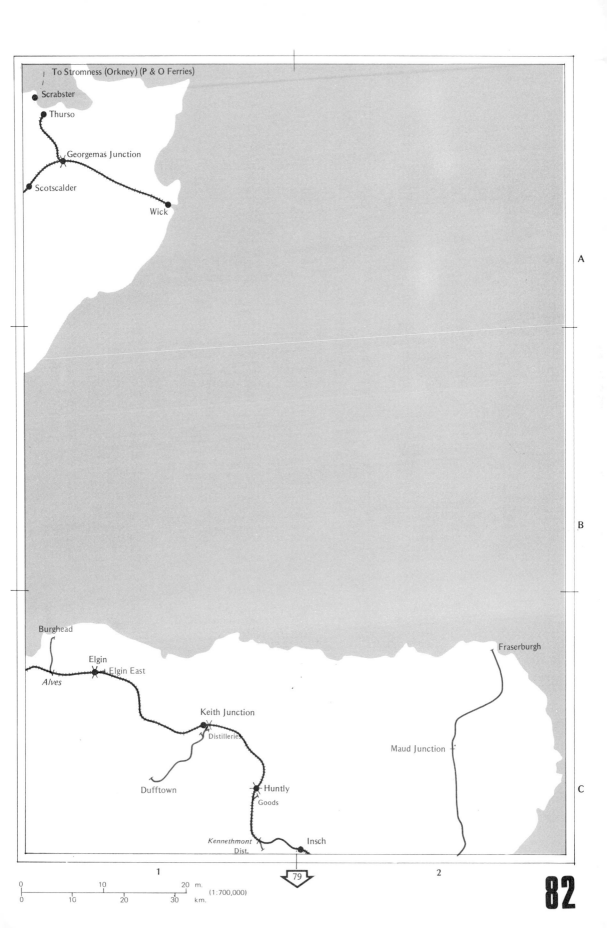

To Stromness (Orkney) (P & O Ferries)

Scrabster

Thurso

Georgemas Junction

Scotscalder

Wick

A

B

Burghead

Fraserburgh

Elgin

Elgin East

Alves

Keith Junction

Distilleries

Maud Junction

Dufftown

Huntly

Goods

C

Kennethmont
Dist.

Insch

1

79

2

0   10   20 m.

(1:700,000)

0   10   20   30   km.

For list of abbreviations see end of Passenger Station Index
(* Indicates unadvertised or excursion station)

Balloch Pier	SC	71	A2		Belle Vue	LM	52	B1
Balmossie	SC	79	B1		Bellgrove	SC	76	B1
Bamber Bridge	LM	54	B2		Bellingham	SO	18	A1
Bamford	LM	47	A1		Bellshill	SC	72	B1
Banavie	SC	78	B1		Belmont	SO	17	C1
Banbury	LM	30	A2		Belper	LM	47	C1
Bangor	LM	43	A2		Belsize Park	LT	21	A1
Bank	SO/LT	21	B2		Beltring & Branbridges	SO	12	A2
Bank Hall	LM	53	B1		Belvedere	SO	32	C2
Bank Foot	TW	69	A1		Bempton	ER	63	C2
Banstead	SO	17	C1		Benfleet	ER	33	C1
Barassie	SC	71	C2		Ben Rhydding	ER	55	A2
Barbican	LM/LT	21	B2		Bentham	LM	55	A1
Bardon Mill	ER	67	C1		Bentley	SO	11	B1
Bare Lane	LM	54	A2		Benton	TW	69	A2
Bargoed	WR	28	B1		Bere Alston	WR	2	B2
Barking	ER/LT	22	B2		Bere Ferrers	WR	2	B2
Barkingside	LT	22	A2		Berkhamsted	LM	31	B2
Barlaston	LM	46	C1		Berkswell	LM	38	B1
Barming	SO	13	A1		Berney Arms	ER	42	A1
Barmouth	LM	34	A2		Berrylands	SO	16	B2
Barmouth Ferry	FB	34	A2		Berwick (Sussex)	SO	12	C2
Barnehurst	SO	32	C2		Berwick-upon-Tweed	ER	74	B2
Barnes	SO	20	C2		Bescar Lane	LM	54	C2
Barnes Bridge	SO	20	C2		Bescot	LM	37	B2
Barnetby	ER	57	C2		Besses o' th' Barn	LM	51	A2
Barnham	SO	11	C2		Betchworth	SO	11	A2
Barnhill	SC	76	B1		Bethnal Green	ER/LT	22	B1
Barnsley	ER	56	C1		Betws-y-Coed	LM	44	B1
Barnstaple	WR	6	B2		Beverley	ER	57	B2
Barnt Green	LM	37	B2		Bewdley	SV	37	B1
Barons Court	LT	21	C1		Bexhill	SO	13	C1
Barrhead	SC	75	C1		Bexley	SO	32	C2
Barrhill	SC	64	B1		Bexleyheath	SO	32	C2
Barrow-in-Furness	LM	54	A1		Bicester	LM	30	A2
Barrow Haven	ER	57	B2		Bickley	SO	18	B2
Barry	WR	7	A2		Bideford*	WR	6	B2
Barry Docks	WR	8	A1		Bidston	LM	45	A1
Barry Island	WR	7	A2		Biggleswade	ER	31	A2
Barry Links	SC	79	B1		Bilbrook	LM	37	A1
Barton-on-Humber	ER	57	B2		Billericay	ER	32	C2
Basildon	ER	32	C2		Billingham	ER	62	A2
Basingstoke	SO	10	A2		Billingshurst	SO	11	B2
Bat & Ball	SO	12	A2		Bingham	LM	48	C1
Bath Spa	WR	9	A1		Bingham Road	SO	17	B2
Batley	ER	56	B1		Bingley	ER	55	B2
Battersby	ER	62	B2		Birchgrove	WR	28	C1
Battersea Park	SO	21	C1		Birchington-on-Sea	SO	14	A1
Battle	SO	13	C1		Birkbeck	SO	18	B1
Battlesbridge	ER	33	C1		Birkdale	LM	54	C1
Bayford	ER	32	B1		Birkenhead Central	LM	53	C1
Bayswater	LT	21	B1		Birkenhead Hamilton Square	LM	53	B1
Beaconsfield	LM	31	C1		Birkenhead North	LM	53	B1
Bearley	LM	38	C1		Birkenhead Park	LM	53	B1
Bearsden	SC	75	A2		Birmingham International	LM	38	B1
Bearsted & Thurnham	SO	13	A1		Birmingham Moor Street	LM	38	B2
Beasdale	SC	77	A2		Birmingham New Street	LM	38	B2
Beaulieu Road	SO	10	C1		Bishop Auckland	ER	62	A1
Bebington & New Ferry	LM	53	C1		Bishopbriggs	SC	76	A1
Beccles	ER	42	B1		Bishops Stortford	ER	32	B2
Beckenham Hill	SO	18	A1		Bishopstone	SO	12	C2
Beckenham Junction	SO	18	A1		Bishopton	SC	71	A2
Beckfoot	RE	60	B1		Bispham	BF	54	B1
Becontree	LT	32	C1		Blackburn	LM	55	B1
Beddington Lane	SO	17	B2		Blackfriars	SO/LT	21	B2
Bede	TW	70	B1		Blackheath	SO	22	C1
Bedford Midland	LM	39	C2		Black Horse Road	ER/LT	22	A1
Bedford St. John's	LM	39	C2		Blackpool North	LM	54	B1
Bedhampton	SO	11	C1		Blackpool South	LM	54	B1
Bedminster	WR	8	B2		Blackrod	LM	54	C2
Bedwyn	WR	10	A1		Blackwater	SO	11	A1
Beeston	LM	47	C2		Blaenau Ffestiniog	LM/FR	44	C1
Bekesbourne	SO	13	A2		Blair Atholl	SC	78	B2
Belgrave & Birstall	ML	37	A2		Blairhill	SC	72	A1
Bellevue	ME	59	B2		Blakedown	LM	37	B1

84

Blake Hall	LT	32	B2		Brimsdown	ER	24	B1
Blake Street	LM	37	A2		Brinnington	LM	52	C2
Blantyre	SC	76	C2		Bristol Parkway	WR	28	C2
Blaydon	ER	69	B1		Bristol Temple Meads	WR	8	B2
Bleasby	LM	48	B1		Brithdir	WR	28	B1
Bletchley	LM	31	A1		British Steel (Redcar)*	ER	62	A2
Blue Anchor	WS	7	B2		Brixton	SO/LT	21	C2
Blundellsands & Crosby	LM	53	A1		Broadbottom	LM	46	A2
Blythe Bridge	LM	46	C2		Broad Green	LM	53	B2
Boat of Garten	SY	78	A2		Broadstairs	SO	14	A1
Bodmin Road	WR	2	B1		Broad Street	LM	21	B2
Bodorgan	LM	43	B2		Brockenhurst	SO	10	C1
Bognor Regis	SO	11	C1		Brockholes	ER	56	C1
Bogston	SC	71	A1		Brocklesby	ER	57	C2
Boldon Colliery	ER	70	B1		Brockley	SO	22	C1
Bolton	LM	55	C1		Bromborough	LM	45	A1
Bolton-on-Dearne	ER	56	C2		Bromley-by-Bow	LT	22	B1
Bond Street	LT	21	B1		Bromley Cross	LM	55	C1
Bookham	SO	11	A2		Bromley North	SO	18	B2
Boothferry Park*	ER	57	B2		Bromley South	SO	18	B2
Bootle (Cumbria)	LM	59	C2		Bromsgrove	WR	37	C2
Bootle New Strand	LM	53	A1		Brondesbury	LM	21	B1
Bootle Oriel Road	LM	53	A1		Brondesbury Park	LM	21	B1
Bordesley	LM	38	B2		Bronwydd Arms	GW	62	A2
Borough	LT	21	B2		Brooklands	LM	51	C2
Borough Green & Wrotham	SO	12	A2		Brookman's Park	ER	32	B1
Borth	LM	34	B2		Brookwood	SO	11	A2
Bosham	SO	11	C1		Broome	WR	36	B2
Boston	ER	49	C1		Broomfleet	ER	57	B1
Boston Lodge	FR	43	C2		Brora	SC	81	B2
Boston Manor	LT	20	C1		Brough	ER	57	B2
Botley	SO	10	C2		Broughty Ferry	SC	79	B1
Bottesford	ER	48	C1		Broxbourne	ER	32	B1
Bounds Green	LT	23	C2		Bruce Grove	ER	23	C2
Bourne End	WR	31	C1		Brundall	ER	42	A1
Bournemouth	SO	5	A2		Brundall Gardens	ER	42	A1
Bournville	LM	37	B2		Bruton	WR	9	B1
Bow Brickhill	LM	31	A1		Bryn	LM	54	C2
Bowes Park	ER	23	C2		Brynglas	TL	34	A2
Bowker Vale	LM	51	A2		Buchanan Street	GG	76	B1
Bowling	SC	75	A1		Buckenham	ER	42	A1
Bow Road	LT	22	B1		Buckfastleigh	DV	3	B1
Boxhill & Westhumble	SO	11	A2		Buckhurst Hill	LT	24	C2
Bracknell	SO	11	A1		Buckley	LM	45	B1
Bradford-on-Avon	WR	8	A1		Bucknell	WR	36	B1
Bradford Exchange	ER	56	B1		Bugle	WR	1	B2
Bradford Forster Square	ER	56	B1		Builth Road	LM	35	C2
Brading	SO	6	A2		Bungalow	ME	59	C1
Braintree	ER	33	A1		Bures	ER	33	A1
Bramhall	LM	46	A1		Burgess Hill	SO	12	C1
Bramley	SO	10	A2		Burley-in-Wharfedale	ER	56	A1
Brampton (Cumbria)	ER	66	C2		Burmarsh Road Halt*	RH	13	B2
Brampton (Suffolk)	ER	42	B1		Burnage	LM	52	C1
Branchton	SC	71	A1		Burneside	LM	60	C2
Brandon	ER	41	B1		Burnham	WR	31	C1
Branksome	SO	5	A2		Burnham-on-Crouch	ER	33	C1
Braystones	LM	59	B2		Burnley Barracks	LM	55	B1
Bredbury	LM	52	C2		Burnley Central	LM	55	B1
Breich	SC	72	B2		Burnside	SC	76	C1
Brent Cross	LT	20	A2		Burntisland	SC	73	A1
Brentford Central	SO	20	C1		Burnt Oak	LT	31	C2
Brentwood	ER	32	C2		Burscough Bridge	LM	54	C2
Bricket Wood	LM	31	B2		Burscough Junction	LM	54	C2
Bridgend	WR	27	C2		Bursledon	SO	10	C2
Bridge of Orchy	SC	78	B1		Burton-on-Trent	LM	47	C1
Bridge of Weir	SC	71	B2		Burton Joyce	LM	47	C2
Bridge Street	GG	76	B1		Bury	LM	55	C1
Bridgeton	SC	76	B1		Bury St. Edmunds	ER	41	C1
Bridgnorth	WR	8	B1		Busby	SC	76	C1
Bridgwater	SV	37	B1		Bushey	LM/LT	31	C2
Bridlington	ER	57	A2		Bush Hill Park	ER	23	B2
Brierfield	LM	55	B1		Butlers Lane	LM	37	A2
Brigg	ER	57	C2		Buxted	SO	12	B2
Brighton	SO	12	C1		Buxton	LM	46	A2
Brightside	ER	50	A1		Byfleet & New Haw	SO	15	C1

Station	Region	Page	Grid		Station	Region	Page	Grid
Byker	TW	69	B2		Chapeltown	ER	50	A1
Bynea	WR	26	B2		Chappel & Wakes Colne	ER	33	A1
Cabin	BF	54	B1		Charing	SO	13	A1
Cadoxton	WR	8	A1		Charing Cross (Glasgow)	SC	76	B1
Caergwrle	LM	45	B1		Charing Cross (London)	SO/LT	21	B2
Caerphilly	WR	28	C1		Charlbury	WR	30	B1
Caersws	LM	35	B2		Charlton	SO	22	C2
Caldicot	WR	28	C2		Chartham	SO	13	A2
Caledonian Road	LT	21	A2		Chassen Road	LM	51	C1
Caledonian Road & Barnsbury	LM	21	B2		Chatham	SO	13	A1
Calstock	WR	2	B2		Chathill	SC	74	A2
Camberley	SO	11	A1		Cheadle Hulme	LM	46	A1
Camborne	WR	1	C1		Cheam	SO	17	C1
Cambridge	ER	40	C1		Cheddington	LM	31	B1
Cambridge Heath	ER	22	B1		Chelford	LM	46	A1
Cambuslang	SC	76	C2		Chelmsford	ER	32	B2
Camden Road	LM	21	B1		Chelsfield	SO	12	A1
Camden Town	LT	21	B1		Cheltenham Spa	WR	29	A2
Canley	LM	38	B1		Chepstow	WR	28	C2
Canning Town	ER	22	B1		Cherry Tree	LM	55	B1
Cannon Street	SO/LT	21	B2		Chertsey	SO	15	B1
Canonbury	LM	21	A2		Chesham	LT	31	B2
Canons Park	LT	31	C2		Cheshunt	ER	24	A1
Canterbury East	SO	13	A2		Chessington North	SO	16	C1
Canterbury West	SO	13	A2		Chessington South	SO	16	C1
Cantley	ER	42	A1		Chester	LM	45	B2
Capel Bangor	LM	33	B2		Chester-le-Street	ER	68	C1
Capenhurst	LM	45	A1		Chesterfield	ER	47	B1
Carbis Bay	WR	1	A1		Chester Road	LM	37	B2
Cardenden	SC	79	C1		Chestfield & Swalecliffe	SO	13	A2
Cardiff Bute Road	WR	28	C1		Chetnole	WR	8	C2
Cardiff Central	WR	28	C1		Chichester (Sussex)	SO	11	C1
Cardiff Queen Street	WR	28	C1		Chichester (Tyne & Wear)	TW	70	B2
Cardonald	SC	75	B2		Chigwell	LT	24	C2
Cardross	SC	71	A2		Chilham	SO	13	A2
Carfin Halt	SC	72	B1		Chillingham Road	TW	69	B2
Cargo Fleet	ER	62	B2		Chilworth & Albury	SO	11	B2
Cark & Cartmel	LM	60	C1		Chingford	ER	24	C1
Carlisle	LM	66	C2		Chinley	LM	46	A2
Carlton	LM	47	C2		Chippenham	WR	29	C2
Carluke	SC	72	B2		Chipstead	SO	12	A1
Carmarthen	WR	26	B2		Chirk	LM	45	C1
Carnforth	LM	60	C2		Chislehurst	SO	18	B2
Carnoustie	SC	79	B1		Chiswick	SO	20	C2
Carntyne	SC	76	B2		Chiswick Park	LT	20	C2
Carpenders Park	LM/LT	31	C2		Cholsey	WR	30	C2
Carr Bridge	SC	78	A2		Chorley	LM	54	C2
Carshalton	SO	17	B1		Chorley Wood	LM/LT	31	C2
Carshalton Beeches	SO	17	C1		Christ's Hospital	SO	11	B2
Carstairs	SC	72	B2		Christchurch	SU	5	A2
Cartsdyke	SC	71	A1		Church & Ostwaldwhistle	LM	55	B1
Castle Bar Park	WR	20	B1		Church Fenton	ER	56	B2
Castle Caereinon	WL	36	A1		Church Stretton	LM	36	B2
Castle Cary	WR	8	B2		Churston	TD	3	B2
Castleford	ER	56	B2		Cilmery	LM	35	C2
Castleton	LM	55	C1		Clacton	ER	33	C2
Castleton Moor	ER	63	B1		Clandon	SO	11	A2
Castletown	ME	59	C1		Clapham	SO	21	C2
Caterham	SO	12	A1		Clapham (Yorks.)	LM	55	A1
Catford	SO	18	A1		Clapham Common	LT	21	C2
Catford Bridge	SO	18	A1		Clapham Junction	SO	21	C1
Cathcart	SC	76	C1		Clapham North	LT	21	C2
Cattal	ER	56	A2		Clapham South	LT	17	A1
Causeland	WR	2	B1		Clapton	ER	22	A1
Cefn-y-Bedd	LM	45	B1		Clarbeston Road	WR	25	A2
Cefn On	WR	28	C1		Clarkston	SC	76	C1
Cei Llydan	LL	43	B2		Claverdon	LM	38	C1
Cessnock	GG	75	B2		Claygate	SO	16	C1
Chadwell Heath	ER	32	C2		Clayton West	ER	56	C1
Chalfont & Latimer	LM/LT	31	C2		Cleethorpes	ER	58	C1
Chalk Farm	LT	21	B1		Cleland	SC	72	B1
Chalkwell	ER	33	C1		Cleveleys	BF	54	B1
Chancery Lane	LT	21	B2		Clifton	LM	51	A2
Chapel-en-le-Frith	LM	46	A2		Clifton Down	WR	8	A2
Chapelton	WR	6	B2		Clitheroe*	LM	55	B1

Clock House	SO	18	B1
Clogwyn	SM	43	B2
Clydebank	SC	75	A1
Clynderwen	WR	26	B1
Coatbridge Central	SC	72	B1
Coatbridge Sunnyside	SC	72	B1
Coatdyke	SC	72	B1
Cobham & Stoke d'Abernon	SO	11	A2
Cockfosters	LT	23	B1
Codsall	LM	37	A1
Cogan	WR	8	A1
Colby	ME	59	C1
Colchester	ER	33	A1
Colindale	LT	31	C2
Collier's Wood	LT	17	A1
Collingham	ER	48	B1
Collington	SO	12	C2
Colne	LM	55	B1
Colwall	WR	29	A1
Colwyn Bay	LM	44	A1
Colyford	ST	4	A1
Colyton	ST	4	A1
Combe (Oxon)	WR	30	B1
Commondale	ER	63	B1
Congleton	LM	46	B1
Conisbrough	ER	56	C2
Connel Ferry	SC	77	B2
Cooden Beach	SO	12	C2
Cookham	WR	31	C1
Cooksbridge	SO	12	C1
Coombe (Cornwall)	WR	2	B1
Coombe Road	SO	17	C2
Copland Road	GG	75	B2
Copplestone	WR	7	C1
Corbridge	ER	67	C2
Corkerhill	SC	75	B2
Corkickle	LM	59	B2
Cornaa	ME	59	B2
Corpach	SC	78	B1
Corrour	SC	78	B1
Coryton	WR	28	C1
Coseley	LM	37	B2
Cosford	LM	37	A1
Cosham	SO	10	C2
Cottingham	ER	57	B2
Coulsdon North	SO	12	A1
Coulsdon South	SO	12	A1
Covent Garden	LT	21	B2
Coventry	LM	38	B1
Cowcaddens	GG	76	B1
Cowden	SO	12	B2
Cowdenbeath	SC	73	A1
Coxlodge	TW	69	A2
Cradley	LM	37	B2
Craigendoran	SC	71	A1
Cramlington	ER	68	B1
Craven Arms	WR	36	B2
Crawley	SO	12	B1
Crayford	SO	32	C2
Crediton	WR	3	A1
Cressing	ER	33	B1
Cressington	LM	53	C2
Crewe	LM	46	B1
Crewkerne	WR	8	C2
Crews Hill	ER	23	A2
Crianlarich	SC	78	C1
Criccieth	LM	43	C2
Cricklewood	LM	20	A2
Croftfoot	SC	76	C1
Crofton Park	SO	18	A1
Cromer	ER	50	C1
Cromford	LM	47	B1
Crookston	SC	75	B2
Cross Gates	ER	56	B1
Crosshill	SC	76	C1
Crossmyloof	SC	75	C2
Croston	LM	54	C2
Crouch Hill	ER	21	A2
Crowborough & Jarvis Brook	SO	12	B2
Crowle	ER	57	C1
Crowthorne	SO	11	A1
Croxley	LT	31	C2
Croxley Green	LM	31	C2
Croy	SC	72	A1
Crumpsall	LM	52	A1
Crystal Palace	SO	17	A2
Cuddington	LM	45	A2
Cuffley	ER	23	A2
Culham	WR	30	C2
Cullercoats	TW	70	A2
Culrain	SC	81	B2
Cumbernauld	SC	72	A1
Cupar	SC	79	C1
Custom House Victoria Dock	ER	22	B2
Cuxton	SO	12	A2
Cwmdwyfran	GW	26	A2
Cyfronydd	WL	36	A1
Cynghordy	WR	27	A1
Dagenham Dock	ER	32	C2
Dagenham East	LT	32	C2
Dagenham Heathway	LT	32	C2
Daisy Hill	LM	55	C1
Dalegarth	RE	60	B1
Dalmally	SC	78	C1
Dalmarnock	SC	76	B1
Dalmeny	SC	73	A1
Dalmuir	SC	75	A1
Dalreoch	SC	71	A2
Dalry	SC	71	B1
Dalston (Cumbria)	LM	66	C2
Dalston (Kingsland Road)	LM	21	A2
Dalston Junction	LM	21	A2
Dalton	LM	60	C1
Dalwhinnie	SC	78	A2
Damems	KW	55	B2
Danby	ER	63	B1
Dane Road	LM	51	C2
Danzey	LM	37	C2
Darlington	ER	62	B1
Darnall	ER	50	B1
Darnley (Proposed)	SC	75	C2
Darsham	ER	42	C1
Dartford	SO	32	C2
Dartmouth Ferry & Kingswear	TD	3	B2
Darton	ER	56	C1
Darwen	LM	55	B1
Datchet	SO	31	C2
Davenport	LM	52	C1
Dawlish	WR	3	A2
Dawlish Warren	WR	3	A2
Dduallt	FR	44	C1
Deal	SO	14	A1
Dean	SO	10	B1
Dean Lane	LM	52	A1
Deansgate	LM	51	B2
Debden	LT	24	B2
Deepdene	SO	11	A2
Deganwy	LM	44	A1
Delamere	LM	45	B2
Denby Dale	ER	56	C1
Denham	LM	19	A1
Denham Golf Club	LM	31	C2
Denmark Hill	SO	21	C2
Dent*	LM	61	C1
Denton	LM	52	B2
Deptford	SO	22	C1
Derby	LM	47	C1
Derby Castle (Douglas)	ME	59	C1
Derby Road (Ipswich)	ER	33	A2

Devil's Bridge	LM	34	B2
Devonport	WR	2	B2
Dewsbury	ER	56	B1
Dhoon	ME	59	C2
Didcot	WR	30	C2
Dilton Marsh	SO	9	A1
Dinas Powis	WR	8	A1
Dinas Rhondda	WR	27	C2
Dingle Road	WR	8	A1
Dingwall	SC	81	C2
Dinsdale	ER	62	B1
Dinting	LM	46	A2
Disley	LM	46	A2
Diss	ER	41	B2
Ditton	LM	45	A2
Dockyard	WR	2	B2
Dolau	WR	36	C1
Doleham	SO	13	C1
Dolgarrog	LM	44	B1
Dolgoch Falls	TL	34	A2
Dollis Hill	LT	20	A2
Dolwyddelen	LM	44	B1
Doncaster	ER	56	C2
Dorchester South	SO	5	A1
Dorchester West	SO	5	A1
Dore	ER	47	A1
Dorking	SO	11	A2
Dorking Town	SO	11	A2
Dormans	SO	12	B1
Dorridge	LM	38	B1
Douglas	ME	59	C1
Dove Holes	LM	46	A2
Dovercourt	ER	33	A2
Dover Marine	SO	14	B1
Dover Priory	SO	14	B1
Dovey Junction	LM	34	A2
Downham	ER	40	A2
Drayton Green	WR	20	B1
Drayton Park	ER	21	A2
Dreemskerrie	ME	59	B2
Drem	SC	73	A2
Driffield	ER	57	A2
Drigg	LM	59	B2
Droitwich Spa	WR	37	C1
Drumchapel	SC	75	A2
Drumry	SC	75	A2
Duddeston	LM	38	B2
Dudley Port	LM	37	B2
Duffield	LM	47	C1
Duirinish	SC	80	C2
Duke Street	SC	76	B1
Dullingham	ER	40	C2
Dumbarton Central	SC	71	A2
Dumbarton East	SC	71	A2
Dumfries	SC	63	B2
Dumpton Park	SO	14	A1
Dunbar	SC	74	A1
Dunblane	SC	78	C2
Dunbridge	SO	10	B1
Duncraig	SC	80	C2
Dundee	SC	79	B1
Dunfermline	SC	73	A1
Dungeness	RH	13	C2
Dunkeld & Birnam	SC	78	B2
Dunlop	SC	71	B2
Dunster	WS	7	B2
Dunton Green	SO	12	A2
Durham	ER	62	A1
Durrington-on-Sea	SO	11	C2
Dyffryn Ardudwy	LM	43	C2
Dymchurch	RH	13	B2
Eaglescliffe	ER	62	B2
Ealing Broadway	WR/LT	20	B1
Ealing Common	LT	20	B2
Eardington	SV	37	B1
Earl's Court	LT	21	C1
Earlestown	LM	45	A2
Earley	SO	11	A1
Earlsfield	SO	17	A1
Earlswood (Surrey)	SO	12	A1
Earlswood (West Midlands)	LM	37	B2
East Acton	LT	20	B2
East Boldon	ER	70	C2
Eastbourne	SO	12	C2
Eastcote	LT	19	A2
East Croydon	SO	17	B2
East Didsbury	LM	52	C1
East Dulwich	SO	21	C2
Easterhouse	SC	76	B2
East Farleigh	SO	13	A1
East Finchley	LT	21	A1
East Grinstead	SO	12	B1
East Ham	LT	22	B2
East Kilbride	SC	72	B1
Eastleigh	SO	10	C2
East Malling	SO	12	A2
East Putney	LT	21	C1
Eastrington	ER	57	B1
East Tilbury	ER	32	C2
East Worthing	SO	11	C2
Eccles	LM	51	B2
Eccles Road	ER	41	B2
Eccleston Park	LM	45	A2
Edale	LM	46	A2
Edenbridge	SO	12	A1
Edenbridge Town	SO	12	B1
Eden Park	SO	18	B1
Edge Hill	LM	53	B2
Edgware	LT	31	C2
Edgware Road	LT	21	B1
Edinburgh	SC	73	A1
Effingham Junction	SO	11	A2
Eggesford	WR	7	C1
Egham	SO	11	A2
Egton	ER	63	B1
Elephant & Castle	SO/LT	21	C2
Elgin	SC	82	C1
Ellesmere Port	LM	45	A2
Elmers End	SO	18	B1
Elm Park	LT	32	C2
Elmstead Woods	SO	18	A2
Elmswell	ER	41	C1
Elsecar	ER	56	C1
Elsenham	ER	32	A2
Elsham	ER	57	C2
Elstree	LM	31	C2
Eltham Park	SO	22	C2
Eltham Well Hall	SO	22	C2
Elton & Orston	ER	48	C1
Ely	ER	40	B2
Embankment	LT	21	B2
Emerson Park	ER	32	C2
Emsworth	SO	11	C1
Enfield Chase	ER	23	B2
Enfield Lock	ER	24	B1
Enfield Town	ER	23	B2
Entwistle	LM	55	C1
Epping	LT	32	B1
Epsom	SO	16	C2
Epsom Downs	SO	12	A1
Erdington	LM	37	B2
Eridge	SO	12	B2
Erith	SO	32	C2
Errol	SC	79	C1
Esher	SO	16	B1
Eskdale Green	RE	60	B1
Essex Road	ER	21	B2
Etchingham	SO	12	B2
Etruria	LM	46	C1
Euston	LM/LT	21	B2

Euston Square	LT	21	B2		Forsinard	SC	81	A2
Evesham	WR	29	A2		Fort Matilda	SC	71	A1
Ewell East	SO	16	C2		Fort William	SC	78	B1
Ewell West	SO	16	C2		Four Oaks	LM	37	A2
Exeter Central	WR	3	A2		Foxfield	LM	60	C1
Exeter St. David's	WR	3	A2		Foxton	ER	40	C1
Exeter St. Thomas	WR	3	A2		Frant	SO	12	B2
Exmouth	WR	3	A2		Fratton	SO	10	C2
Exton	WR	3	A2		Freshfield (Merseyside)	LM	54	C1
Eylsham	SO	13	A2		Freshfield Halt (Sussex)	BL	12	B1
Eynsford	SO	12	A2		Freshford	WR	9	A1
Failsworth	LM	52	A1		Frimley	SO	11	A1
Fairbourne	LM/FB	34	A2		Frinton	ER	33	B2
Fairfield	LM	52	B2		Frodsham	LM	45	A2
Fairlie	SC	71	B1		Frome	WR	9	B1
Fairlop	LT	24	C2		Fulham Broadway	LT	21	C1
Fairy Cottage	ME	59	C2		Fulwell	SO	16	A1
Falconwood	SO	22	C2		Furness Vale	LM	46	A2
Falkirk Grahamston	SC	72	A2		Furze Platt	WR	31	C1
Falkirk High	SC	72	A2		Gainsborough Central	ER	48	A1
Falmer	SO	12	C1		Gainsborough Lea Road	ER	48	A1
Falmouth	WR	1	C2		Gants Hill	LT	22	A2
Fambridge	ER	33	B1		Garelochhead	SC	71	A1
Fareham	SO	10	C2		Garforth	ER	56	B2
Farnborough	SO	11	A1		Gargrave	LM	55	A2
Farnborough North	SO	11	A1		Garrowhill	SC	76	B2
Farncombe	SO	11	B2		Garscadden	SC	75	B2
Farnham	SO	11	B1		Garsdale*	LM	61	C1
Farningham Road & Sutton-at-					Garston (Herts)	LM	31	B2
Hone	SO	12	A2		Garston (Merseyside)	LM	53	C2
Farnworth	LM	51	A1		Garswood	LM	54	C2
Farringdon	LM/LT	21	B2		Garth	LM	35	C2
Fauldhouse	SC	72	B2		Garve	SC	81	C1
Faversham	SO	13	A2		Garwick Glen	ME	59	C2
Fawdon	TW	69	A1		Gateshead	TW	69	B2
Faygate	SO	12	B1		Gathurst	LM	54	C2
Fazakerley	LM	53	A2		Gatley	LM	52	C1
Fearn	SC	81	B2		Gatwick Airport	SO	12	B1
Felixstowe	ER	34	A1		Georgemas Junction	SC	82	A1
Felling	TW	69	B2		Gerrards Cross	LM	31	C2
Feltham	SO	15	A2		Giffnock	SC	75	C2
Fenchurch Street	ER	21	B2		Giggleswick	LM	55	A1
Feniton	WR	3	A2		Gilberdyke	ER	57	B1
Fenny Stratford	LM	31	A1		Gilfach Ddu (Llanberis)	LL	43	B2
Ferriby	ER	57	B2		Gilfach Fargoed	WR	28	B1
Ferryside	WR	26	B2		Gillingham (Dorset)	WR	9	B1
Ffairfach	WR	27	B1		Gillingham (Kent)	SO	13	A1
Filey	ER	63	C2		Gipsy Hill	SO	17	A2
Filton	WR	28	C2		Girvan	SC	64	A1
Finchley Central	LT	23	C1		Glaisdale	ER	63	B1
Finchley Road & Frognal	LT	21	A1		Glan Conway	LM	44	A1
Findfuck	LM	21	A1		Glanrafon	LM	33	B2
Finnieston	SC	76	B1		Glasgow Central	SC	76	B1
Finsbury Park	ER/LT	21	A2		Glasgow Queen Street	SC	76	B1
Finstock	WR	30	B1		Glazebrook	LM	46	A1
Fishbourne	SO	11	C1		Glen Mona	ME	59	C2
Fishersgate	SO	12	C1		Gleneagles	SC	78	C2
Fishguard Harbour	WR	25	A2		Glenfinnan Loch Shiel	SC	77	A2
Fiskerton	LM	48	B1		Glengarnock ·	SC	71	B2
Five Ways	LM	38	B2		Glossop	LM	46	A2
Fleet	SO	11	A1		Gloucester	WR	29	B1
Fleetwood	BF	54	A1		Gloucester Road	LT	21	C1
Flimby	LM	59	A2		Glynde	SO	12	C1
Flint	LM	45	A1		Goathland	NY	63	B1
Flitwick	LM	31	A2		Gobowen	LM	45	C1
Flixton	LM	51	C1		Godalming	SO	11	B2
Folkestone Central	SO	13	B2		Godley	LM	52	B2
Folkestone Harbour	SO	13	B2		Godstone	SO	12	A1
Folkestone Warren*	SO	13	B2		Gogarth	LM	34	A2
Folkestone West	SO	13	B2		Golders Green	LT	21	A1
Ford	SO	11	C2		Goldhawk Road	LT	20	C2
Forest Gate	ER	22	A2		Golf Street Halt	SC	79	B1
Forest Hill.	SO	18	A1		Golspie	SC	81	B2
Formby	LM	54	C1		Gomshall & Shere	SO	11	A2
Forres	SC	81	C2		Goodge Street	LT	21	B2

89

Goodmayes	ER	32	C1	Halling	SO	12	A2
Goodrington Sands	TD	3	B2	Hall Road	LM	53	A1
Goole	ER	57	B1	Haltwhistle	ER	67	C1
Goostrey	LM	46	B1	Hamble	SO	10	C2
Gordon Hill	ER	23	B2	Hamilton Central	SC	72	B1
Goring & Streatley	WR	30	C2	Hamilton West	SC	72	B1
Goring-by-Sea	SO	11	C2	Hammersmith	LT	20	C2
Gorton	LM	52	B1	Hammerton	ER	56	A2
Gospel Oak	LM	21	A1	Hampden Park	SO	12	C2
Gourock	SC	71	A1	Hampstead	LT	21	A1
Govan Cross	GG	75	B2	Hampstead Heath	LM	21	A1
Gowerton	WR	26	C2	Hampton	SO	15	B2
Goxhill	ER	57	B2	Hampton-in-Arden	LM	38	B1
Grange-over-Sands	LM	60	C2	Hampton Court	SO	16	B1
Grange Hill	LT	24	C2	Hampton Loade	SV	37	B1
Grange Park	ER	23	B2	Hampton Wick	SO	16	B1
Grangetown (Cleveland)	ER	62	A2	Hamstead	LM	37	B2
Grangetown (S. Glam)	WR	28	C1	Ham Street	SO	13	B2
Grantham	ER	48	C1	Hamworthy	SO	5	A2
Grateley	SO	10	B1	Handborough	WR	30	B2
Gravelly Hill	LM	37	B2	Handforth	LM	46	A1
Gravesend	SO	32	C2	Hanger Lane	LT	20	B1
Grays	ER	32	C2	Hanwell	WR	20	B1
Great Ayton	ER	62	B2	Hapton	LM	55	B1
Great Bentley	ER	33	B2	Harlech	LM	43	C2
Great Chesterford	ER	32	A2	Harlesden	LM/LT	20	B2
Great Coates	ER	58	C1	Harling Road	ER	41	B1
Greatham	ER	62	A2	Harlington	LM	31	A2
Great Malvern	WR	29	A1	Harlow Mill	ER	32	B2
Great Missenden	LM	31	B1	Harlow Town	ER	32	B1
Great Orme	GO	44	A1	Harold Wood	ER	32	C2
Great Portland Street	LT	21	B1	Harpenden	LM	31	B2
Greatstone	RH	13	B2	Harrietsham	SO	13	A1
Greenbank	LM	46	A1	Harringay	ER	21	A2
Greenfield	LM	55	C2	Harringay Stadium	ER	21	A2
Greenford	WR/LT	20	B1	Harrington	LM	59	A2
Greenhithe	SO	32	C2	Harrogate	ER	56	A1
Green Lane	LM	53	C1	Harrow & Wealdstone	LM/LT	20	A1
Greenock Central	SC	71	A1	Harrow-on-the-Hill	LM/LT	20	A1
Greenock West	SC	71	A1	Hartford	LM	45	B2
Green Park	LT	21	B1	Hartlebury	LM	37	C1
Green Road	LM	60	C1	Hartlepool	ER	62	A2
Greenwich	SO	22	C1	Hartwood	SC	72	B2
Grimsby Docks	ER	58	C1	Harwich Parkeston Quay	ER	33	A2
Grimsby Town	ER	58	C1	Harwich Town	ER	33	A2
Grindleford	LM	47	A1	Haslemere	SO	11	B1
Groombridge	SO	12	B2	Hassocks	SO	12	C1
Grosmont	ER/NY	63	B1	Hastings	SO	13	C1
Groudle Glen	ME	59	C2	Hatch End	LM/LT	31	C2
Grove Park	SO	18	A2	Hatfield	ER	32	B1
Guide Bridge	LM	52	B2	Hatfield Peverel	ER	33	B1
Guildford	SO	11	A2	Hathersage	LM	47	A1
Guiseley	ER	56	B1	Hattersley	LM	46	A2
Gunnersbury	SO/LT	20	C2	Hatton	LM	38	C1
Gunnislake	WR	2	B2	Hatton Cross	LT	19	C2
Gunton	ER	50	C2	Havant	SO	11	C1
Gwersyllt	LM	45	B1	Havenhouse	ER	49	B2
Gypsy Lane	ER	62	B2	Havenstreet	IW	6	A2
Habrough	ER	57	C2	Haverfordwest	WR	25	B2
Hackbridge	SO	17	B1	Haverthwaite	LH	60	C1
Hackney (Mare St.)	ER	22	A1	Hawarden	LM	45	B1
Hackney Downs	ER	22	A1	Hawarden Bridge	LM	45	B1
Haddiscoe	ER	42	A1	Haworth	KW	55	B2
Hadfield	LM	46	A2	Haydon Bridge	ER	67	C1
Hadley Wood	ER	23	B1	Haydons Road	SO	17	A1
Hadrian Road	TW	70	B1	Hayes (Kent)	SO	18	B2
Hagley	LM	37	B1	Hayes & Harlington	WR	19	C2
Hainault	LT	24	C2	Hayle	WR	1	A1
Hairmyres	SC	72	B1	Haymarket (Edinburgh)	SC	73	A1
Hale	LM	46	A1	Haymarket (Newcastle)	TW	69	B2
Halesworth	ER	42	B1	Haywards Heath	SO	12	B1
Halfway (Great Orme)	GO	44	A1	Hazel Grove	LM	46	B2
Halfway (Snowdon)	SM	43	B2	Headcorn	SO	13	B1
Halifax	ER	55	B2	Headingley	ER	56	B1
Hall Green	LM	37	B2	Headstone Lane	LM/LT	31	C2

Heald Green	LM	46	A1	Holton Heath	SO	5	A2
Healing	ER	58	C1	Holyhead	LM	43	A1
Heath High Level	WR	28	C1	Holytown	SC	72	B1
Heath Low Level	WR	28	C1	Homerton	ER	22	A1
Heathrow Central	LT	19	C1	Honiton	WR	8	C1
Heaton	ER	69	B2	Honley	ER	55	C2
Heaton Chapel	LM	52	C1	Honor Oak Park	SO	18	A1
Heaton Park	LM	51	A2	Hook	SO	11	A1
Hebburn	TW	70	B1	Hoo Staff Halt*	SO	32	C2
Hebden Bridge	ER	55	B2	Hooton	LM	45	A1
Hebron	SM	43	B2	Hope (Clwyd)	LM	45	B1
Heckington	ER	48	C2	Hope (Derbyshire)	LM	47	A1
Heighington	ER	62	A1	Hopton Heath	WR	36	B1
Helensburgh Central	SC	71	A1	Horley	SO	12	B1
Helensburgh Upper	SC	71	A1	Hornchurch	LT	32	C2
Hellifield	LM	55	A1	Hornsey	ER	21	A2
Helmsdale	SC	81	B2	Horsforth	ER	56	B1
Helsby	LM	45	A2	Horsham	SO	11	B2
Hemel Hempstead	LM	31	B2	Horsley	SO	11	A2
Hendon	LM	20	A2	Horsted Keynes	BL	12	B1
Hendon Central	LT	20	A2	Horton*	LM	61	C1
Hengoed	WR	28	C1	Hoscar	LM	54	C2
Heniarth	WL	35	A2	Hough Green	LM	45	A2
Henley-in-Arden	LM	37	C2	Hounslow	SO	20	C1
Henley-on-Thames	WR	31	C1	Hounslow Central	LT	19	C2
Hensall	ER	56	B2	Hounslow East	LT	20	C1
Hereford	WR	28	A2	Hounslow West	LT	19	C2
Herne Bay	SO	13	A2	Houston	SC	71	B2
Herne Hill	SO	17	A2	Hove	SO	12	C1
Hersham	SO	15	B2	Howden	ER	57	B1
Hertford East	ER	32	B1	Howdon	TW	70	B1
Hertford North	ER	32	B1	Howstrake	ME	59	C2
Hessle	ER	57	B2	Hoylake	LM	45	A1
Heswall	LM	45	A1	Hubbert's Bridge	ER	49	C1
Hever	SO	12	B1	Huddersfield	ER	55	C2
Heworth	ER/TW	69	B2	Hull	ER	57	B2
Hexham	ER	67	C2	Huncoat	LM	55	B1
Heyford	WR	30	A2	Hungerford	WR	10	A1
Heysham (Proposed)	LM	54	A2	Hunmanby	ER	63	C2
Higham	SO	32	C2	Huntingdon	ER	40	C1
Highams Park	ER	24	C1	Huntly	SC	82	C1
High Barnet	LT	23	B1	Hunt's Cross	LM	45	A2
Highbridge	WR	8	B1	Hurst Green	SO	12	A1
High Brooms	SO	12	B2	Hutton Cranswick	ER	57	A2
Highbury & Islington	ER/LT	21	A2	Huyton	LM	45	A2
Highgate	LT	21	A1	Hyde Central	LM	52	B2
Highley	SV	37	B1	Hyde North	LM	52	B2
High Shields	ER	70	B2	Hyde Park Corner	LT	21	B1
High Street (Glasgow)	SC	76	B1	Hykeham	ER	48	B2
High Street, Kensington	LT	21	C1	Hyndland	SC	75	B2
Hightown	LM	54	C1	Hythe (Essex)	ER	33	A2
High Wycombe	LM	31	C1	Hythe (Kent)	RH	13	B2
Hildenborough	SO	12	A2	IBM Halt*	SC	71	A1
Hillfoot	SC	75	A2	Ickenham	LT	19	A1
Hillhead	GG	75	B2	Ifield	SO	12	B1
Hillingdon	LT	19	A1	Ilford	ER	22	A2
Hillington East	SC	75	B2	Ilford Road	TW	69	B2
Hillington West	SC	75	B2	Ilkley	ER	55	A2
Hillside	LM	54	C1	Ince (Greater Manchester)	LM	54	C2
Hilsea	SO	10	C2	Ince & Elton	LM	45	A2
Hinchley Wood	SO	16	B1	Ingatestone	ER	32	B2
Hinckley	LM	38	B2	Ingrow	KW	55	B2
Hindley	LM	54	C2	Insch	SC	82	C2
Hinton Admiral	SO	6	A1	Invergordon	SC	81	C2
Hitchin	ER	31	A2	Invergowrie	SC	79	B1
Hither Green	SO	18	AT	Inverkeithing	SC	73	A1
Hockley	ER	33	C1	Inverkip	SC	71	A1
Holborn	LT	21	B2	Inverness	SC	81	C2
Holborn Viaduct	SO	21	B2	Invershin	SC	81	B2
Holland Park	LT	21	B1	Inverurie	SC	79	A2
Hollingbourne	SO	13	A1	Ipswich	ER	33	A2
Hollinwood	LM	52	A1	Irlam	LM	51	C1
Holloway Road	LT	21	A2	Irton Road	RE	60	B1
Holmes Chapel	LM	46	B1	Irvine	SC	71	C2
Holmwood	SO	11	B2	Isleworth	SO	20	C1

91

Iver	WR	19	B1		Kirkham & Wesham	LM	54	B2
Jarrow	TW	70	B1		Kirkhill	SC	76	C2
Jesmond	TW	69	B2		Kirton Lindsey	ER	57	C2
Johnston	WR	25	B2		Kiveton Bridge	ER	47	A2
Johnstone	SC	71	B2		Kiveton Park	ER	47	A2
Jordanhill	SC	75	B2		Knaresborough	ER	56	A1
Kearsley	LM	51	A1		Knebworth	ER	32	B1
Kearsney	SO	14	B1		Knighton	WR	36	C1
Keighley	ER/KW	55	B2		Knightsbridge	LT	21	C1
Keith Junction	SC	82	C1		Knockholt	SO	12	A2
Kelvedon	ER	33	B1		Knottingley	ER	56	B2
Kelvin Bridge	GG	76	B1		Knucklas	WR	36	B1
Kelvin Hall	GG	75	B2		Knutsford	LM	46	A1
Kemble	WR	29	C2		Kyle of Lochalsh	SC	80	C2
Kempston Hardwick	LM	31	A2		Ladbroke Grove	LT	21	B1
Kempton Park*	SO	15	A2		Lade Halt	RH	13	C2
Kemsing	SO	12	A2		Ladybank	SC	79	C1
Kemsley	SO	13	A1		Ladywell	SO	22	C1
Kemsley Down	SK	13	A1		Laindon	ER	32	C2
Kendal	LM	60	C2		Lairg	SC	81	B2
Kenley	SO	17	C2		Lakenheath	ER	40	B2
Kennett	ER	40	C2		Lakeside	LH	60	C1
Kennington	LT	21	C2		Lambeth North	LT	21	C2
Kennishead	SC	75	C2		Lamphey	WR	25	B2
Kensal Green	LM/LT	20	B2		Lanark	SC	72	C2
Kensal Rise	LM	20	B2		Lancaster	LM	54	A2
Kensington Olympia	LM/LT	21	C1		Lancaster Gate	LT	21	B1
Kent House	SO	18	A1		Lancing	SO	11	C2
Kentish Town	LM	21	A1		Langbank	SC	71	A2
Kenton	LM/LT	20	A1		Langley	WR	31	C2
Kenton Bank Foot	TW	69	A1		Langley Green	LM	37	B2
Kents Bank	LM	60	C2		Langside	SC	76	C1
Kettering for Corby	LM	39	B1		Langwathby*	LM	60	A2
Kew Bridge	SO	20	C2		Lapford	WR	7	C1
Kew Gardens	SO/LT	20	C2		Lapworth	LM	38	C1
Keyham	WR	2	B2		Larbert	SC	72	A2
Keynsham	WR	9	A1		Largs	SC	71	B1
Kidbrooke	SO	22	C2		Latimer Road	LT	20	B2
Kidderminster	LM	37	B1		Lawrence Hill	WR	8	A2
Kidsgrove	LM	46	B2		Laxey	ME	59	C2
Kidwelly	WR	26	B2		Layton	LM	54	B1
Kilburn	LT	21	A1		Lazonby*	LM	60	A2
Kilburn High Road	LM	21	B1		Lea Bridge	ER	22	A1
Kilburn Park	LT	21	B1		Leagrave	LM	31	A2
Kildale	ER	62	B2		Lea Hall	LM	37	B2
Kildonan	SC	81	B2		Lealholm	ER	63	B1
Kilgetty	WR	26	B1		Leamington Spa	LM	38	C1
Kilmacolm	SC	71	A2		Leasowe	LM	45	A1
Kilmarnock	SC	71	C2		Leatherhead	SO	11	A2
Kilpatrick	SC	75	A1		Ledbury	WR	29	A1
Kilwinning	SC	71	B1		Lee	SO	18	A2
Kinbrace	SC	81	A2		Leeds	ER	56	B1
King's Cross	ER/LT	21	B2		Leicester	LM	38	A2
King's Langley	LM	31	B2		Leicester Square	LT	21	B2
King's Lynn	ER	40	A2		Leigh	SO	12	B2
King's Norton	LM	37	B2		Leigh-on-Sea	ER	33	C1
King's Nympton	WR	7	C1		Leighton Buzzard	LM	31	A1
King's Park	SC	76	C1		Lelant	WR	1	A1
King's Sutton	LM	30	A2		Lelant Saltings	WR	1	A1
Kingham	WR	30	B1		Lenham	SO	13	A1
Kinghorn	SC	73	A1		Lenzie	SC	76	A2
Kingsbury	LT	20	A2		Leominster	WR	36	C2
Kingsknowe	SC	73	A1		Letchworth	ER	32	A1
Kingston	SO	16	B1		Leuchars	SC	79	C1
Kingswood	SO	12	A1		Levenshulme	LM	52	C1
Kingussie	SC	78	A1		Levisham	NY	63	C1
Kinning Park	GG	75	B2		Lewaigue	ME	59	B2
Kintbury	WR	10	A1		Lewes	SO	12	C1
Kirby Cross	ER	33	B2		Lewisham	SO	22	C1
Kirkby (Merseyside)	LM	53	A2		Leyland	LM	54	B2
Kirkby-in-Furness	LM	60	C1		Leyton	LT	22	A1
Kirkby Stephen*	LM	61	B1		Leyton Midland Road	ER	22	A1
Kirkcaldy	SC	73	A1		Leytonstone	LT	22	A1
Kirkconnel	SC	63	A1		Leytonstone High Road	ER	22	A1
Kirkdale	LM	53	B1		Lichfield City	LM	37	A2

92

Lichfield Trent Valley	LM	37	A2	Longton	LM	46	C2
Lidlington	LM	31	A2	Looe	WR	2	B1
Lincoln Central	ER	48	B2	Lostock Gralam	LM	46	A1
Lincoln St. Marks	ER	48	B2	Lostwithiel	WR	2	B1
Lingfield	SO	12	B1	Loughborough	LM	38	A2
Linlithgow	SC	72	A2	Loughborough Central	ML	38	A2
Liphook	SO	11	B1	Loughborough Junction	SO	21	C2
Liskeard	WR	2	B1	Loughton	LT	24	B2
Liss	SO	11	B1	Lowdham	LM	47	C2
Little Bispham	BF	54	B1	Lower Edmonton	ER	23	C2
Littleborough	LM	55	C2	Lower Sydenham	SO	18	A1
Littlehampton	SO	11	C2	Lowestoft	ER	42	B2
Littlehaven	SO	11	B2	Ludgershall*	SO	10	A1
Little Kimble	LM	31	B1	Ludlow	WR	36	B2
Littleport	ER	40	B2	Luton	LM	31	B2
Little Sutton	LM	45	A1	Luxulyan	WR	1	B2
Liverpool Central	LM	53	B1	Lydney	WR	28	B2
Liverpool James Street	LM	53	B1	Lye	LM	37	B2
Liverpool Lime Street	LM	53	B1	Lymington Pier	SO	6	A1
Liverpool Moorfields	LM	53	B1	Lymington Town	SO	6	A1
Liverpool Street (London)	ER/LT	21	B2	Lympstone	WR	3	A2
Llanaber	LM	34	A2	Lympstone Commando	WR	3	A2
Llanbadarn	LM	34	B2	Lyndhurst Road	SO	10	C1
Llanbedr	LM	43	C2	Lytham	LM	54	B1
Llanberis	SM	43	B2	Macclesfield	LM	46	A2
Llanbister Road	WR	36	C1	Machynlleth	LM	34	A2
Llanbradach	WR	28	C1	Maddieson's Camp	RH	13	C2
Llandaff for Whitchurch	WR	28	C1	Magdalen Road	ER	40	A2
Llandanwg	LM	43	C2	Maghull	LM	54	C2
Llandecwyn	LM	44	C1	Maida Vale	LT	21	B1
Llandeilo	WR	27	A1	Maidenhead	WR	31	C1
Llandovery	WR	27	A1	Maiden Newton	WR	4	A2
Llandrindod Wells	LM	35	C2	Maidstone Barracks	SO	13	A1
Llandudno	LM	44	A1	Maidstone East	SO	13	A1
Llandudno Junction	LM	44	A1	Maidstone West	SO	13	A1
Llandudno Victoria	GO	44	A1	Malden Manor	SO	16	B2
Llandybie	WR	27	B1	Mallaig	SC	77	A2
Llanelli	WR	26	B2	Malton	ER	63	C1
Llanfair Caereinion	WL	35	A2	Malvern Link	WR	37	C1
Llanfairfechan	LM	44	A1	Manchester Oxford Road	LM	52	B1
Llanfairpwll	LM	43	A2	Manchester Piccadilly	LM	52	B1
Llangadog	WR	27	A1	Manchester Square	BF	54	B1
Llangammarch Wells	WR	27	A2	Manchester United Football			
Llangelynin	LM	33	A2	Ground*	LM	51	B2
Llangennech	WR	26	B2	Manchester Victoria	LM	52	B1
Llangower	BA	44	C2	Manea	ER	40	B2
Llangunllo	WR	36	B1	Manningtree	ER	33	A2
Llanishen	WR	28	C1	Manorbier	WR	25	B2
Llanuwchllyn	BA	44	C2	Manor House	LT	21	A2
Llanrwst	LM	44	B1	Manor Park	ER	22	A2
Llanwrda	WR	27	A1	Manor Road	LM	45	A1
Llanwrtyd Wells	WR	27	A2	Manors	ER/TW	69	B2
Llwyngwril	LM	34	A2	Mansion House	LT	21	B2
Llwynpia	WR	27	C2	Marble Arch	LT	21	B1
Lochailort	SC	77	A2	March	ER	40	B1
Locheilside	SC	78	A1	Marden	SO	13	B1
Lochgelly	SC	79	C1	Margate	SO	14	A1
Lochluichart	SC	81	C1	Market Bosworth	SH	38	A1
Lochside	SC	71	B2	Market Harborough	LM	39	B1
Lochty	LY	79	C1	Market Rasen	ER	48	A2
Lockerbie	SC	66	B1	Markinch for Glenrothes	SC	79	C1
Lockwood	ER	55	C2	Marks Tey	ER	33	A1
London Bridge	SO/LT	21	B2	Marlow	WR	31	C1
London Fields	ER	22	B1	Marple	LM	52	C2
London Road (Brighton)	SO	12	C1	Marsden	ER	55	C2
London Road (Guildford)	SO	11	A2	Marske	ER	62	A2
Longbenton	TW	69	A2	Marston Green	LM	38	B1
Longbridge	LM	37	B2	Martin Mill	SO	14	B1
Long Buckby	LM	38	C2	Maryland	ER	22	A1
Longcross	SO	11	A2	Marylebone	LM/LT	21	B1
Long Eaton	LM	47	C2	Maryport	LM	59	A2
Longfield	SO	12	A2	Matlock	LM	47	B1
Longniddry	SC	73	A2	Matlock Bath	LM	47	B1
Longport	LM	46	B1	Mauldeth Road	LM	52	C1
Long Preston	LM	55	A1	Maxwell Park	SC	75	B2

93

Maybole	SC	64	A1	Motherwell	SC	72	B1
Maze Hill	SO	22	C1	Motspur Park	SO	16	B2
Meldreth	ER	32	A1	Mottingham	SO	18	A2
Melton*	ER	57	B2	Mottram Staff Halt*	LM	46	A2
Melton Mowbray	LM	39	A1	Mouldsworth	LM	45	B2
Menheniot	WR	2	B1	Mount Florida	SC	76	C1
Menston	ER	56	B1	Mountain Ash*	WR	27	B2
Meols	LM	45	A1	Muirend	SC	76	C1
Meols Cop	LM	54	C1	Muir of Ord	SC	81	C1
Meopham	SO	12	A2	Muncaster Mill	RE	59	B2
Merstham	SO	12	A1	Mytholmroyd	ER	55	B2
Merthyr	WR	27	B2	Nafferton	ER	57	A2
Merthyr Vale	WR	27	B2	Nailsea and Backwell	WR	8	A2
Merton Park	SO	17	A1	Nairn	SC	81	C2
Metheringham	ER	48	B2	Nant Gwernol	TL	34	A2
Mexborough	ER	56	C2	Nantwich	LM	46	B2
Micheldever	SO	10	B2	Nantyronen	LM	34	B2
Micklefield	ER	56	B2	Narberth	WR	26	B1
Midcalder	SC	73	B1	Narborough	LM	38	A2
Middlesbrough	ER	62	B2	Navigation Road	LM	51	C2
Middlewood	LM	46	A2	Neasden	LT	20	A2
Midgham	WR	10	A2	Neath	WR	27	C1
Mile End	LT	22	B1	Needham Market	ER	41	C2
Miles Platting	LM	52	B1	Neilston	SC	75	C1
Milford (Surrey)	SO	11	B2	Nelson	LM	55	B1
Milford Haven	WR	25	B2	Neston	LM	45	A1
Millbrook (Beds)	LM	31	A2	Netherfield	LM	47	C2
Millbrook (Hants)	SO	10	C1	Netherton	LM	59	B2
Mill Hill (Lancs)	LM	55	B1	Netley	SO	10	C2
Mill Hill Broadway	LM	31	C2	Newark Castle	ER	48	B1
Mill Hill East	LT	23	C1	Newark Northgate	ER	48	B1
Millom	LM	60	C1	New Barnet	ER	23	B1
Milngavie	SC	75	A2	New Beckenham	SO	18	A1
Milnrow	LM	55	C2	New Brighton	LM	53	B1
Milton Keynes (Proposed)	LM	31	A1	Newbury	WR	10	A2
Minehead	WS	7	B2	Newbury Park	LT	22	A2
Minffordd	LM/FR	43	C2	Newbury Racecourse*	WR	10	A2
Minorca	ME	59	C2	Newby Bridge	LH	60	C1
Minster	SO	14	A1	Newcastle (Central)	ER/TW	69	B2
Mirfield	ER	56	C1	New Clee	ER	58	C1
Mistley	ER	33	A2	New Cross	SO/LT	22	C1
Mitcham	SO	17	B1	New Cross Gate	SO/LT	22	C1
Mitcham Junction	SO	17	B1	New Eltham	SO	18	A2
Mobberley	LM	46	A1	New Hadley	LM	37	A1
Monifieth	SC	79	B1	Newhaven Harbour	SO	12	C1
Monkseaton	TW	70	A1	Newhaven Town	SO	12	C1
Monks Risborough	LM	31	B1	New Hey	LM	55	C2
Montpelier	WR	8	A2	New Holland Pier	ER	57	B2
Montrose	SC	79	B2	New Holland Town	ER	57	B2
Monument (London)	LT	21	B2	New Hythe	SO	12	A2
Monument (Newcastle)	TW	69	B2	Newington	SO	13	A1
Moorgate	ER/LT	21	B2	New Lane	LM	54	C2
Moor Park	LM/LT	31	C2	New Malden	SO	16	B2
Moorside	LM	51	A1	Newmarket	ER	40	C2
Moorthorpe	ER	56	C2	New Mills Central	LM	46	A2
Morar	SC	77	A2	New Mills Newtown	LM	46	A2
Morchard Road	WR	7	C1	New Milton	SO	6	A1
Morden	LT	17	B1	Newport (Essex)	ER	32	A2
Morden Road	SO	17	B1	Newport (Gwent)	WR	28	C1
Morden South	SO	17	B1	New Pudsey	ER	56	B1
Morecambe	LM	54	A2	Newquay	WR	1	B2
Moreton (Dorset)	SO	5	A1	New Romney	RH	13	B2
Moreton (Merseyside)	LM	45	A1	New Southgate	ER	23	C1
Moreton-in-Marsh	WR	30	A1	Newton (Greater Glasgow)	SC	76	C2
Morfa Mawddach	LM	34	A2	Newton (Greater Manchester)	LM	52	B2
Morley	ER	56	B1	Newton-le-Willows	LM	45	A2
Mornington Crescent	LT	21	B1	Newton-on-Ayr	SC	71	C2
Morpeth	ER	68	B1	Newton Abbot	WR	3	B2
Mortimer	SO	10	A2	Newton Aycliffe	ER	62	A1
Mortlake	SO	20	C2	Newtonmore	SC	78	A2
Moses Gate	LM	51	A1	Newton St. Cyres	WR	3	A1
Mossley	LM	55	C2	Newton	LM	35	B2
Mossley Hill	LM	53	C2	Ninian Park*	WR	28	C1
Mosspark	SC	75	B2	Nitshill	SC	75	C2
Moston	LM	52	A1	Norbiton	SO	16	B2

94

Norbury	SO	17	B2		Oxenholme	LM	60	C2
Norman's Bay	SO	12	C2		Oxenhope	KW	55	B2
Normanton	ER	56	B1		Oxford	WR	30	B2
North Acton	LT	20	B2		Oxford Circus	LT	21	B1
Northallerton	ER	62	C1		Oxshott	SO	16	C1
Northampton	LM	39	C1		Oxted	SO	12	A1
North Berwick	SC	73	A2		Paddington	WR/LT	21	B1
North Camp	SO	11	A1		Paddock Wood	SO	12	B2
North Dulwich	SO	17	A2		Padgate	LM	45	A2
North Ealing	LT	20	B2		Paignton	WR	3	B2
Northfield	LM	37	B2		Paignton (Queen's Park)	TD	3	B2
Northfields	LT	20	C1		Paisley Canal	SC	75	B1
North Filton Platform*	WR	28	C2		Paisley Gilmour Street	SC	75	B1
Northfleet	SO	32	C2		Paisley St. James	SC	75	B1
North Harrow	LT	19	A2		Palmers Green	ER	23	C2
Northolt	LT	19	B2		Pangbourne	WR	30	C2
Northolt Park	LM	20	A1		Pannal	ER	56	A1
North Queensferry	SC	73	A1		Pantyffynon	WR	27	B1
North Road	ER	62	B1		Par	WR	2	B1
North Sheen	SO	20	C2		Parbold	LM	54	C2
North Shields	TW	70	A1		Park	LM	52	B2
Northumberland Park	ER	24	C1		Park Royal	LT	20	B2
North Walsham	ER	50	C2		Parkstone	SO	5	A2
North Weald	LT	32	B2		Park Street	LM	31	B2
North Wembley	LM/LT	20	A1		Parsons Green	LT	21	C1
Northwich	LM	46	A1		Parson Street	WR	8	B2
Northwick Park	LT	20	A1		Partick	SC/GG	75	B2
Northwood (Greater London)	LT	31	C2		Parton	LM	59	B2
Northwood (Worcs)	SV	37	B1		Patchway	WR	28	C2
Northwood Hills	LT	31	C2		Patricroft	LM	51	B1
North Woolwich	ER	22	B2		Patterton	SC	75	C2
Norton Bridge	LM	46	C1		Peartree	LM	47	C1
Norwich	ER	41	A2		Peckham Rye	SO	21	C2
Norwood Junction	SO	17	B2		Pegswood	ER	68	B1
Nottingham	LM	47	C2		Pemberton	LM	54	C2
Notting Hill Gate	LT	21	B1		Pembrey & Burry Port	WR	26	B2
Nuneaton	LM	38	B1		Pembroke	WR	25	B2
Nunhead	SO	22	C1		Pembroke Dock	WR	25	B2
Nunthorpe	ER	62	B2		Penally	WR	26	B1
Nutbourne	SO	11	C1		Penarth	WR	8	A1
Nutfield	SO	12	A1		Pendleton	LM	51	B2
Oakengates	LM	37	A1		Pengam	WR	28	C1
Oakham	LM	39	A1		Penge East	SO	18	A1
Oakleigh Park	ER	23	B1		Penge West	SO	18	A1
Oakwood	LT	23	B2		Penhelig	LM	34	B2
Oakworth	KW	55	B2		Penistone	ER	56	C1
Oban	SC	77	B2		Penkridge	LM	37	A2
Ockendon	ER	32	C2		Penmaenmawr	LM	44	A1
Ockley & Capel	SO	11	B2		Penmere	WR	1	C1
Okehampton*	WR	3	A1		Penrhiwceiber*	WR	27	B2
Oldbury	LM	37	B2		Penrhyn (Gwynedd)	FR	44	C1
Oldfield Park	WR	9	A1		Penrhyndeudraeth	LM	44	C1
Oldham Mumps	LM	52	A2		Penrith	LM	60	A2
Oldham Werneth	LM	52	A2		Penryn (Cornwall)	WE	1	C1
Old Fold	TW	69	B2		Pensarn (Gwynedd)	LM	43	C2
Old Hill	LM	37	B2		Penshurst	SO	12	B2
Old Roan	LM	53	A2		Pentrebach	WR	27	B2
Old Street	ER/LT	21	B2		Penybont	LM	35	C2
Old Trafford	LM	51	B2		Penychain	LM	43	C2
Olton	LM	37	B2		Penyffordd	LM	45	B1
Onchan Head	ME	59	C1		Penzance	WR	1	A1
Ongar	LT	32	B2		Percy Main	TW	70	B1
Ore	SO	13	C2		Perivale	LT	20	B1
Ormesby	ER	62	B2		Perranwell	WR	1	C1
Ormskirk	LM	54	C2		Perry Barr	LM	37	B2
Orpington	SO	12	A1		Pershore	WR	37	C2
Orrell	LM	54	C2		Perth	SC	79	C1
Orrell Park	LM	53	A2		Peterborough	ER	39	A2
Orton Mere	NV	39	A2		Petersfield	SO	11	B1
Osterley	LT	20	C1		Petts Wood	SO	18	B2
Otford	SO	12	A2		Pevensey & Westham	SO	12	C2
Oulton Broad North	ER	42	B2		Pevensey Bay	SO	12	C2
Oulton Broad South	ER	42	B2		Pewsey	WR	9	A2
Oval	LT	21	C2		Piccadilly Circus	LT	21	B2
Overton	SO	10	A2		Pickering	NY	63	C1

Pilning	WR	28	C2		Queen's Park (London)	LM/LT	21	B1
Pimlico	LT	21	C2		Queen's Road, Battersea	SO	21	C1
Pinner	LT	19	A2		Queen's Road, Peckham	SO	22	C1
Pitlochry	SC	78	B2		Queensbury	LT	31	C2
Pitsea	ER	33	C1		Queensway	LT	21	B1
Plaistow	LT	22	B2		Quintrel Downs	WR	1	B2
Pleasington	LM	54	B2		Quorn & Woodhouse	ML	38	A2
Pleasure Beach	BF	54	B1		Radcliffe (Greater Manchester)	LM	55	C1
Plockton	SC	80	A2		Radcliffe (Notts)	LM	47	C2
Pluckley	SO	13	B1		Radipole	SO	5	A1
Plumley	LM	46	A1		Radlett	LM	31	B2
Plumpton	SO	12	C1		Radley	WR	30	B2
Plumstead	SO	22	C2		Radyr	WR	28	C1
Plymouth	WR	2	B2		Rainford	LM	54	C2
Pokesdown	SO	5	A2		Rainham (Essex)	ER	32	C2
Polegate	SO	12	C2		Rainham (Kent)	SO	13	A1
Polesworth	LM	38	A1		Rainhill	LM	45	A2
Pollokshaws East	SC	75	C2		Ramsey	ME	59	B2
Pollokshaws West	SC	75	C2		Ramsgate	SO	14	A1
Pollokshields East	SC	76	B1		Rannoch	SC	78	B1
Pollokshields West	SC	76	B1		Rauceby	ER	48	C2
Polmont	SC	72	A2		Ravenglass	LM/RE	59	C2
Polsloe Bridge	WR	3	A2		Ravensbourne	SO	18	A1
Ponders End	ER	24	B1		Ravenscourt Park	LT	20	C2
Pontardulais	WR	26	B2		Ravensthorpe	ER	56	C1
Pontefract Baghill	ER	56	B2		Rawcliffe	ER	57	B1
Pontefract Monkhill	ER	56	B2		Rayleigh	ER	33	C1
Pontlottyn	WR	27	B2		Rayners Lane	LT	19	A2
Pont-y-Pant	LM	44	B1		Raynes Park	SO	16	B2
Pontypool	WR	28	B1		Reading	WR	31	C1
Pontypridd	WR	27	C2		Reading West	WR	31	C1
Poole	SO	5	A2		Rectory Road	ER	21	A2
Poppleton	ER	56	A2		Redbridge (Greater London)	LT	22	A2
Portchester	SO	10	C2		Redbridge (Hants)	SO	10	C1
Port Erin	ME	59	C1		Redcar Central	ER	62	A2
Port Glasgow	SC	71	A2		Redcar East	ER	62	A2
Porth	WR	27	C2		Reddish North	LM	52	B1
Porthmadog	LM/FR	43	C2		Reddish South	LM	52	C1
Portslade & West Hove	SO	12	C1		Redditch	LM	37	C2
Portsmouth & Southsea	SO	10	C2		Redhill	SO	12	A1
Portsmouth Arms	WR	7	C1		Redland	WR	8	A2
Portsmouth Harbour	SO	10	C2		Redruth	WR	1	C1
Port Soderick	ME	59	C1		Reedham (Norfolk)	ER	42	A1
Port St. Mary	ME	59	C1		Reedham (Surrey)	SO	17	C2
Port Sunlight	LM	53	C1		Regent Centre	TW	69	A2
Port Talbot	WR	27	C1		Regent's Park	LT	21	B1
Potters Bar	ER	23	A1		Reigate	SO	12	A1
Poulton-le-Fylde	LM	54	B1		Renton	SC	71	A2
Poynton	LM	46	A2		Retford	ER	48	A1
Prees	LM	45	C2		Rheidol Falls	LM	34	B2
Prescot	LM	45	A2		Rhiwbina	WR	28	C1
Prestatyn	LM	44	A2		Rhiwfron	LM	34	B2
Prestbury	LM	46	A2		Rhosneigr	LM	43	A1
Prestbury Park (Racecourse)*	WR	29	A2		Rhydyronen	TL	34	A2
Preston	LM	54	B2		Rhyl	LM	44	A2
Prestonpans	SC	73	A2		Rhymney	WR	27	B2
Preston Park	SO	12	C1		Ribblehead*	LM	61	C1
Preston Road (Greater London)	LT	20	A1		Richmond	SO/LT	20	C1
Preston Road (Merseyside)	LM	53	A2		Rickmansworth	LM/LT	31	C2
Prestwich	LM	51	A2		Riddlesdown	SO	17	C2
Prestwick	SC	71	C2		Ridgmont	LM	31	A2
Primrose Hill	LM	21	B1		Riding Mill	ER	67	C2
Princes Risborough	LM	31	B1		Rishton	LM	55	B1
Prittlewell	ER	33	C1		Robertsbridge	SO	13	B1
Prudhoe	ER	67	C2		Roby	LM	45	A2
Pulborough	SO	11	C2		Rochdale	LM	55	C1
Purfleet	ER	32	C2		Roche	WR	1	B2
Purley	SO	17	C2		Rochester	SO	13	A1
Purley Oaks	SO	17	C2		Rochford	ER	33	C1
Putney	SO	20	C2		Rock Ferry	LM	53	C1
Putney Bridge	LT	21	C1		Roding Valley	LT	24	C2
Pwllheli	LM	43	C2		Rogart	SC	81	B2
Quaker's Yard	WR	27	C2		Rolleston	LM	48	B1
Queenborough	SO	33	C1		Rolvenden	KS	13	B1
Queen's Park (Glasgow)	SC	76	C1		Roman Bridge	LM	44	B1

Romford	ER	32	C2	Salhouse	ER	42	A1
Romiley	LM	52	C2	Salisbury	SO	9	B2
Romsey	SO	10	C1	Saltash	WR	2	B2
Roose	LM	54	A1	Saltburn	ER	62	A2
Ropley	MH	10	B2	Saltcoats	SC	71	C1
Rose Grove	LM	55	B1	Saltmarshe	ER	57	B1
Rose Hill (Marple)	LM	52	C2	Salwick	LM	54	B2
Rossall	BF	54	B1	Sandbach	LM	46	B1
Rosyth Halt	SC	73	A1	Sanderstead	SO	17	C2
Rosyth Dockyard*	SC	73	A1	Sandhills	LM	53	B1
Rotherham	ER	50	A2	Sandhurst	SO	11	A1
Rotherhithe	LT	22	C1	Sandling for Hythe	SO	13	B2
Rothley	ML	38	A2	Sandown	SO	6	A2
Rowland's Castle	SO	11	C1	Sandplace	WR	2	B1
Rowley Regis	LM	37	B2	Sandwich	SO	14	A1
Rowntree Halt*	ER	56	A2	Sandy	ER	39	C2
Royal Oak	LT	21	B1	Sankey for Penketh	LM	45	A2
Roy Bridge	SC.	78	A1	Santon	ME	59	C1
Roydon	ER	32	B1	Saundersfoot	WR	26	B1
Royston	ER	32	A1	Saunderton	LM	31	C1
Royton	LM	52	A2	Sawbridgeworth	ER	32	B2
Ruabon	LM	45	C1	Saxilby	ER	48	A1
Rufford	LM	54	C2	Saxmundham	ER	42	C1
Rugby	LM	38	B2	Scarborough	ER	63	C2
Rugeley	LM	37	A2	Scotscalder	SC	82	A1
Ruislip	LT	19	A2	Scotstounhill	SC	75	B2
Ruislip Gardens	LT	19	A2	Scunthorpe	ER	57	C1
Ruislip Manor	LT	19	A2	Seaburn	ER	70	C2
Runcorn	LM	45	A2	Seaford	SO	12	C2
Ruskington	ER	48	B2	Seaforth & Litherland	LM	53	A1
Russell Square	LT	21	B2	Seaham	ER	68	C2
Ruswarp	ER	63	B1	Seamer	ER	63	C2
Rutherglen	SC	76	C1	Sea Mills	WR	28	C2
Ryde Esplanade	SO	6	A2	Seascale	LM	59	B2
Ryde Pier Head	SO	6	A2	Seaton	ST	4	A1
Ryde St. John's Road	SO	6	A2	Seaton Carew	ER	62	A2
Rye	SO	13	C1	Seer Green	LM	31	C2
Rye House	ER	32	B1	Selby	ER	56	B2
St. Albans Abbey	LM	31	B2	Selhurst	SO	17	B2
St. Albans City	LM	31	B2	Sellafield	LM	59	B2
St. Andrews Road	WR	28	C2	Selling	SO	13	A2
St. Annes-on-the-Sea	LM	54	B1	Selly Oak	LM	37	B2
St. Austell	WR	1	B2	Selsdon	SO	17	C2
St. Bees	LM	59	B2	Settle	LM	55	A1
St. Botolphs	ER	33	A2	Seven Kings	ER	32	C1
St. Budeaux (Ferry Road)	WR	2	B2	Sevenoaks	SO	12	A2
St. Budeaux (Victoria Road)	WR	2	B2	Seven Sisters	ER/LT	21	A2
St. Columb Road	WR	1	B2	Severn Beach	WR	28	C2
St. Denys	SO	10	C1	Severn Tunnel Junction	WR	28	C2
St. Enoch	GG	76	B1	Shackerstone	SH	38	A1
St. Erth	WR	1	A1	Shadwell	LT	22	B1
St. George's Cross	GG	76	B1	Shalford	SO	11	B2
St. Germans	WR	2	B2	Shanklin	SO	6	A2
St. Helens Junction	LM	45	A2	Shaw	LM	55	C2
St. Helens Shaw Street	LM	45	A2	Shawford	SO	10	B2
St. Helier	SO	17	B1	Shawlands	SC	75	C2
St. Ives	WR	1	A1	Sheerness-on-Sea	SO	33	C1
St. James' Park (London)	LT	3	A2	Sheffield	ER	50	B1
St. James' Park (Newcastle)	TW	69	B2	Sheffield Park	BL	12	B1
St. James' Street, Walthamstow	ER	22	A1	Shelford	ER	40	C1
St. John's	SO	22	C1	Shenfield	ER	32	C2
St. John's Wood	LT	21	B1	Shenstone	LM	37	A2
St. Keyne	WR	2	B1	Shepherd's Bush	LT	20	B2
St. Leonards Warrior Square	SO	13	C1	Shepherd's Well	SO	14	A1
St. Margaret's (Herts)	ER	32	B1	Shepley	ER	56	C1
St. Margaret's (Middlesex)	SO	16	A1	Shepperton	SO	15	B1
St. Mary's Bay	RH	13	B2	Shepreth	ER	40	C1
St. Mary Cray	SO	12	A1	Sherborne	WR	8	C2
St. Michaels	LM	53	C2	Sheringham	ER/NN	50	C1
St. Neots	ER	39	C2	Shettleston	SC	76	B2
St. Pancras	LM	21	B2	Shields Road	GG	76	B1
St. Paul's	LT	21	B2	Shifnal	LM	37	A1
Sale	LM	51	C2	Shildon	ER	62	A1
Salford	LM	51	B2	Shiplake	WR	31	C1
Salfords	SO	12	B1	Shipley	ER	56	B1

Shippea Hill	ER	40	B2
Shipton	WR	30	B1
Shirehampton	WR	28	C2
Shiremoor	TW	70	A1
Shireoaks	ER	47	A2
Shirley	LM	37	B2
Shoeburyness	ER	33	C1
Sholing	SO	10	C2
Shoreditch	LT	21	B2
Shoreham (Kent)	SO	12	A2
Shoreham-by-Sea	SO	12	C1
Shortlands	SO	18	B1
Shotton	LM	45	B1
Shrewsbury	LM	36	A2
Sidcup	SO	32	C1
Silecroft	LM	60	C1
Silverdale	LM	60	C2
Silver Street	ER	23	C2
Silvertown	ER	22	B2
Sinfin Central	LM	47	C1
Sinfin North	LM	47	C1
Singer	SC	75	A1
Sittingbourne	SO/SK	13	A1
Skegness	ER	49	B2
Skelmanthorpe	ER	56	C1
Skipton	LM	55	A2
Slade Green	SO	32	C2
Slateford	SC	73	A1
Sleaford	ER	48	C2
Sleights	ER	63	B1
Sloane Square	LT	21	C1
Slough	WR	31	C2
Small Heath	LM	38	B2
Smethwick Rolfe Street	LM	37	B2
Smethwick West	LM	37	B2
Smitham	SO	12	A1
Smith's Park	TW	70	A1
Snaefell	ME	59	C1
Snaith	ER	56	B2
Snaresbrook	LT	22	A2
Snodland	SO	12	A2
Snowdon Summit	SM	43	B2
Snowdown & Nonington	SO	13	A2
Sole Street	SO	12	A2
Solihull	LM	37	B2
Somerleyton	ER	42	B1
South Acton	LM	20	C2
Southall	WR	19	C2
Southampton	SO	10	C1
Southampton Airport	SO	10	C2
Southampton Docks	SO	10	C1
South Bank	ER	62	A2
South Beach	SC	71	C1
South Bermondsey	SO	22	C1
Southbourne	SO	11	C1
Southbury	ER	24	B1
South Cape	ME	59	C2
South Croydon	SO	17	C2
South Ealing	LT	20	C1
Southease & Rodmell	SO	12	C1
South Elmsall	ER	56	C2
Southend Airport (Proposed)	ER	33	C1
Southend Central	ER	33	C1
Southend East	ER	33	C1
Southend Victoria	ER	33	C1
Southfields	LT	17	A1
Southgate	LT	23	C2
South Gosforth	TW	69	A2
South Greenford	WR	20	B1
South Hampstead	LM	21	B1
South Harrow	LT	20	A1
South Kensington	LT	21	C1
South Kenton	LM/LT	20	A1
South Merton	SO	17	B1
South Milford	ER	56	A2

Southminster	ER	33	B1
Southport	LM	54	C1
South Ruislip	LM/LT	19	A2
South Shields	TW	70	B2
South Tottenham	ER	21	A2
Southwick	SO	12	C1
South Wimbledon	LT	17	A1
South Woodford	LT	24	C2
Sowerby Bridge	ER	55	B2
Spalding	ER	49	C1
Spean Bridge	SC	78	A1
Spital	LM	53	C1
Spondon	LM	47	C1
Spooner Row	ER	41	B2
Springburn	SC	76	B1
Springfield	SC	79	C1
Spring Road	LM	37	B2
Squires Gate	LM	54	B1
Stafford	LM	46	C2
Staines	SO	15	A1
Stainforth & Hatfield	ER	56	C2
Stallingborough	ER	58	C1
Stalybridge	LM	52	B2
Stamford	ER	39	A2
Stamford Brook	LT	20	C2
Stamford Hill	ER	21	A2
Stanford-le-Hope	ER	32	C2
Stanlow & Thornton	LM	45	A2
Stanmore	LT	31	C2
Stansted	ER	32	A2
Staplehurst	SO	13	B1
Stapleton Road	WR	8	A2
Starbeck	ER	56	A1
Starcross	WR	3	A2
Starr Gate	BF	54	B1
Staveley	LM	60	B2
Staverton Bridge	DV	3	B1
Stechford	LM	37	B2
Stepney East	ER	22	B1
Stepney Green	LT	22	B1
Stevenage	ER	32	A1
Stevenston	SC	71	C1
Stewartby	LM	31	A2
Stewarton	SC	71	B2
Stirling	SC	78	C2
Stockport	LM	52	C1
Stocksfield	ER	67	C2
Stocksmoor	ER	56	C1
Stockton	ER	62	B2
Stockwell	LT	21	C2
Stogumber	WS	7	B2
Stoke-on-Trent	LM	46	C1
Stoke Mandeville	LM	31	B1
Stoke Newington	ER	21	A2
Stone	LM	46	C1
Stonebridge Park	LM/LT	20	B2
Stone Crossing	SO	32	C2
Stonegate	SO	12	B2
Stonehaven	SC	79	A2
Stonehouse	WR	28	B1
Stoneleigh	SO	16	C2
Stourbridge Junction	LM	37	B2
Stourbridge Town	LM	37	B1
Stowmarket	ER	41	C2
Stranraer Harbour	SC	64	C1
Stratford	ER/LT	22	B1
Stratford-upon-Avon	LM	38	C1
Strathcarron	SC	80	A2
Strawberry Hill	SO	16	A1
Streatham	SO	17	A2
Streatham Common	SO	17	A2
Streatham Hill	SO	17	A2
Stretford	LM	51	C2
Strines	LM	46	A2
Stromeferry	SC	80	A2

Strood	SO	13	A1		Thornton Gate	BF	54	B1
Stroud	WR	29	B1		Thorntonhall	SC	72	B1
Sturry	SO	13	A2		Thornton Heath	SO	17	B2
Styal	LM	46	A1		Thorpe Bay	ER	33	C1
Sudbury (Suffolk)	ER	33	A1		Thorpe Culvert	ER	49	B2
Sudbury & Harrow Road	LM	20	A1		Thorpe-le-Soken	ER	33	B2
Sudbury Hill	LT	20	A1		Three Bridges	SO	12	B1
Sudbury Hill, Harrow	LM	20	A1		Three Oaks & Guestling	SO	13	C1
Sudbury Town	LT	20	A1		Thurgarten	LM	48	B1
Sunbury	SO	15	A2		Thurso	SC	82	A1
Sunderland	ER	70	C2		Thurston	ER	41	C1
Sundridge Park	SO	18	A2		Tilbury Riverside	ER	32	C2
Sunningdale	SO	11	A1		Tilbury Town	ER	32	C2
Sunnymeads	SO	31	C2		Tile Hill	LM	38	B1
Surbiton	SO	16	B1		Tilehurst	WR	30	C2
Surrey Docks	LT	22	C1		Timperley	LM	51	C2
Sutton	SO	17	C1		Tipton	LM	37	B2
Sutton Coldfield	LM	37	B2		Tir Phil	WR	28	B1
Sutton Common	SO	17	B1		Tisbury	WR	9	B2
Swale	SO	13	A1		Tiverton Junction	WR	7	C2
Swanley	SO	12	A2		Todmorden	LM	55	B2
Swanscombe	SO	32	C2		Tolworth	SO	16	B2
Swansea	WR	27	C1		Tonbridge	SO	12	B2
Swanwick	SO	10	C2		Tonfanau	LM	33	A2
Sway	SO	10	C1		Tonypandy	WR	27	C2
Swaythling	SO	10	C1		Tooting	SO	17	A1
Swinderby	ER	48	B1		Tooting Bec	LT	17	A1
Swindon	WR	29	C2		Tooting Broadway	LT	17	A1
Swineshead	ER	49	C1		Topsham	WR	3	A2
Swinton	LM	51	A2		Torquay	WR	3	B2
Swiss Cottage	LT	21	B1		Torre	WR	3	B2
Sydenham	SO	18	A1		Totnes	WR	3	B1
Sydenham Hill	SO	17	A2		Totnes Riverside	DV	3	B1
Sylfaen	WL	36	A1		Tottenham Court Road	LT	21	B2
Syon Lane	SO	20	C1		Tottenham Hale	ER/LT	21	A2
Tackley	WR	30	B2		Totteridge & Whetstone	LT	23	C1
Tadworth	SO	12	A1		Totton	SO	10	C1
Taffs Well	WR	28	C1		Tower	BF	54	B1
Tain	SC	81	B2		Tower Hill	LT	21	B2
Talbot Square	BF	54	B1		Town Green	LM	54	C2
Talsarnau	LM	43	C2		Trafford Park	LM	51	B2
Talybont	LM	33	A2		Treforest	WR	27	C2
Tal-y-Cafn	LM	44	A1		Treforest Estate	WR	27	C2
Tamworth	LM	37	A1		Trehafod	WR	27	C2
Tan-y-Bwlch	FR	44	C1		Treherbert	WR	27	C2
Tan-y-Grisiau	FR	44	C1		Treorchy	WR	27	C2
Taplow	WR	31	C1		Trimley	ER	34	A1
Tattenham Corner	SO	12	A1		Tring	LM	31	B1
Taunton	WR	8	B1		Troedyrhiw	WR	27	B2
Taynuilt	SC	77	B2		Troon	SC	71	C2
Teddington	SO	16	A1		Trowbridge	WR	9	A1
Tees-side Airport	ER	62	B1		Truro	WR	1	C2
Teignmouth	WR	3	B2		Tufnell Park	LT	21	A1
Telford Central (Proposed)	LM	37	A1		Tulloch	SC	78	A1
Temple	LT	21	B2		Tulse Hill	SO	17	A2
Tenby	WR	26	B1		Tunbridge Wells Central	SO	12	B2
Tenterden Town	KS	13	B1		Tunbridge Wells West	SO	12	B2
Teynham	SO	13	A1		Turkey Street	ER	24	B1
Thames Ditton	SO	16	B1		Turnham Green	LT	20	C2
Thatcham	WR	10	A2		Turnpike Lane	LT	23	C2
Thatto Heath	LM	45	A2		Twickenham	SO	16	A1
Theale	WR	10	A2		Twyford	WR	31	C1
The Dell (Falmouth)	WR	1	C1		Ty Croes	LM	43	A1
The Lakes	LM	37	B2		Tygwyn	LM	43	C2
Theobalds Grove	ER	24	A1		Tyndrum Lower	SC	78	B1
The Pilot Halt	RH	13	C2		Tyndrum Upper	SC	78	B1
Thetford	ER	41	B1		Tyne Dock	TW	70	B2
Theydon Bois	LT	32	B1		Tynemouth	TW	70	A2
Thirsk	ER	62	C2		Tyseley	LM	37	B2
Thornaby	ER	62	B2		Tywyn	LM	34	A2
Thorne North	ER	57	C1		Tywyn Pendre	TL	34	A2
Thorne South	ER	57	C1		Tywyn Wharf	TL	34	A2
Thornford	WR	8	C2		Uckfield	SO	12	C2
Thornliebank	SC	75	C2		Uddingston	SC	76	C2
Thornton Abbey	ER	57	C2		Ulceby	ER	57	C2

99

Ulleskelf	ER	56	B2		Weeley	ER	33	B2
Ulverston	LM	60	C1		Weeton	ER	56	A1
Umberleigh	WR	7	C1		Welling	SO	32	C1
University (Birmingham)	LM	37	B2		Wellingborough	LM	39	C1
Upholland	LM	54	C2		Wellington	LM	37	A1
Upminster	ER/LT	32	C2		Wellworthy Ampress Works			
Upminster Bridge	LT	32	C2		Halt*	SO	6	A1
Upney	LT	32	C1		Welshpool	LM	36	A1
Upper Halliford	SO	15	B2		Welwyn Garden City	ER	32	B1
Upper Holloway	LM	21	A2		Welwyn North	ER	32	B1
Upper Warlingham	SO	12	A1		Wem	LM	45	C2
Upton	LM	45	A1		Wembley Central	LM/LT	20	A1
Upton-by-Chester	LM	45	B2		Wembley Complex	LM	20	A2
Upton Park	LT	22	B2		Wembley Park	LT	20	A2
Upwey & Broadwey	SO	5	A1		Wemyss Bay	SC	71	A1
Urmston	LM	51	C1		Wendover	LM	31	B1
Uttoxeter	LM	46	C2		Wennington	LM	54	A2
Uxbridge	LT	19	B1		West Acton	LT	20	B2
Vauxhall	SO/LT	21	C2		West Allerton	LM	53	C2
Victoria	SO/LT	21	C1		Westbourne Park	WR/LT	21	B1
Virginia Water	SO	11	A2		West Brompton	LT	21	C1
Waddon	SO	17	C2		Westbury	WR	9	A1
Waddon Marsh	SO	17	B2		West Byfleet	SO	15	C1
Wadhurst	SO	12	B2		West Calder	SC	72	B2
Wadsley Bridge*	ER	47	A1		Westcliff	ER	33	C1
Wainfleet	ER	49	B2		Westcombe Park	SO	22	C2
Wakefield Kirkgate	ER	56	C1		West Croydon	SO	17	B2
Wakefield Westgate	ER	56	C1		West Drayton	WR	19	B1
Walkden	LM	51	A1		West Dulwich	SO	17	A2
Walkergate	TW	69	B2		West Ealing	WR	20	B1
Wallasey Grove Road	LM	53	B1		Westenhanger	SO	13	B2
Wallasey Village	LM	53	B1		Westerfield	ER	33	A2
Wallington	SO	17	C1		Westerton	SC	75	A2
Wallsend	TW	70	B1		West Finchley	LT	23	C1
Walmer	SO	14	A1		Westgate-on-Sea	SO	14	A1
Walsall	LM	37	A2		West Ham	LT	22	B1
Waltham Cross	ER	24	A1		West Hampstead	LM/LT	21	A1
Walthamstow Central	ER/LT	22	A1		West Hampstead Midland	LM	21	A1
Walthamstow Queen's Road	ER	22	A1		West Harrow	LT	20	A1
Walton (Merseyside)	LM	53	A2		West Horndon	ER	32	C2
Walton-on-Naze	ER	33	B2		Westhoughton	LM	55	C1
Walton-on-Thames	SO	15	C2		West Jesmond	TW	69	B2
Wanborough	SO	11	A1		West Kensington	LT	21	C1
Wansford	NV	39	A2		West Kilbride	SC	71	B1
Wandsworth Common	SO	17	A1		West Kirby	LM	45	A1
Wandsworth Road	SO	21	C2		West Malling	SO	12	A2
Wandsworth Town	SO	21	C1		Westminster	LT	21	B2
Wansbeck Road	TW	69	A2		West Monkseaton	TW	70	A1
Wanstead	LT	22	A2		West Norwood	SO	17	A2
Wanstead Park	ER	22	A2		Weston Milton	WR	8	A1
Wapping	LT	22	B1		Weston-super-Mare	WR	8	A1
Warblington	SO	11	C1		West Ruislip	LM/LT	19	A2
Ware	ER	32	B1		West Runton	ER	50	C1
Wareham	SO	5	A2		West St. Leonards	SO	13	C1
Wargrave	WR	31	C1		West Street	GG	76	B1
Warminster	SO	9	B1		West Sutton	SO	17	C1
Warnham	SO	11	B2		West Wickham	SO	18	B1
Warren Street	LT	21	B2		West Worthing	SO	11	C2
Warrington Bank Quay	LM	45	A2		Weybourne	NN	50	C1
Warrington Central	LM	45	A2		Weybridge	SO	15	C1
Warwick	LM	38	C1		Weymouth	SO	5	A1
Warwick Avenue	LT	21	B1		Weymouth Quay	SO	5	A1
Warwick Road	LM	51	B2		Whaley Bridge	LM	46	A2
Washford Halt	WS	7	B2		Whatstandwell	LM	47	B1
Watchet	WS	7	B2		Whimple	WR	3	A2
Wateringbury	SO	12	A2		Whitby	ER	63	B1
Waterloo (London)	SO/LT	21	B2		Whitchurch (Hants)	SO	10	A2
Waterloo (Merseyside)	LM	53	A1		Whitchurch (Salop)	LM	45	C2
Water Orton	LM	38	B1		Whitchurch (South Glam)	WR	28	C1
Watford	LT	31	C2		Whitechapel	LT	22	B1
Watford High Street	LM/LT	31	C2		White City	LT	20	B2
Watford Junction	LM/LT	31	C2		Whitecraigs	SC	75	C2
Watford North	LM	31	B2		Whitefield	LM	51	A2
Watford West	LM	31	C2		White Hart Lane	ER	23	C2
Wedgwood	LM	46	C1		Whitehaven	LM	59	B2

White Notley	ER	33	B1
Whitland	WR	26	B1
Whitley Bay	TW	70	A2
Whitley Bridge	ER	56	B2
Whitlock's End	LM	37	B2
Whitstable & Tankerton	SO	13	A2
Whittlesea	ER	40	B1
Whittlesford	ER	32	A2
Whitton	SO	16	A1
Whyteleafe	SO	12	A1
Whyteleafe South	SO	12	A1
Wick	SC	82	A1
Wickford	ER	33	C1
Wickham Market	ER	42	C1
Widdrington	ER	68	B1
Widnes	LM	45	A2
Widney Manor	LM	37	B2
Wigan North Western	LM	54	C2
Wigan Wallgate	LM	54	C2
Wigton	LM	66	C1
Willesden Green	LT	20	A2
Willesden Junction	LM/LT	20	B2
Williamwood	SC	75	C2
Williton	WS	7	B2
Wilmcote	LM	38	C1
Wilmslow	LM	46	A1
Wilnecote	LM	38	A1
Wimbledon	SO/LT	17	A1
Wimbledon Chase	SO	17	B1
Wimbledon Park	LT	17	A1
Wimbledon Staff Halt*	SO	17	A1
Winchelsea	SO	13	C1
Winchester	SO	10	B2
Winchfield	SO	11	A1
Winchmore Hill	ER	23	C2
Windermere	LM	60	B2
Windsor & Eton Central	WR	31	C2
Windsor & Eton Riverside	SO	31	C2
Winnersh	SO	11	A1
Winsford	LM	46	B1
Wishaw	SC	72	B1
Wistaston Road (Crewe Wks.)*	LM	46	C1
Witham	ER	33	B1
Witley	SO	11	B2
Wittersham Road	KS	13	B1
Witton	LM	37	B2
Wivelsfield	SO	12	C1
Wivenhoe	ER	33	B2
Woburn Sands	LM	31	A1
Woking	SO	11	A2
Wokingham	SO	11	A1
Woldingham	SO	12	A1
Wolverhampton	LM	37	A2
Wolverton	LM	31	A1
Wombwell	ER	56	C1

Woodbridge	ER	42	C1
Wood End	LM	37	C2
Woodford	LT	24	C2
Woodgrange Park	ER	22	A2
Wood Green	ER/LT	23	C2
Woodhall	SC	71	A2
Woodham Ferrers	ER	33	B1
Woodhouse	ER	50	B2
Woodlands Road	LM.	52	A1
Woodlesford	ER	56	B1
Woodley	LM	52	C2
Woodmansterne	SO	12	A1
Woodside	SO	18	B1
Woodside Park	LT	23	C1
Wood Street Walthamstow	ER	22	A1
Wool	SO	5	A1
Woolston	SO	10	C2
Woolwich Arsenal	SO	22	C2
Woolwich Dockyard	SO	22	C2
Wootton	IW	6	A2
Wootton Wawen	LM	37	C2
Worcester Foregate Street	WR	37	C1
Worcester Park	SO	16	B2
Worcester Shrub Hill	WR	37	C1
Workington	LM	59	A2
Worksop	ER	47	A2
Worplesdon	SO	11	A2
Worstead	ER	50	C2
Worthing	SO	11	C2
Wrabness	ER	33	A2
Wraysbury	SO	31	C2
Wrenbury	LM	45	B2
Wressle	ER	57	B1
Wrexham Central	LM	45	B1
Wrexham Exchange	LM	45	B1
Wrexham General	LM	45	B1
Wroxham	ER	42	A1
Wye	SO	13	A2
Wylam	ER	67	C2
Wylde Green	LM	37	B2
Wymondham	ER	41	A2
Wythall	LM	37	B2
Yalding	SO	12	A2
Yardley Wood	LM	37	B2
Yarmouth	ER	42	A2
Yatton	WR	8	A2
Yeoford	WR	3	A1
Yeovil Junction	WR	8	C2
Yeovil Pen Mill	WR	8	C2
Yetminster	WR	8	C2
Yoker	SC	75	A2
York	ER	56	A2
Yorton	LM	45	C2
Ystrad Mynach	WR	28	C1
Ystrad Rhondda	WR	27	C2

INDEX TO BRITISH RAIL DEPOTS AND STABLING POINTS

102

INDEX TO FREIGHT TERMINALS AND YARDS

Burrelton	79	B1	Cumwhinton Gypsum Works	66	C2
Burtonwood	45	A2	Curzon Street (Birmingham)	38	B2
Bush - on - Esk (Longtown)	66	C2	Cwm Bargoed Colliery	27	B2
Butterley Works	47	B1	Cwm Colliery	27	C2
Butterwell Colliery	68	A1	Cwmmawr Colliery	26	B2
Buxton South Goods	46	A2	Cynheidre Colliery	26	B2
Cadder Yard	76	A2	Dairycoates	57	B2
Cadeby Colliery	56	C2	Dalkeith Colliery	73	A1
Cadley Hill Colliery	38	A1	Dalzell - BSC	72	B1
Caerwent	28	C2	Danygraig FLT	27	C1
Caldon Low Quarry	46	B2	Darfield Main Colliery	56	C1
Callerton - ICI	69	A1	Dawdon Colliery	68	C2
Calvert	31	A1	Daw Mill Colliery (Whitacre)	38	B1
Calvert Lane (Hull)	57	B2	Dean Hill	10	B1
Calverton Colliery	47	B2	Dean Road	70	B2
Cameron Bridge	79	C1	Dearne Valley Colliery	56	C2
Canada Dock (Liverpool)	53	B1	Deep Navigation Colliery	27	C2
Cannock Colliery	37	A2	Denaby NCB Workshops	56	C2
Carbis Wharf	1	B2	Denby Colliery	47	B1
Cardowan Colliery (Stepps)	76	B2	Deptford	70	C2
Carlton Sidings (Cudworth)	56	C1	Dereham	41	A1
Carmarthen Bay P.S.	26	B2	Derwenthaugh Coking Plant	69	B1
Carmyle Yard	76	C2	Desford Colliery	38	A2
Carne Point	2	B1	Dewsbury Railway Street	56	B1
Carville	70	B1	Dewsnap Sidings	52	B2
Castle Donington P.S.	47	C1	Dibles Wharf	10	C1
Castle Foregate (Shrewsbury)	36	A2	Didcot P.S.	30	C2
Castle Steelworks — GKN	28	C1	Didcot Distribution Centre	30	C2
Cattewater	2	B2	Dinnington Colliery	47	A2
Celynen North Colliery	28	C1	Dinsdale P.W. Depot	62	B1
Celynen South Colliery	28	C1	Dinton	9	B2
Chacewater	1	C1	Dodworth Colliery	56	C1
Chadderton P.S.	52	A1	Doe Hill	47	B2
Chaddesden	47	C1	Donisthorpe Colliery	38	A1
Channelsea Sidings	22	B1	Donnington	37	A1
Chatham Docks	13	A1	Dora Colliery	73	A1
Cheadle	46	C2	Dowlais — BSC	27	B2
Chelsea Basin	21	C1	Drakelow P.S.	38	A1
Chesterton P.W. Depot	40	C1	Drax P.S.	56	B2
Chilmark	9	B2	Draycott	47	C2
Chilwell	47	C2	Drayton Gravel Terminal	11	C1
Chinnor Quarry	31	B1	Dringhouses Yard (York)	56	A2
Chipping Sodbury	29	C1	Drinnick Mill	1	B2
City Basin (Exeter)	3	A2	Dudley FLT	37	B2
Clatchard Craig Quarry	79	C1	Dudley Hill	56	B1
Clay Cross Foundry	47	B1	Dufftown	82	C1
Claydon	41	C2	Dungeness P.S.	13	C2
Clegg Street (Oldham)	52	A2	Dunstable	31	A2
Cliffe	32	C2	Dunston P.S.	69	B1
Cliffe Hill	38	A2	Dunston Staithes	69	B2
Clifton C.S.	56	A2	Earley P.S.	31	C1
Clipstone Colliery	47	B2	Easington Colliery	62	A2
Clydach—on—Tawe	27	B1	Eassie	79	B1
Clyde's Mill P.S.	76	C2	East Caudledown	1	B2
Clydebridge — BSC	76	C1	East Heela Steelworks	50	A1
Clydeport FLT	71	A1	East Hetton Colliery	62	A1
Clydesdale — BSC	72	B1	East Leake	47	C2
Coalville	38	A1	Eastgate	61	A2
Cockenzie P.S.	73	A2	Eastriggs	66	C1
Cockshute Sidings	46	C1	Ebbw Vale — BSC	28	B1
Codnor Park	47	B2	Eccles Colliery	70	A1
Coed Bach Colliery	26	B2	Ecclesfield	50	A1
Coed Ely Colliery	27	C2	Edwalton	47	C2
Cofton Hackett — BL	37	B2	Eggborough P.S.	56	B2
Coity Goods (Bridgend)	27	C2	Eight Ash Green	33	A1
Colnbrook	19	C1	Eldon St. (Gateshead)	69	B2
Colthrop Board Mill	10	A2	Eling Wharf	10	C1
Coltishall	42	A1	Elland P.S.	55	B2
Coltness	72	B1	Ellington Colliery	68	B1
Colwick	47	C2	Elmham	41	A1
Comrie Colliery (Saline)	72	A2	Elsecar Main Colliery	56	C1
Conington South	39	B2	Emley Moor Colliery	56	C1
Connah's Quay P.S.	45	B1	Ernesettle	2	B2
Consett	67	C2	Eskmeals	59	B2
Corby	39	B1	Etherley	62	A1
Corringham Oil Ref.	32	C2	Evanton	81	C2
Corton Wood Colliery	56	C1	Exeter Riverside Yard	3	A2
Coryton Oil Ref.	33	C1	Exmouth Junction Coal Depot	3	A2
Cotgrave Colliery	47	C2	Fakenham	50	C1
Coton Hill Yard (Shrewsbury)	36	A2	Falkland Yard	71	C2
Cottam P.S.	48	A1	Farnley	56	B1
Coundon Road (Coventry)	38	B1	Faslane	71	A1
Coupar Angus	79	B1	Fawcett St. (Sunderland)	70	C2
Courthouse Green — BL (Cov.)	38	B1	Fawley Oil Ref.	10	C2
Coventry Colliery (Keresley)	38	B1	Fazakerley P.W. Depot	53	A2
Cowley Hill Wks. — Pilkingtons	54	C2	Felixstowe Docks & FLT	34	A1
Coxhoe Quarry	62	A1	Ferguslie	75	B1
Coxlodge	69	A1	Ferrybridge P.S.	56	B2
Craig—y—Nos Quarry	27	B1	Ferryhill (Aberdeen)	79	A1
Craigentinny C.S. & HST Depot	73	A1	Ferryhill (Co. Durham)	62	A1
Craiginches Yard (Aberdeen)	79	A1	Ferry Road (Grangetown)	28	C1
Craigneuk — BSC	72	B1	Fiddlers Ferry P.S.	45	A2
Cranmore	9	B1	Fighting Cocks	62	B1
Creekmouth P.S.	32	C2	Finedon	39	B1
Cresswell Colliery	47	B2	Fishburn Coking Plant	62	A1
Croes Newydd Sidings	45	B1	Flax Bourton	8	A2
Croft Quarry	38	B2	Fleetwood P.S.	54	A1
Croft Sidings (Darlington)	62	B1	Fletton	39	A2
Crofton P.W. Depot	56	C1	Flixborough Wharf	57	C1
Crombie	72	A2	Florence Colliery	46	C2
Cronton Colliery	45	A2	Foley — British Sugar	37	B1
Croxley Mill	31	C2	Follingsby FLT	70	C1
Cruiks Quarry	73	A1	Folly Lane	45	A2
Culloden Moor	81	C2	Forfar	79	B1
			Fort Dunlop	37	B2